In the *Fullness of* Time

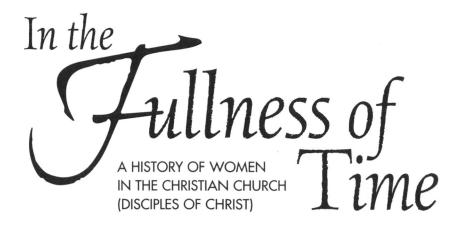

In the Fullness of Time

A HISTORY OF WOMEN
IN THE CHRISTIAN CHURCH
(DISCIPLES OF CHRIST)

Fran Craddock • Martha Faw • Nancy Heimer

Chalice Press®

St. Louis, Missouri

Biblical quotations, unless otherwise noted, are from the *New Revised Standard Version Bible*, copyright 1989, Division of Christian Education of the National Council of Churches of Christ in the United States of America. Used by permission. All rights reserved.

Cover Art: Glenda Dietrich, "Resurrection Dance"
Cover Design: Lynne Condellone
Art Director: Michael Domínguez
Interior design: Wynn Younker

This book is printed on acid-free, recycled paper.

Visit Chalice Press on the World Wide Web at
www.chalicepress.com

10 9 8 7 6 5 4 3 2 1   99 00 01 02 03 04

Library of Congress Cataloging–in–Publication Data

Craddock, Fran.
    In the Fullness of Time : a history of women in the Christian Church (Disciples of Christ) / by Fran Craddock, Martha Faw, and Nancy Heimer.
        p.   cm.
    Includes bibliographical references.
    ISBN 0-8272-1618-1
    1. Christian Church (Disciples of Christ)—History 2. Women in church work—Christian Church (Disciples of Christ)—History.   I. Faw, Martha. II. Heimer, Nancy. III. Title.
    BX7315 .C73   1999   99–043443
    286.6′3—dc21

Printed in the United States of America

Contents

Foreword

by
Anthony Dunnavant

Language is powerful. It is sometimes ironic. For decades the Disciples of Christ referred to their denominational organization and community as "the Brotherhood." Yet the reality was that the most vital, persistent, and significant locus of mission in that community was among the "sisters." Having been raised in a Disciples home, I shall never be able to hear "fellow" as a masculine word. The "fellowship" I grew up hearing the most about and seeing in vigorous activity was the Christian Women's Fellowship. The Christian Woman's Board of Missions and its successors, most notably the Christian Women's Fellowship, have reflected on, organized for, educated for, and raised funds for missionary and benevolent outreach for a century and a quarter.

What follows is a richly detailed account of that century-and-a-quarter's activity. Certain themes persist: the sense of a calling to participate in the mission of God that demanded response, the willingness to struggle against obstacles to make that response, the commitment to enlarging the church's missionary vision, the commitment to deepening the church's sense of benevolent compassion, the flexibility that embraced change as creative possibility, and a constancy of purpose in the midst of extraordinary changes in both the understandings of Christian mission and of women's roles in church and society.

This is a story of Disciples women responding to God's Spirit in mission, in the ministry of the gospel of Jesus Christ, and in faithful relationships to one another and to the whole church ("the Sisterhood!"). It is a story, therefore, that belongs to the whole church. I commend it to you.

Acknowledgments

While there are only three of us pictured on the back of this book, many brought it into being. Like so many women, we work better together than alone. Collaboration and community were the foundation of this work and therefore those mentioned here are but a partial list of those partners who made this book possible.

For their wisdom, support, and affirmation, we thank the members of the sponsoring body for the project, the 1986–1998 ICWF Cabinets and especially the ICWF Executive Committees.

Our grateful acknowledgment is extended to all the following persons:

To the members of the editorial advisory committee who not only shared the vision but helped us to build on it: Alice Langford, who researched women's giving; Janice Newborn, who researched the story of African American Disciples women; Gloria Hernandez, who sought information on the history of Hispanic women; and Ellen Frost, whose assistance, support, and encouragement were invaluable in the struggle to complete the book.

To all the staff of the Office of Disciples Women and its predecessor, the Department of Church Women, who were willing to give of their time and knowledge to be interviewed that this work might be as accurate as possible.

To Tracy Bee, who worked with Nancy to write and edit Part II. This work could not have been completed without her assistance.

A word of profound gratitude to Marilyn Moffett, who not only shared her experiences in a day-long interview but also taped the contents of so many valuable documents and articles for Nancy.

To our husbands, Jim Craddock, Judson Faw, and Roger Heimer, who not only tolerated our obsession with this task but also assisted us with their time and wisdom.

To Julia Dadds, Nancy's daughter, who shared her fresh perspective and journalistic ability and whose insightful wisdom gave clarity to her mother's writing.

To Ann Updegraff Spleth and Joyce Coalson of Homeland Ministries who took time from their very busy schedules to share their thoughts, experiences, and insights.

Hazel Rudduck, the first elected Vice President of the ICWF in 1953, is the oldest living officer, celebrating her 103rd birthday on July 21, 1999. She writes, "In my long lifetime, my most cherished moments come from the work I did for the ICWF Quadrennial Assembly, when people of many nations met and learned to work together for the good of all."

To all those who so graciously agreed to be interviewed: Pauline Johnson Askin, Luz Bacerra, Carnella Barnes, Anne J. Beach, Hilda Beachin, Virginia Bell, Doris Bennett, Majorie Black, Catherine Broadus, Jackie Bunch, Ann Burns, Evelyn Cartmill, Eliza Cave, Lucille Cole, Minnie Dorman, Edith Evans, Bonnie Frazier, Ellen Frost, Giley Griffith, Elizabeth Hartsfield, Alice Langford, Betty Mohney, Ernestine Mrozinski, Janice Newborn, Arlene Pimentel, Greta Brown Plopper, Odatta Redd, Norma Roberts, Mary Louise Rowand, Hazel Rudduck, Helen Spaulding, Marilyn Taylor, Sybel Thomas, and Jessie Trout.

To May Reed at the Disciples of Christ Historical Society for all her help in securing old photographs, magazine articles, official documents, and bits of memorabilia.

To Newell Williams and Tony Dunnavant for their guidance and consultations, and to Tony for his willingness to write a foreword even when the manuscript was so late.

To David Polk, Michael Domínguez, and Sally Smith at Christian Board of Publication and Chalice Press. We are most grateful for their patient partnership guiding us through the labyrinth of authorship.

And finally, to all those who have made valuable contributions to the story of Disciples women but whose names do not appear in this book, we offer both our gratitude and our apology.

Introduction

"Disciples women should recognize and remember their heritage for this sets the stage for the future…They feel a high sense of achievement for their share in molding the past and look forward with a deep sense of responsibility to shaping the future."[1]

Betty Fiers, former ICWF president

"These women of the past will live among us. Their fantastically successful efforts in the face of equally fantastic obstacles will be recounted and young members of the church will learn for the first time of their heritage."[2]

Helen Spaulding, former executive
Department of Church Women

"In the fullness of time…" These are audacious words of power and promise, reminding us of the biblical claim that "In the fullness of time God sent forth his son…" Now, the Holy Spirit is poured out on all our daughters and sons. That too is a biblical claim spoken by the apostle Peter on the first Christian Pentecost in the fulfillment of the earlier prophet Joel (Acts 2:17).

This is our specific assertion: In the last century and a half, God has blessed the daughters and the mothers of this special people, the Christian Church (Disciples of Christ). As in the Bible's *kairos*[3] moment, the perception of the rightness and fullness of this era moves us to inquire how God wed secular history and church institutions to do "a new thing." This brief history is but the beginning of that inquiry.

As in ancient times the "sons of the prophet" claimed God's communal blessing, so our own fellowship of prophets, in their fullness of time, required the ordering of spiritual life as a visible community for mutual support and for the Holy Spirit's blessing and direction.

The nature of God's tangible favor is in the Christian Women's Fellowship, which during its first fifty years can be remembered in the personalities of individual leaders or in the scores of millions of dollars devoted to Christ's missions. A more complex but more important part of the story of God's visible gifts must be sought in a description of this and other communities of women.

The sharing of history is an important exercise of every community that expects a future. It is no less important for those groups that find their reason for being, not in a projected future, but in the mission that gives them life. Such groups are not concerned so much about their future as they are about the fulfillment of their mission. Christian Women's Fellowship is such a group. Its future is rooted in its past and nurtured by its present. By renaming the women and tracing the development of their particular ministries from the beginning of organized work in 1874, we are better able to chart the course of their achievements and to see our own mission as we approach a new century.

No one group of us has the whole truth, but we share what we know of the truth. With it as their foundation, our daughters and granddaughters may seek their own truth to pass on to the generations that will come after them. This, too, is the vitality of the movement of Disciples women. We tell this history as forthrightly as we can. It is our story as we read it and our story as we lived it. We hope it encourages others to uncover the past and create the future.

This book was written in conjunction with the fiftieth anniversary celebration of the Christian Women's Fellowship. While inevitably the women's organization is central in such a history, as women today seek to understand the power of Disciples women, they need first to comprehend the essential, foundational place of CWF—its history, its present struggles, and its potential for the future. More than the story of an organization, it is the story of a movement. Yet it remains incomplete, for our diversity creates our stories. Residing both in Canada and the United States, Disciples women are clergy, lay, African American, Hispanic, Asian, and Caucasian. Some belong to the CWF or its ethnic counterparts and some do not. All have a story to tell.

It is important to keep the story alive and, true to our heritage, to keep church people well informed. To know the story is to tell it, and to tell it is to strengthen it, and to strengthen it is to empower women, and to empower women is to empower the whole church.

Part I
1874–1968

Martha Faw

THE *Venturing Years*
1874–1919

THE VISION

April 10, 1874, had all the marks of a typical spring day in Iowa City, Iowa. The day had begun veiled with heavy fog, but rain was expected to move in from the west and rinse away the last remnants of snow still lingering on cobblestoned streets.

Caroline Neville Pearre (pronounced Pa-ree) began her day as usual, preparing breakfast to share with her husband, the Reverend Doctor Sterling Elwood Pearre, before sending him off to the church office. They had come to Iowa City in 1872 when he assumed duties as pastor of First Christian Church. This day, Friday, held promise of being filled with preparations for the Eastertide prayer service in the evening, an appointment with several church leaders, and receiving unexpected but welcome persons needing assistance and counsel.

After starting preparation for the noon meal when her husband would come home, perhaps bringing an unannounced guest with him, Caroline Pearre sat down in her favorite chair for her daily time of Bible reading and prayer. What followed changed the direction of Mrs. Pearre's life and began a new era for women in the Christian Church, also known as the Disciples of Christ.

As she reached for her Bible, memories of the previous Sunday flooded over her. Easter services never failed to thrill Caroline Pearre, and this Easter Sunday had been no exception. The music had been especially inspiring, and Dr. Pearre's sermon was most eloquent. She recalled his passionate declaration of the redemptive grace of God aimed toward drawing all of humanity into a new relationship through the risen Christ. Her own concern for the lack of evangelizing and serving unchurched persons at home and around the world welled up inside her once again.

The American Christian Missionary Society (ACMS) had existed for twenty-five years, having been formed under the leadership of Alexander Campbell in 1849, and this Society had begun work in three areas overseas. However, it had not been able to secure enough funds to continue the missionary efforts it had started, and it had to discontinue its enterprises in Jerusalem, Liberia, and Jamaica.

At the 1869 General Convention of the Christian Church, a report was submitted from a committee of twenty church leaders that called for a structured approach to missions, providing for better congregational participation and control of missionary work. Dubbed "The Louisville Plan," named after the location of the 1869 convention, this plan was received with apparent enthusiasm, but in reality it was ignored by most of the very individuals and groups who had hailed its introduction. The result was that receipts for missionary work plunged to an all-time low, and it was this failure, coupled with a later report from the "Committee on the Cooperation of Women in the Missionary Work," given at the Indianapolis Convention in 1870 by chairman James Challen and footnoted by Thomas Munnell, that weighed heavily on Caroline Pearre's heart as she completed her devotional time.

James Challen, a longtime leader in the now almost defunct ACMS, said in his report:

> They [women] may become missionaries at home and abroad like the Judsons and others…They may organize and sustain a chosen field of labor, on which they can bestow their offerings and prayers…The Women's Boards of Missions in certain denominations around us have demonstrated this, and set a noble example to our sisters…We feel assured that there is an element of power here, almost unknown to us, and unemployed, which needs to be called into active labor.[1]

Thomas Munnell, another longtime leader in ACMS and Corresponding Secretary of the convention, added these words:

> Recognizing that, as a people we have never opened the way for the women of our churches to unite in any broad enterprise with us, we propose to invite their vast, though unemployed, abilities to "labor with us in the gospel," both as solicitors among ourselves and as missionaries in suitable fields.

As Caroline Neville Pearre rose from her knees that April day in Iowa City,[2] about ten o'clock in the morning, the thought came to her to become involved in organizing the women of the church for missionary work. Her prayer had been for God to send a leader, and when the question formed in her mind, "Why cannot you do it?" she felt a great throb of joy and release as she said aloud, "I will!"[3]

Although her forty-third birthday celebration would take place on the fifteenth, only five days away, Mrs. Pearre brushed aside all involvements of lesser importance to her and immediately began laying groundwork for what would ultimately become a $1.5 million enterprise, organized and managed exclusively by women. Aware of the keen interest of Thomas Munnell in having women share in the missionary efforts of the total church, she wrote first to him, then in quick succession she penned letters to personal acquaintances in six different states. Their responses were immediate and very encouraging.

Historians of the nineteenth century have indicated that the Civil War years formed a time of enormous discovery for women. One such writer, R. Pierce Beaver, indicates that women on both sides of that struggle were driven to new experiences and new sources of power. In his opinion, women were

> driven to organize, forced to cooperate by their passion of pity and patriotism, and in the management of the Great Commission for raising and distributing aid to the soldiers. Thus they discovered powers of which they themselves and the nation had been quite unconscious.[4]

Perhaps the dawning realization that women were finding ways of expressing their deepest concerns for humanity had an effect on Mrs. Pearre's meditation time that April morning.

Perhaps it was the conviction that the great commission was extended to her time in history as well as to the time in which it was first issued by Jesus of Nazareth. Perhaps it was an emerging vision of the advancement of the kingdom of heaven over the whole earth. Perhaps it was a melding of all three.

Caroline Pearre's Letters

A closer look at some of the recipients of Mrs. Pearre's handwritten letters reveals her keen sensitivity to the importance of strategic planning in order to achieve the desired ends. Of the eight women mentioned in her three-part essay published in the summer 1899 issues of *Missionary Tidings*, each has been easily identified as a woman of prominence in her church and community, and in every instance married to men of high esteem in the leadership of the

Disciples of Christ. Among the women to whom she wrote were Mrs. R. M. Bishop, Mrs. O. A. Burgess, Mrs. Enos Campbell, Mrs. B. F. Coleman, Mrs. Joseph King, Mrs. L. S. Major, Mrs. J. K. Rogers, and Mrs. R. R. Sloan.

The first woman Mrs. Pearre wrote to after her communication with Thomas Munnell was Mrs. L. S. Major of Chicago, whose husband was a well-known doctor. Together they had united with a group of "Campbellites" in 1848 and had continued to be active in establishing Chicago area congregations. While little more has been found concerning Mrs. Major, it is a safe assumption that she was a good friend and likely a person of influence. She sent an immediate and enthusiastic response to Mrs. Pearre and was present in Cincinnati at the organizing meeting of the women. She was elected there to serve on the first Board of Managers for the Christian Woman's Board of Missions (CWBM).

Living in Indianapolis and married to the president of North Western Christian University (renamed Butler College in 1877), Nannie L. Burgess received Caroline Pearre's letter with deep excitement. Raised in a strong Christian family, she had invested her almost forty years in the Disciples of Christ, first in her native Illinois and later as wife of the minister of the prestigious Central Christian Church in Indianapolis, before moving to the suburban campus of North Western where she received Mrs. Pearre's letter. Mrs. Burgess was in full agreement with the proposal of her childhood friend to organize a society whose objective would be "to cultivate a missionary spirit" in the churches, starting with the women, and she promised to lend her considerable influence to this enterprise. Mrs. Burgess was elected to serve as the first national treasurer when CWBM was organized. Still later, she was to become a vice president, then president, a position she held from 1890 until her death in 1902.

Mrs. Enos Campbell was married to the pastor of First Christian Church in Jacksonville, Illinois, when she heard from Caroline Pearre. She and her husband had worked long and hard in promoting the cause of missions, and they were successful in leading a former congregation, First Christian Church in Hopkinsville, Kentucky, in initiating a project to send a remarkably skilled slave preacher, Alexander Cross, as a missionary to Liberia. With the help of other congregations in the Green River Cooperation, they had purchased his freedom in 1853 for $530, and Mr. Campbell trained him for a period of six months while Mrs. Campbell helped prepare his wife for service in Africa. The elders of the Hopkinsville church "set him apart" to go to Africa, and he went under the auspices of ACMS in the latter part of 1853. Mrs. Campbell, whose husband was a cousin of Alexander Campbell, knew intimately the difficulties that Disciples leaders had in trying to get their first major missionary organization off the ground, so she was greatly relieved and very encouraged when she received the news from Caroline Pearre that the women of the churches would soon be organized to assist in this effort so dear to her own heart.

Representing women from Kentucky at the organizing meeting for CWBM on October 21, 1874, were four women, one of whom was Mrs. B. F. Coleman of Lexington. News of the projected plan to organize had reached her in a letter from Mrs. Pearre several months earlier, and she immediately endorsed the plan and began to direct her energies toward its passage. A great barrier of conservatism among the Kentucky congregations made it necessary for the women to move more slowly toward organized work than their sisters in other states. When the Woman's Kentucky Christian Missionary Society was organized in 1875, it grew out of a report from a four-man committee that recommended the enterprise and even specified that each member would pay ten cents monthly. Further, this all-male group required that all the income would be expended in the state of Kentucky, mostly for the education of young men, including "young colored men," for the Christian ministry. With such endorsement from the men, Kentucky women organized themselves, produced a basic constitution and elected officers. Mrs. Coleman was chosen corresponding secretary for the new group, thus occupying a position that enabled her to keep directly in touch with the leaders of the general organized work.

Charlotte McGrew King received her letter from Mrs. Pearre as she was deeply involved in the missionary efforts of First Christian Church in Allegheny, Pennsylvania, where her husband was enjoying a twenty-one-year pastorate. Together they had given leadership and insight into the establishment of several new congregations in the Pittsburgh area. Upon receipt of the news that the women would meet to organize for greater missionary activity when the General Convention met in October, Mrs. King, along with her illustrious and highly respected husband, began to make plans to be present in Cincinnati. She became a charter member of CWBM and devoted herself to organizing mostly children's missionary groups, not only in her own church in 1877 but in churches throughout the eastern seaboard. She received the blessing of CWBM as she pioneered in the training of children and youth in the knowledge and work of missions. When CWBM added a Young People's Department in 1884, Charlotte King was chosen as the first national superintendent. There were 20 "mission bands" for children the first year of her term, and one year later the reported number was 120. In another two years, the number had more than doubled to 272.

While yet a student at Christian College in Columbia, Missouri, Mrs. J. K. Rogers knew Caroline Neville as her teacher, then in later years as a coworker at the school where Dr. Rogers, president of the college, administered the school's affairs with wisdom and success. When in the summer of 1874 a letter from her friend and mentor reached Mrs. Rogers, the sequence of events that followed helped launch the move toward missions among the Disciples of Christ. Mrs. Rogers believed the news it contained—plans for organizing church women for mission education and action—was too great to keep to a few.

Quickly she forwarded Caroline Pearre's letter to J. H. Garrison, editor of *The Christian*, one of the outstanding journals of the Christian Church. He immediately joined Isaac Errett, editor of the Ohio-based *The Christian Standard*, in endorsing Mrs. Pearre's proposal, and both used their pages to issue a call for a meeting of women at the General Missionary Convention in Cincinnati in October. Mrs. Rogers became a charter member CWBM, an enterprise whose message, through her thoughtfulness, had been rapidly and forcefully disseminated to homes and churches in every state and territory where Christian Churches were located.

Mrs. R. R. Sloan was chosen to preside at the women's meeting that took place in the basement of the Richmond Street Christian Church in Cincinnati on Wednesday, October 21, 1874. The wife of a Cleveland minister, Jane Sloan had received a letter from her friend, Caroline Pearre, in June and had responded with strong approval of her plan. She was invited to be the presiding officer, but insisted that Mrs. Pearre should have that honor. It was pointed out that Mrs. Pearre's participation would be more effective as a speaker, so Mrs. Sloan consented to preside and did so with much enthusiasm for the work that was before them.

Caroline Pearre was greatly encouraged by the responses she received from each woman. She had chosen very carefully those persons who would be likely to consider her proposal favorably and be willing to use their influence in its development. All but one responded as promptly as circumstances would permit. Mrs. R. M. Bishop of Cincinnati did not reply initially, but later in the summer she and her husband gave their full endorsement. Mr. Bishop, as the

third elected president of ACMS, presided over sessions of the
General Convention, a position that enabled him to cultivate
considerable support from his all-male Board for the proposed
women's organization. It was more than mere coincidence that four
members of the Board were married to four of the eight women cited
above!

"A Flame of the Lord's Kindling"

Ida Withers Harrison's book *Forty Years of Service* was published
as "the history of the Christian Woman's Board of Missions, 1874–
1914," and in it she wrote:

> The first thing to do before entering on any enterprise is to
> convert oneself thoroughly to it, and this our pioneers had
> done with their fixed purpose "to do something in the mis-
> sionary field." The second step was to bring the great body
> of women in the church to a like state of mind.

Bringing women to a like state of mind was the object of Mrs.
Pearre's efforts for the six months between her inspired commitment
on an April morning and the gathering of approximately seventy-
five women on an October afternoon. Already there were reports of
women in local congregations who were responding to the demands
for social and educational improvements for women on every continent. The Women's Rights Movement of 1848 laid the groundwork;
the 1861 Woman's Union Missionary Society movement gained
widespread endorsement for the great awakening among women.
Following the 1861–1865 war, many changes took place as women
embraced new areas of interest and education, and many Disciples
of Christ congregations were ready to help in this advancement.

As women gained wider acceptance in formal education institutions, they were drawn to areas of service: teaching, medicine, and
social reform, thus acquiring skills and training that were precisely
those required in missionary service. Caroline Pearre was quick to
recognize this and moved rapidly to implement her vision of an organized constituency of the Disciples of Christ that would respond
in new and creative ways.

Iowa City church women rallied around Caroline Pearre's desire
to begin an organizational structure for missions in their local
congregation. On the second Sunday in May, only thirty-two days
after her historic morning of commitment to the vision of missions,
the women of First Christian Church met and formally organized a
missionary society. Women in other locations also began to organize
missionary groups. Some were prompted by the concerns expressed

in the 1872 General Convention's resolution for reestablishing mission work. Some were prompted by Mrs. Pearre's correspondence. All were endorsed by J. H. Garrison's editorial in *The Christian* and by Isaac Errett's editorial "Help Those Women" in *The Christian Standard* which Erett wrote during a visit to the Pearre home in June. Errett's editorial, perhaps more than any other, provided strong endorsement for the women's efforts and played a significant role in moving toward the national organizational meeting in October 1874. Both church papers used their pages to issue the call for a meeting of Christian Church women at the time of the General Missionary Convention in October in Cincinnati.

Years later, Caroline Pearre wrote an article that appeared in three installments in *Missionary Tidings* magazine. "Our Beginning" revealed interesting details of her struggles with the obstacles she encountered as she began to develop the plans for organizing, not the least of which was inexperience. Her article mentioned her correspondence with Thomas Munnell, seeking his opinion about whether the church was ready for such a move. His reply was returned with great promptness:

> I am writing through tears of thankfulness. Yes, go on; this is a flame of the Lord's kindling, and no man can extinguish it.

In her articles she wrote appreciatively of the endorsement she received:

> It was a great strength and comfort to have my earnest wish and settled purpose fortified by counsel so worthy of consideration, and to be assured that the way was open.

She referred to the lack of knowledge and experience among the women who voluntarily took on the reins of leadership.

> A great work—how great no one is able even yet to forecast—was now ready to be begun, but with what appalling lack of equipment in the workers. It was as if a noble ship were ready to put to sea without chart or compass and a totally inexperienced hand upon the helm. We had no knowledge of missions. Not many of us knew anything about organized work; very few had even so much training in managing a business meeting as is furnished by a school literary society...The missionary societies of the older churches (Baptists, Congregationalists, Methodists, Presbyterians), with their experienced central boards, network of auxiliaries, and strong rallying points of long-established missions,

furnished no precedents for us…We had nothing to start with. We were to find our willing workers, gather them into societies, create our Board, and select a rallying point.[5]

By the time the arrangements for the 1874 General Convention were completed, women across several states had met in local groups, affirmed the call to organize missionary societies, and had begun to collect offerings for spreading the good news even though there was not yet a national treasury or even a stated enterprise to forward the work.

The convention met at the Richmond Street Christian Church in Cincinnati. Approximately seventy-five women from nine different states[6] gathered in the basement on the afternoon of Wednesday, October 21, 1874, to hear convention president Richard R. Sloan's wife, Jane, call the meeting to order and ask Caroline Pearre to make a statement regarding the purpose of the meeting. There were three or four men in attendance, and one of them, F. D. Power, a leading minister from Washington, later reported that "hardly any of them took part in the proceedings."

In addition to Mrs. Pearre's eloquent introduction to the concept of organized work, four other women spoke, including Mrs. Pearre's lifelong friend from Eureka, Illinois, Elmira Dickinson, who had spent the summer organizing women's groups in numerous Illinois towns. She was to play a very prominent role as field worker for the new women's national board. Caroline Pearre, Maria Jameson, and Marcia Goodwin were appointed to draft a constitution.

Attention had already been given to such a document by these women, with the agreement endorsed by all that it should be brief and simple. And brief it was, consisting of only eight articles and thirty-one lines of type. Its simple wording was readily understood by all. The proposed constitution was presented to the women's session the following morning and adopted article by article.

A second item of business dealt with that morning was the report of the committee on nominations. Again, it is obvious that prior attention had been given to this slate, which included six of the eight women to whom Mrs. Pearre had written following her April morning experience. Others, notably Maria Jameson, Elmira Dickinson, Zerelda Wallace, Marcia Goodwin, Nancy Atkinson, and Sarah Wallace, had also been contacted by her during the months prior to this meeting and had agreed to accept designated positions of leadership on the first board. The nominees were unanimously elected as follows:

President

Mrs. Maria Jameson
Indianapolis, Indiana

Vice Presidents

Mrs. J. B. Thomas
Baltimore, Maryland

Mrs. Joseph King
Allegheny City, Pennsylvania

Mrs. W. T. Moore
Cincinnati, Ohio

Mrs. N. E. Atkinson
Wabash, Indiana

Mrs. S. E. Jones
Newtown, Kentucky

Miss E. J. Dickinson
Eureka, Illinois

Mrs. Enos Campbell
St. Louis, Missouri

Mrs. James E. Garton
Des Moines, Iowa

Mrs. T. F. Campbell
Monmouth, Oregon

Recording Secretary

Mrs. Sarah Wallace
Indianapolis, Indiana

Corresponding Secretary

Mrs. C. N. Pearre
Indianapolis, Indiana

Treasurer

Mrs. O. A. Burgess
Indianapolis, Indiana

State Secretaries

Miss Rebecca Sitler
Baltimore, Maryland

Mrs. W. C. Weedon
Cleveland, Ohio

Mrs. M. F. Streator
New Castle, Pennsylvania

Mrs. J. T. Dye
Indianapolis, Indiana

Mrs. B. F. Coleman
Lexington, Kentucky

Miss Ella Myers
Eureka, Illinois

Mrs. J. K. Rogers
Columbia, Missouri

Mrs. G. T. Carpenter
Oskaloosa, Iowa

Mrs. S. C. Adams
Salem, Oregon

Board of Managers

Mrs. Charles Phillips
New Castle, Pennsylvania

Mrs. C. H. Gould
Cincinnati, Ohio

Mrs. Henry Pearce
Cincinnati, Ohio

Mrs. Ryland T. Brown
Indianapolis, Indiana

Mrs. Mary Radcliffe Butler
Louisville, Kentucky

Mrs. William T. Withers
Lexington, Kentucky

Mrs. L. S. Major
Chicago, Illinois

Mrs. Johnson Hatch
Chicago, Illinois

Mrs. John G. Allen
St. Louis, Missouri

Mrs. M. M. B. Goodwin
Indianapolis, Indiana

Mrs. Alfred Sanders
Davenport, Iowa

In the afternoon session, the newly organized board met with the full convention. The new officers were graciously received, and the following resolution was adopted with a standing vote:

> *Resolved*, That this Convention extends to the Christian Woman's Board of Missions recognition and hearty approval, assured that it opens a legitimate field of activity and usefulness, in which Christian women may be active co-operants of ours in the great work of sending the Gospel to the world. We pledge ourselves to "help those women, who propose to favor with us in the Lord."[7]

With this strong affirmation of their beginning, the Board convened once more in separate session to consider the type and location of their first work. Appeals for four projects were given, and each one was considered with careful attention. One was for work among the recently freed slaves in the South; one was for evangelistic work in the West, which was rapidly being populated following the opening of new territories. Another urged the women to reopen the work begun in Jamaica by ACMS in 1858 but abandoned for lack of funds; and yet another plea was for female workers among women in India who because of cultural restrictions were not open to receiving the gospel from male missionaries. All these proposals were valid and fell within the stated range of concern.

After thorough deliberation and two votes, it was determined that the day's offering of $430 would be invested and other receipts added to it until sufficient funds of "at least $1,000" might be secured to send a missionary to Jamaica. It took fifteen months to accomplish this, and Dr. William H. Williams, along with his wife and baby, sailed from New York late in January 1876. Dr. Williams was a medical doctor whose major assignment in Jamaica was the planting of self-sustaining congregations.

The women left Cincinnati with much excitement and anticipation. Their courage, combined with optimistic caution, was typical of the approach they would make to future plans and decisions. There was no ambiguity about their intent and purpose; the purpose stated in the CWBM was clear:

> Its object shall be to cultivate a missionary spirit, to encourage missionary effort in our churches, to disseminate missionary intelligence, and to secure systematic contributions for missionary purposes.[8]

The word *missionary* appeared four times in the same sentence intentionally. Mrs. Pearre's focus was totally on the great challenge that lay before Disciples of Christ women—to join with their sisters in other American denominations, notably Congregationalists, Methodists, Presbyterians, Baptists, and Episcopalians, in winning the world for Jesus Christ. Caroline Pearre felt the best way to do this was to create an institution through which women might be recruited, educated, and challenged to resource a carefully planned missionary work at home and abroad.

Ida Withers Harrison, CWBM's historian, wrote, "At that time (1874), there was no woman among them experienced in public work; they were untrained in speech, in the conduct of business, and in audible, articulate prayer."[9] Looking back on their recorded accomplishments over one hundred years later, one is led to believe that this is not altogether true. Many, if not most, of these leaders had attended schools and colleges, and some of them were teachers and writers. Many of them had successfully assumed management of family businesses when their fathers and husbands had been called into the war between the North and South. Even if they were inexperienced, they were, nevertheless, capable and quickly developed reasonable plans to accomplish their goals.

Years later, Nannie Burgess, the second president of CWBM, addressed the World's Congress of Representative Women at the 1893 Chicago World's Fair. In explaining the working of the Board, she said, "So far as I know, our Board is unique in that its business is managed entirely by women, and we have our own methods of organizing the states and of raising money...we select our mission field and employ both men and women."

THE FLAME GROWS BRIGHTER

Weeks of intensive planning followed the Cincinnati meeting. The telegraph and postal services were kept busy with the correspondence exchanged between state vice presidents who were charged with "the interests of the work within their jurisdiction" and developing resources for that work, and other members of the executive committee, each of whom had specific tasks to complete for the first meeting. The committee was required to meet on the first Monday of every month for the transaction of business, and its first meeting was called for January 4, 1875, in Indianapolis.

CWBM's first president was Maria Jameson, a daughter of Ovid Butler, for whom Butler University was named. He had encouraged his daughter to enlarge her interests beyond that of a homemaker, for he believed strongly that women had minds capable of high thinking and executive action, and he was eager for women to bring their unique gifts to prominent places of leadership in church and community. Likewise, Mrs. Jameson encouraged her daughter, Sarah Jameson Wallace, to take a leadership role as recording secretary in the first organization of CWBM. Mrs. Jameson's first address, made at the January 1875 executive committee meeting, is included here because of the "wise and statesmanlike policy as the plan of work of the Board" as it began its monumental contribution to the development of the Christian Church.[10]

> We meet today for the first time in our official capacity as the Executive Committee of the Christian Woman's Board of Missions. One thing stands out clearly, and that is our firm purpose to do something in the mission field, and with this in our hearts, we can hardly fail of finding the way to accomplish it. We have decided to work this year for Jamaica, and let us concentrate our thoughts, efforts and influence upon raising sufficient money for that object. Let prayerful anxiety stimulate our ingenuity, let us carry it in our thoughts, and what our minds find there to do, let us do with all our might.
>
> The outline of our machinery is in these nine States represented at the Cincinnati Convention, and from each of these we have chosen a Vice-President, a Secretary, the Recording and Corresponding Secretaries, and the Treasurer, the Executive Committee, five of whom form a quorum, and who are fully empowered to transact business. The absent members, however, know the time of meeting, and have the right to send suggestions, or proxy votes, upon any question that is before us.
>
> The State Secretaries are to go to work immediately in their various states, by obtaining from the State Evangelist as complete a list as possible of all churches in the state; she is then to write, explaining the work, and urging the organization of an auxiliary society in every church, receiving quarterly reports from these societies, and transmitting these in her regular reports to our Corresponding Secretary—so that we may keep constantly in touch with the progress and prospects of the work in every part of the country. In all of this, the State Secretary is to be constantly assisted by the State Vice-President—who is to give the work her best thought and attention, gain information that may be useful to it, devise plans of operation, and arrange to hold meetings at the same time and place as the regular State Meetings, and preside over them herself. So, we propose to work for this year.

As little rivulets from hidden springs, running together make the larger stream, which hurrying on with swollen waters bears its steady contribution to the great river—so with the mites of the poor widow, the pennies of the children, the dollars of the salaried women, and the larger gifts from those of independent income, flowing together makes one great stream, whose waters shall refresh the field of missionary labor.

To find and release the smaller sources of income is a special object with us, partly because in a country like ours, where few are very rich, and few abjectly poor, it is the most natural and effective way to raise money, and partly that all may share in the reactive benefits that come to those who contribute to a great cause.

I would recommend as our means of creating more general interest in our work, the distribution of some good current literature devoted to this subject; for this, we must at present look to our religious neighbors; as they have been for two or three years in the field we wish to enter, their experience will bring to us valuable practical lessons in the best modes of operation.

Finally, I have the encouraging fact to report that contributions were sent us at the Cincinnati Convention from Richmond, Virginia, from West Virginia, and messages of warmest sympathy from Kansas, from Savannah, Georgia, and from Detroit, Michigan, though none of these states were formally represented in our Association. And now, feeling conscious that this effort to lay our work before you has been necessarily long, I pledge myself to do for it this year, with the divine blessing, and your co-operation, all that I can to advance the cause of organized missionary effort among the women of the Christian Church.

Following Mrs. Jameson's address, the executive committee sat quietly for a long moment, so moved were they by her words and the convincing manner of her delivery. Finally one of them responded, "I, for one, join you in this pledge to do all I can to advance our cause." Others quickly joined in, and "cultivating a missionary spirit," called for by the CWBM constitution, was prayerfully and carefully launched.

Other subjects of concern were also discussed that day. The committee on by-laws gave its report, and the eight articles it presented were meticulously considered and unanimously adopted.[11]

They were:

1. The Executive Committee shall meet in Indianapolis for the transaction of business on the first Monday in each month. Five members of the Committee shall reside in Indianapolis or vicinity. The non-resident members shall be entitled to a proxy vote on all questions of importance.
2. The President shall prepare programs for and take charge of the meetings of the Board, and of the Executive Committee. She shall use all wise endeavors to promote the interests of the Board.
3. The Vice-Presidents shall prepare programs for and preside over State meetings, take charge of the interests of the work within their jurisdiction, and, in harmony with the President, develop the resources of same.
4. The State Secretaries shall receive all reports from auxiliary societies, and transmit the same quarterly to the Board, and take charge of all books and papers belonging to the same. They shall make all notifications to officers and committees.
5. The Corresponding Secretary shall attend to the correspondence of the Board, keep the same on file, shall receive all reports from State Secretaries, and make a report to the Board at its annual meeting of the work done.
6. The Treasurer shall receive all money sent to the treasury of the Board, and disburse the same according to its order. She shall make a report to the Board at its annual meeting. No money shall be disbursed, except upon the written order of the President and Secretary. The President, with the concurrence of the Secretary, shall be authorized to defray the current expenses of the Board. The Treasurer's account shall be audited annually by a committee appointed by the Board.
7. The Managers shall co-operate with the Vice-Presidents and State Secretaries in their work of organization and development.
8. These By-Laws may be amended at any meeting of the Executive Committee by a vote of two-thirds of the members present.

Missionary literature was an immediate need as vice presidents and state secretaries took charge of the work across the land. The decision was made to accept the offer of three pages in the monthly women's magazine *The Christian Monitor*, being published by Marcia M. B. Goodwin of Indianapolis. Thus the communication between the national Board and individuals in the many local communities could be obtained for twenty-five cents annually. Mrs. Goodwin was immensely successful in providing a first-rate periodical, and she was chosen in 1883 to edit the four-page newsletter, *The Missionary Tidings*. Articles for *The Christian Monitor* were written or chosen by Board members, and it was determined that, when appropriate, the corresponding secretary would submit reports to the *The Christian Standard* and *The Christian* as well.

While there was much affirmation of the new women's Board, especially by those who attended the General Convention in 1874, all was not smooth sailing. Many voices were raised in opposition when the news was received in congregations, resulting in sermons, letters, and stands against this new freedom for women. Already there had been serious debate about the missionary societies, national and state. Those who wanted a model of the New Testament church for all the ways a church functioned could find no justification in the Bible for societies. The failures of ACMS merely added fuel to the ongoing debate. Certainly the widening social and economic gaps between rural and urban church members contributed to the rising opposition to missionary socities on any level, and one organized and operated solely by women was beyond acceptance by those who firmly believed a woman's place was in the home, period.

Women were also exploring other areas of interest outside thier home duties, and this was cause for attack by the general press and ridicule in cartoons and lectures. The Women's Rights Convention, held at Seneca, New York, in 1848 had spawned an outpouring of satire and sarcasm, and each annual convention until 1862 succeeded only in muddying the troubled waters. By the end of the Civil War, a groundswell of activities on all fronts—social, political, educational, industrial, and legal—was evident among women, and an uneasiness crept across the male-dominated systems and institutions.

In his doctoral dissertation, defended in 1979, Fred Arthur Bailey declared:

> The Disciples of Christ in the 1870s was a troubled church splitting into ecumenical and evangelistic wings. As the church's schism widened, the movement's attitudes toward woman's role divided as well. Liberal, ecumenical ministers were much more inclined to allow their sisters to engage in a variety of reform activities than were their more conservative brethren…[12]

He went on to say that following the creation of CWBM, the Disciples of Christ underwent a steady openness to their theology concerning women's place within the church. He indicated that the Board's success in raising funds and recruiting missionaries, along with the "modest decorum" of its leaders, led male Disciples to be more open to expanded female participation by women outside church structures as well. A case in point was the anti-saloon campaign of 1873–1874 and the founding of the Woman's Christian Temperance Union in the fall, precisely during the birthing stage of CWBM!

It is interesting to note that many Disciples women were involved in the temperance movement, two in particular who approached the drive to reform from quite different vantage points. Carry Nation gained notoriety by her fierce aggression toward saloons, an aggression based on her childhood memories of a drunken, abusive father, and a first husband who also had a drinking problem. Later, when she met David Nation, she had already begun to have problems with mental depression. After several business ventures failed, he became pastor of the Christian Church in Medicine Lodge, Kansas, and it was from this point that Carry Nation attempted to shut down the illegal but flourishing alcohol industry in Kansas by passive resistance; namely, praying outside the saloon doors. Appeals to law enforcement personnel also failed, so she tried more aggressive tactics. She became known throughout the Midwest for her hatchet-swinging destruction of bars and saloons which, of course, landed her in jail many times.

In stark contrast was Zerelda Wallace, another Disciples woman, whose passion for reform of alcohol abuses was equal to that of Carry Nation, but found expression in a different way. Writer Debra Hull describes her as "gentle, refined and traditional." She was the oldest of five daughters, an advantage that created many opportunities for her to enjoy lively conversations with her physician father about literature, politics, and scientific matters. She married David Wallace, a widower with three small children, then serving as lieutenant governor of Indiana. He went on to become governor, then a member of the United States House of Representatives. It was not until her children were grown that Mrs. Wallace confessed to her friend Maria Jameson that she had no experience in public speaking, yet something inside was driving her to speak out against the practice observed in most Protestant churches, including the Disciples, of using wine in the communion service.

Opposition to the sale and use of any intoxicants was a cause that liberals and conservatives alike could join in. Disciples of Christ were active leaders in state and local efforts to curtail the liquor traffic and even moved into the forefront of total prohibition. Mrs. Wallace was so opposed to any use of alcohol that she refused for several weeks to take the communion cup. She rose from her seat one Sunday and gave her reasons for declining the wine in a short speech which was "the death knell to the use of spirituous liquor in churches. A meeting of the church board was called. The energetic woman renewed her warfare on spirits with a vigor that carried everything before it, and she won the day."[13] This from a fifty-seven-year-old woman who had not spoken in public before!

In due time, Zerelda Wallace was recognized as the foremost woman orator of Indiana and continued to speak out against the evils of alcohol as well as for the advantages of giving women the right to vote. These two causes, however, took second place with Mrs. Wallace. Her first concern was for the missionary efforts sparked by friends at a meeting in her home in July of 1874, and culminating in CWBM. As Lorraine Lollis points out in her book, *The Shape of Adam's Rib,* our chief interest in Zerelda Wallace lies in that she went to Cincinnati to help organize CWBM and there was elected to membership on its first board of managers. Accompanying her was Sarah Jameson Wallace, the wife of her stepson William. Sarah was elected recording secretary, a position she held at two different times for a total of four years, and from 1875 to 1880 she was corresponding secretary, following Caroline Neville Pearre.

Those who were caught up in the challenge of the new missionary enterprise did not let the harsh criticism or the public ridicule deter them. Taking to heart the endorsement of Thomas Munnell—"this is a flame of the Lord's kindling, and no man can extinguish it"—Disciples of Christ women set about, in quiet and unostentatious ways, to make Caroline Pearre's vision a reality.

Under the leadership of Maria Jameson, CWBM laid a substantive base for its future, being careful to plan thoroughly each step it should take in its forward movement. The early leaders were very frugal, as evidenced by their first annual report at the 1875 General Convention in Louisville. The reported expense account totaled $27.50! All officers, national and state, and all field workers took care of their own expenses when such were not covered by the host auxiliaries and congregations.

Outstanding among those who were giving so freely of their time and resources for the cause was Elmira J. Dickinson, a former schoolmate and lifelong friend of Mrs. Pearre, and an ardent coworker in rousing the women to the work of missions. Miss Dickinson had dreamed of being a missionary, but there was no agency to send her and no money available among the Disciples when she completed work on her master's degree in 1869 at Eureka College in Illinois. She was on the faculty of Eureka when she learned of her friend's proposal to organize the women of the church. In July 1874, she organized a Woman's Missionary Society in her home church. Two months later, she attended the Illinois State Convention and took a leading role in organizing what is thought to be the first state Woman's Missionary Society.

The time was ripe for women's organizations, and especially was this true for Disciples and other Protestant churches. CWBM quickly became the vehicle by which the Disciples accepted larger church and social roles for their women. By participating in the local and state societies or auxiliaries, women learned about the need for organized missionary work, gained the courage to speak out on social issues in and beyond church settings, and eventually secured the right of pulpit preaching.

For almost the next decade, CWBM escaped effective criticism because it emphasized the conventional concepts of what was generally regarded as "true womanhood," as opposed to "the new woman" concept of aggressive women who were seeking equal rights, which would, in turn, remove wives and mothers from their intended sphere of home and family life. CWBM provided an avenue for Disciples women by which they could make an active contribution to society at large. By means of this organization, many Christian Church women gained the experiences of both men and women, and in increasing numbers they were sent to domestic and foreign lands as social workers, Bible teachers, and medical evangelists.

BACK TO JAMAICA

Having determined at their organizational meeting in Cincinnati that Jamaica would be their first missionary project, the officers and the rapidly growing membership worked long and hard to enlist as many active supporters as possible and to gather offerings for the support of their work in Jamaica. Within fifteen months they had collected enough money to begin the work.

Early in January 1876, advertisements were placed in the two major church weeklies seeking applicants for missionary service in Jamaica. Very quickly, CWBM received applications from a dozen inquirers, Dr. and Mrs. W. H. Williams of Platte City, Missouri, among them. Upon their acceptance by the executive committee, this couple passed through Indianapolis to receive a brief orientation, along with letters of introduction, before sailing from New York City.

The Williams family arrived in Kingston on February 5, where they were warmly welcomed by people who had waited many years for the work, abandoned by ACMS, to be renewed.[14] A small nucleus of Disciples of Christ was found in the capital city of Kingston, and the Williams family soon gathered a good many individuals who had remained faithful. Victims of poverty and natural disasters, these islanders were, nevertheless, eager to start the rebuilding process. While the Jamaica work progressed more slowly than had been envisioned, it did show steady and orderly growth.

Even as the CWBM executive committee worked to strengthen the financial support for the Jamaican mission, it was reminded over and over of the urgent request for work among the freedmen of the southern United States. ACMS had accepted the assignment for evangelistic and educational work among black people, and for this reason CWBM leaders refrained from advancing any formal work among this, or any other, special group.

An experimental effort, however, was made in the spring of 1881 when Mr. and Mrs. Randall Faurot were employed by CWBM to set up a preaching-teaching ministry in Jackson, Mississippi. The ACMS board had begun the Southern Christian Institute at Edwards, a short distance away. The Faurots resigned after one year in Jackson to take a position at Southern Christian Institute, and CWBM did nothing more among black people in the South until 1900, when that assignment was formally turned over to CWBM. (This will be dealt with in greater detail in a later section.)

Not long after CWBM was organized, its leaders began to lay plans for expanding the financial basis for the work. A major step in this direction was taken in February 1880 when articles of incorporation were taken out. By this act, they gained existence and recognition in law, and thus secured the permanency of the endowment fund and the safe handling of bequests and donations. As the national economy was improving and people were becoming more generous with increased incomes, offerings to all national church agencies were improving. Mrs. Burgess, as treasurer in 1877, led in the creation that year of the CWBM Endowment Fund, with the agreement that interest earned for the first five years would not be used. This fund was made up of life memberships, individual donations, and bequests. Assurances were given to many who had taken life memberships that "from time to time we shall appropriate the interest to the establishment of missions in a heathen land." After all, this had been the burning challenge of Caroline Pearre's vision in 1874 and continued as the motivating drive behind all the endeavors of CWBM.

The concern for heathen peoples of the world was mounting within the entire church population during the early days of the 1880s. As women learned at their missionary meetings about needs for Christian teaching, medical and housing services, and basic educational training, they shared with their families and friends many of their concerns. Entire families, as well as major segments of towns and villages, became aware of the plight of millions of people in many parts of the known world, and most were responsive to any call for help.

At the Louisville convention in 1880, James H. Garrison, editor of *The Christian*, made a stirring address in which he told of an incident that had occurred in his home the previous evening. During their family devotional time, Dr. Garrison explained to his two young sons and a niece that he would speak at the convention on missions, and he invited the children to suggest how he might urge the convention to take steps to help tell the world about Jesus. When prayers were concluded, the children left the room, put their savings banks money together, a total of $1.13, and presented it to Dr. Garrison with the urgent request that it be used "to send the gospel to children who have never heard of Jesus."

Dr. Garrison, an eloquent and persuasive orator, used this story to move the convention audience to unheard-of heights of commitment to missions. They adopted a motion to ask local Sunday schools to receive a special offering every year for foreign missions, on a day to be known as "Children's Day." Disciples historians note that from this time onward, missionary receipts by the three major boards showed a general and rapid improvement.

INTO INDIA WITH THE FOREIGN CHRISTIAN MISSIONARY SOCIETY

As a result of the new emphasis on Children's Day offerings, the increased interest among church leaders generally, the growth of children's and young people's mission bands or groups, and the continuing numerical growth of women's auxiliary groups, foreign missions among Disciples of Christ took on a higher priority. CWBM decided to open a new work, this time in a land distinctly pagan, and its leaders proposed to the Foreign Christian Missionary Society (FCMS) that the two unite in establishing a mission in a field to be decided on jointly. The proposal was readily accepted by the

Foreign Society, and a joint committee was set up to decide on the destination.

The committee's decision to send the first group of missionaries to India came only after long and arduous study of several strong possibilities: Japan, India, and Turkey among them. Also taken into account was the difficulty of finding qualified persons who were willing to undertake a work in a distant land where language and scant knowledge of the customs of the people would be decided drawbacks. It would be especially difficult for an unmarried woman to enter such an uncharted career, yet women were essential to the success of the enterprise because of cultural restrictions in each of the three countries under consideration.

According to Ida Withers Harrison, the young women who were pioneers in foreign missionary work deserved to have their names written high in the hearts of Disciples of Christ everywhere. The Misses Mary (or Maria) Graybiel, Ada Boyd, Mary Kingsbury, and Laura Kinsey left home on September 16, 1882, in the company of Mr. and Mrs. Albert Norton and Mr. and Mrs. G. L. Wharton of the Foreign Society, bound for Bombay, India. The four young women had offered to work without a stipulated salary the first year, asking only for CWBM to pay their travel expenses. With no prior missionary efforts by the Disciples of Christ in India to build on, this first joint effort was begun slowly and carefully. The Wharton family lived at Harda, the first permanent mission station.

In 1885, a station was opened at Bilaspur, where Mary Kingsbury and Mary Graybiel, assisted by the other two women, started with the women and children, first a Bible school, then a weekday school, then zenana work (visitation and teaching women in that part of their homes where only women were allowed). This was an essential part of missionaries' attempts to reach families; without it missionary efforts in India, as well as other places where cultural traditions prohibited contact between women and men who were not their husbands, would surely have failed. Their work soon included the care and feeding of children orphaned by extended famines and extreme poverty.

The joint planning and management of the India mission quickly showed results at home as well as abroad. Congregations became enthused about the progress so quickly made and responded to early reports from the two mission boards with increased financial support, which, in turn, provided added encouragement to the missionaries. Additional staff were sent overseas, including the first women doctors, Dr. Olivia Baldwin and Dr. Arabella Merrill. They were the first in a long line of medical missionaries to work in India, many of them women, and they played a significant part in encouraging the demand for higher education for India's women.

A Paper of Its Own

Maria Jameson had indicated in her inaugural address to the organizational meeting of CWBM's executive committee in January of 1875 that a publication for that group would be launched as soon as there were available resources to support it. Resources became available in 1883, and plans were developed to publish and distribute the first issue in May. Marcia Goodwin was named editor of the four-page monthly, but the publication itself was still without a name when the copy for the first issue was ready to go to the printer. Mrs. Goodwin hurriedly suggested *The Missionary Tidings*. The executive committee approved it with similar haste, and the magazine bore that title until it was merged in 1919 with four other periodicals into *World Call* magazine.

Marcia Goodwin had been instrumental in promoting CWBM from its beginning. She offered four pages of each issue of her magazine *The Christian Monitor*, for use by CWBM officials for the first nine years of its life. When CWBM leaders responded to a steady pressure to start a paper of its own, the subscription price was set at twenty-five cents per year. The newsletter format was used for several months, then changed to a magazine style that grew to an average of forty pages per issue. Sadly, Marcia Goodwin was editor for only five months, forced by a serious illness to give up the work in its infancy.

Sarah E. Shortridge, serving in 1883 as corresponding secretary, took charge of the magazine, though she never listed her name as editor on the masthead. All communications and correspondence came to her desk, so it was appropriate for her to assume the task of editing a magazine that included news of local and state auxiliaries, reports from the mission stations, and minutes of the executive committee. She continued until her health failed in late 1888. Upon her death in January 1889, a memorial fund was started and resulted in the building of a church in Butte, Montana, the first home evangelism project of CWBM, in 1893.

The Shape of Adam's Rib,[15] by Lorraine Lollis, records a detailed accounting of the growth and development of *The Missionary Tidings*, including its listing of editors and prolific writers over the span of thirty-six years. When the publications of six major agencies of the Disciples of Christ merged in 1919 to become *World Call*, Effie L.

Cunningham, who had been *Missionary Tidings* editor from 1909 through 1918, became associate editor of *World Call*. Although *Tidings* had brought its subscriber list of sixty thousand to the merger (more than all the other publications together), there was only one time that a woman served as editor. Bess White, later married to Disciples writer Louis B. Cochran, succeeded W. R. Warren in 1929 and left in 1932 to become publicity director and editor for the National Benevolent Association.

Christian Woman's Board of Missions surrendered control over a large segment of its work when it finally agreed to enter into the formation of The United Christian Missionary Society. This will be addressed more fully in a later chapter, but it is important to note here that the voice of world missions lost much of its vigor, and the message, while not garbled, was nevertheless muffled. The result was a diminishing of the impact that organized work among women was able to make on the church.

CHILDREN AND MISSIONS

It was only natural that women of the Disciples of Christ felt that their children should be trained in the knowledge and work of missions as part of their Christian upbringing. From the early days of CWBM's formation, children's groups were organized in local congregations. Mrs. Alonzo M. (Nancy) Atkinson, of Wabash, Indiana, invited the children of First Christian Church to meet together to hear stories of children in other lands, learning how to relate to them and developing a "missionary spirit." This pioneer group was named "Willing Workers." They, and many similar groups formed during the mid-1870s, were encouraged to engage in systematic self-denial not only to train them in the practice of Christian stewardship but also to increase their ownership of mission efforts.[16] As women became aware of the needs of the world, it was an easy next step to relate what they had learned to their husbands and families. "Mission Bands" sprang up in several states along with the organization of CWBM women's auxiliaries as the movement gained momentum. Indeed, the following resolution was adopted at the CWBM session of the General Convention in 1876:

> This Convention requests all its members to give special attention to the instruction of the children under their care, at home and in the Sunday school, in missionary work; it asks them to devise means for the accomplishment of this work, teaching them to give, and, through self-denial, further the work of Christ.

Nancy Atkinson's work with children in Wabash is thought to be the first formed with the encouragement of the Woman's Board. Disciples historian Debra B. Hull writes:

> This and other children's missionary societies were the pre-cursors of Christian education and missionary education for children. Children progressed from Little Light Bearers (a society for babies who were given life memberships in CWBM), through the Willing Workers, into Triangle Clubs, and then into Mission Circles (for young women). In the last year of the Christian Woman's Board of Missions' existence, there were thirty thousand child members in more than one hundred twenty societies who had raised half a million dollars for mission work.[17]

Another strong advocate of missionary education for children and young people was Charlotte M. King, married to Joseph King, a prominent pastor in Pennsylvania. Like Nancy Atkinson, Charlotte King was a charter member of CWBM and in 1884 became the first director of its Young People's Department, which included all younger children's involvement. *Missionary Tidings* gave generously of its pages for stories of children's work for the next six years. Mrs. King was delighted to learn, at the conclusion of her first year in the work, that twenty mission bands had been recorded as auxiliaries to CWBM. She urged the executive committee to assign some special work to the children, and this was done, perhaps sooner than anyone had dared hope. Word came from Akita, Japan, of the death of Josephine Smith, the first Disciples missionary to die on foreign soil. It was decided that a fitting memorial for Mrs. Smith would be the erection of a home and chapel in Japan, to be financed by the offerings of the mission bands. The children's eager response was reflected in Mrs. King's report of July 1886, indicating that the number of local bands had grown from twenty to one hundred and twenty, and funds for the Josephine Smith Memorial were in hand.

Immediately, the children accepted a second building project, a home for the pioneer missionaries in India, and over a period of thirty-three years they were responsible for resourcing seventy-five other buildings in India, Jamaica, Mexico, Japan, Puerto Rico, and the United States. They became known as the "Little Builders" or "Junior Builders" and soon had a magazine of their own, which grew from eight pages in 1890 to forty pages in 1914. Over its life, this publication went through a series of name changes until 1908 when it became *The King's Builders*, a title it retained for the rest of its existence.

CWBM's missionaries in India opened work for orphans in 1888 in Bilaspur, where Mary Kingsbury and Mary Graybiel served for many years. In addition, orphanages were built by the children's auxiliaries in a wide range of places as CWBM opened mission stations in Mexico in 1895, in Puerto Rico in 1900, in Argentina in 1905, and in Paraguay in 1908.

Into All the World

Supporters of CWBM have often been quoted as saying that one of the glories of CWBM was that it knew no distinction between home and foreign missions—its field was the world. Surely this was a major factor in all the decisions made by its leaders during the years of its phenomenal growth. While establishing fields of endeavor in remote locations around the globe, CWBM was also hard at work advancing its missionary thrust in the United States. The western frontier was being pushed toward the Pacific Ocean with an intensity that sometimes reached head-spinning proportions.

Railroads began to appear with increasing frequency after the Civil War, mostly westward bound. Already the United States was the world's largest industrial power, and the end of this expansion was not in sight. Three new inventions—the telephone, the electric lightbulb, and the automobile—were impacting businesses and homes all across the land. The pioneering spirit was challenged once more by opportunities of expansion and of acquiring new land in the territories beyond the Mississippi River. Disciples of Christ leaders were not unmindful of all this. On the contrary, many were urgent in their requests to send evangelists and educators with the settlers, recognizing the accompanying opportunities for gaining new members and building new churches on the frontier.

ACMS was already at work in the West, but its resources of men and money were limited. The leaders requested that CWBM join with them in evangelizing efforts, and CWBM chose to respond to requests for help in Montana first. An authorized survey of conditions was made in 1881, and the following year two men and their families were sent to Helena and Deer Lodge, charged to develop congregations there and then to move on and build churches in other places when the work was well established. This pattern was followed again and again as CWBM evangelists went later to Colorado, Idaho, North Dakota, Washington, California, Arizona, and Oklahoma.

An unequaled opportunity presented itself to early Christian settlers up and down the Pacific Coast as they encountered unevangelized Asians whose presence was often a surprise. Portland,

Oregon, was still a mission point when the newly established congregation began to work among the Chinese of that city in 1891. San
Francisco provided a similar setting a few years later. Just after the
turn of the century, the Japanese Christian Institute opened its doors
in Los Angeles. For all of these, and many others as well, CWBM
was instrumental in providing leaders and financial resources that
would spread the gospel in ever-widening circles.

Calls for help seemed to come from every part of the globe as
the nineteenth century was winding down. At times there appeared
to be more demands than the women's leaders could manage. After
its inception in 1874, the offices of CWBM existed only in the homes
of its administrators until 1888, when a three-room suite was rented
at 160 North Delaware Street in downtown Indianapolis. The front
room was used for monthly meetings of the executive committee,
and the more solemn and sacred the moment, the more likely that a
man or boy would arrive to make a delivery. If he happened to find
the members on their knees, and this did occur with noted frequency,
he usually withdrew quietly until a more convenient time. The offices were relocated a few years later at 152 East Market Street, where
they remained until 1910, when they were moved to the College of
Missions Building at 222 South Downey Avenue.

While still answering correspondence, recording offerings,
publishing *Missionary Tidings,* and producing missionary literature
in makeshift home offices, CWBM executives maintained a steady
commitment to engaging in mission work at stations far and near.
In addition to the preaching and teaching effort in Jackson,
Mississippi, reported earlier in this chapter, there were other isolated
work stations among southern blacks. Christian Woman's Board of
Missions officials were reticent to launch a major campaign because
this responsibility had been assigned to ACMS shortly after the Civil
War. Leaders of both groups worked cooperatively in several
ventures to evangelize and educate; however, during the 1870s, as
much evangelistic work was carried on outside ACMS as through
it. For example, individuals and congregations were responsible for
such activities as the frequent visits of leading white preachers to
southern states for tent meetings; the financial support of a black
state evangelist; the formation of a society to support the work; and
attempts to establish schools and training centers. Most efforts were
abandoned for lack of support until the Woman's Board was asked
by ACMS to assume the work totally in 1900. During the twenty
years in which CWBM administered the black program, there was
no more important home mission field than this, in its judgment.

The ministry among the ten to fifteen million black Americans who were still learning how to live in a free society was focused on education and social services. The Board inherited a capable superintendent of the work in the personage of Clayton C. Smith, whose administrative abilities helped set Southern Christian Institute (SCI) and two smaller schools, one in Lum, Alabama, and the other in Louisville, Kentucky, on a firmer financial and vocational training footing. By the end of the century, it was apparent that evangelistic efforts among black communities by white church leaders were not as effective as had been hoped for. Disciples turned their focus toward the improvement of educational opportunities, and used SCI, the oldest and largest of the black schools, as the major training ground for future leaders of the church and for society in general. The school educated hundreds of students at the elementary and secondary levels, and provided advanced training for some of the indigenous staff from mission stations in Jamaica and Africa. Many persons, male and female, received their initial training at SCI, and later gave distinguished service to the Disciples of Christ as preachers, administrators, teachers, and leaders of women's missionary auxiliaries on state and national levels. Among its graduates were Sarah Lue Bostick, Rosa Bracy Brown, and Rosa Page Welch, whose stories are included later in this book.

VENTURES IN EDUCATION

The Board's earliest venture in educational work in the homeland occurred in the Appalachian area in Kentucky. It was in 1886 that CWBM assumed the ownership and control of a six-year-old school, Hazel Green Academy, which provided elementary and high school education for young people in the area. This institution continued as one of the major home missions projects of the Disciples of Christ for almost one hundred years. During the years of CWBM's management, thousands of young people went through its training programs and into places of useful citizenship, throughout the East and South especially. There were other mountain schools conducted by CWBM, smaller in size and of less duration.

The establishment of four Bible Chairs at state universities was yet another pioneering effort of the Woman's Board. As early as 1882, Leonard W. Bacon, a Congregational minister in New England, proposed that denominations begin to sponsor and undergird the teaching of religion at state universities. The authors of the Disciples of Christ history *Journey in Faith* suggest that Charles A. Young, pastor at Ann Arbor, Michigan, "no doubt persuaded the CWBM's national

officers to back him in launching an experimental program."[18] On
the other hand, Ida Withers Harrison, CWBM historian, writes that
the first Bible Chair "was placed at the University of Michigan, at
Ann Arbor, where the Board had already built a beautiful church"[19]
in 1891. This fact suggests that the reverse might be more accurate,
that CWBM had already envisioned the establishment of a Bible
Chair in Ann Arbor and had taken steps to provide for a building in
which classes might be held. This argument is furthered by Nannie
Burgess, CWBM President, at the 1892 Convention:

> The way is open, if we have the courage to undertake it, for
> the establishment of an English Bible Chair at...the Univer-
> sity of Michigan, where the courtesies of that great institu-
> tion are offered to us.[20]

Mrs. Burgess was successful in her proposal, and the women in attendance voted their hearty approval to endow a Chair and "put a
competent teacher in charge."

The records of CWBM show that this new project met with criticism from some of the Disciples college administrators who felt it
would create unfair competition with church-related schools. Some
even suggested that CWBM was going beyond its bounds as a "missionary board" to encroach on territory beyond its ken. By and large,
however, the support from Disciples of Christ was strong, and in
1893 Herbert L. Willett and Clinton Lockhart, two very "competent
teachers," began classes in biblical instruction, meeting in the Ann
Arbor church. In this same year, an endowment fund of almost
$38,000 was raised, and a house was given, located across the street
from the main entrance to the state university campus, to house the
classes and provide a social setting for the students.

This initial project was followed by the inauguration of Bible
Chairs at three other state universities—Virginia, Kansas, and
Texas—which were very successful. Attempts were made in several
other states but were short-lived when adequate endowments were
not raised.

The Bible Chair work, designed and resourced by CWBM, continued as an inspiration and model for numerous other denominations well into the twentieth century, and provided the basis for the
development of student ministries on college and university cam-
puses across the North American continent to the present time.

In the last quarter of the nineteenth century, and more particularly the last decade, the American society was caught up in an
optimistic outlook that declared that for every problem there was a

solution, for every need there was a resource. Individualism gave way to group involvement, and persons began to look beyond themselves as the major solution to social and institutional needs. Disciples were caught up in this new trend, resulting in a flurry of new organizations, agencies, and societies.

Women did not confine their participation to CWBM, with its work on local and state levels and its missionary endeavors abroad. Along with their male counterparts, Disciples women were actively confronting the challenges of new times. Tucker and McAllister observed that the latter part of the nineteenth century

> became an era of agencies and institutions as Disciples shared in the boundless drive of an expanding nation. Disciples seemed to have accomplished all they could through the old instrumentalities of crusading periodicals, debate, and, with a few exceptions, poorly educated preachers. Future growth depended on a new evangelism, professional leadership in the ministry, settled pastors, better buildings, and improved cooperation among themselves and with other religious bodies.[21]

Mention has already been made of the origin and development of the Woman's Christian Temperance Union and Disciples women's part in the campaign against alcohol. A second battle, not totally unrelated, was waged against the plight of poor and orphaned children. Led by Mattie Younkin and six other women whom she enlisted, a prayer group met in February 1886 in a basement room of Central Christian Church in St. Louis to seek guidance for ways Disciples of Christ might care for the needy. The following year, the women formed a permanent organization, the (National) Benevolent Association of the Christian Church.[22]

Efforts to minister to orphans had been made in several states prior to the Civil War, but without lasting success. Organized benevolence grew slowly among Disciples, perhaps due to the anti-institutionalism preached by early Disciples leaders. This practice alone had a lasting impact on the church and drew a strong negative reaction among the more conservative congregations well into the next century. In fact, its impact could be readily identified in the break in fellowship that took place in the Christian Church and was thus reflected when the conservatives took the name Church of Christ and listed themselves as a distinct group in the Federal Religious Census of 1906. This group pulled away from the Disciples of Christ for yet another reason: they opposed the use of musical instruments in the church. They held firmly to the stance that because neither missionary societies nor organs were used in the New Testament church, both were to be eliminated from a restorationist church.

Notable among those who managed to establish work among orphans and widows in spite of great opposition were the Midway Orphans School and the Widows and Orphans Home in Kentucky, and the Christian Orphan School in Missouri. Mattie Younkin, Donie Hansborough, Rowena Mason, Emily Meier, and Judith Garrison were prominent among those who participated in the benevolent work that began in a church basement prayer meeting and resulted in the Christian Orphans' Home in St. Louis, the first facility established by the National Benevolent Association, in 1889.

Because of opposition to institutions beyond the congregation, many state conventions refused to grant even a hearing, and the Benevolent Association was denied the opportunity of presenting its work for many years. Unable to secure a hearing at the General Convention, the women held a well-attended convention of their own in 1892. This meeting generated considerable interest and increased revenue, and the purpose of the agency was widely heralded. Finally, in 1899, after two earlier attempts that were tabled, the Benevolent Association was officially recognized as a part of the organized work of the Disciples of Christ.[23] Following this official recognition, men took over the reins of leadership, thus controlling the work of National Benevolent Association until Cindy Dougherty became president in 1996.

Other Disciples agencies sprang up during this period. Some of them had a direct impact on the work of CWBM, while others did not. Included were the Church Extension Committee (1883), The Board of Ministerial Relief (1895), National Convention of the (black) Church of Christ (1887), and the Board of Negro Education and Evangelization (1890). Two of these agencies dealt with concerns that CWBM was also addressing: evangelism and new congregations, and work among black congregations and individuals. In some cases, CWBM worked closely with the agencies, and in others it did not expand to continue its involvement.

The addition of these new enterprises to the cadre of boards of institutions vying for endorsement and financial support played a major role in the movement toward unification that was first suggested in the 1890s, encouraged by the Centennial Convention planning committee in 1909, demonstrated successfully by the Men and Millions Movement inaugurated in 1913, and culminated in the formation of The United Christian Missionary Society in 1919–1920.

UNIFICATION BEGINNINGS

When Thomas Campbell published his *Declaration and Address* in 1809, he had no idea that his document would so impact the religious thinking of his time, nor that it would merit a nine-day celebration of an entire community of faith. Such a celebration did take place, however, in Pittsburgh, Pennsylvania. Called the Centennial Convention because it was planned to coincide with the hundredth anniversary of the original publication date of the *Declaration and Address*, this assembly was like none other held among Disciples of Christ prior to that time or since.

Disciples of Christ congregations were well accustomed to an annual national meeting of four to six days in duration, during which all the recognized agencies of the church made reports, elected officers, and presented their work. Each succeeding assembly provided fellowship, addresses, and sermons from persons of prominence, mostly men, and challenges of evangelism and service to humanity. At the close of each convention, new officers would be installed and they would begin planning for the next annual meeting.

CWBM followed this plan each year after its organizational meeting in 1874, as did each new board or society as it came into being in successive years. Once the decision had been made to celebrate the anniversary of the *Declaration and Address*, a document that Disciples regarded as the mission statement of the movement, it became clear to the leaders of all the recognized societies that holding a mass assembly planned by representative leaders of each group would make a statement to the world of the Disciples' plea for the union of all Christians. A gathering of such monumental proportions would be the vehicle for reviewing the immense progress made by the religious world in general and the Disciples in particular in the areas of education, evangelism, missionary enterprises, and compassionate stewardship. Above all, it would be wrapped in the clarion call for individual spiritual growth, and highlighted around a mass celebration of the Lord's supper.

Enthusiasm mounted as local congregations became aware of the centennial plans and challenges. Individuals were asked to participate in daily devotions and personal evangelism, to tithe, and to make every home an anti-saloon domain. Likewise, congregations were urged to set goals for their Sunday schools, to cooperate more fully with state societies, and to work for Christian unity in their communities. Various boards and societies likewise were asked to set long-range goals and projects, some of which became joint efforts across agency boundaries. Planning for the 1909 celebration took on the character of cooperative planning, and the plea for union of all Christians began to manifest itself among the Disciples themselves.

Two books were published in 1909 dealing with the history of the movement. James H. Garrison prepared *The Story of a Century*, while William T. Moore produced *A Comprehensive History of the Disciples of Christ*, in which he wrote:

> It is probably certain that the Disciples will have, at least, to make the experiment of centralizing their forces much more than has been the case during their past history…They have reached an era where such centralization is absolutely necessary in order that they may achieve the triumphs that are awaiting them in the near future…Undoubtedly there is great danger in this very thing, but there is always danger where life is at its best.[24]

For CWBM, the planning of long-range goals and aims was not new. This had been a practice of CWBM administrators from its beginning. The brilliant leadership of Helen E. Moses, serving first as corresponding secretary (1899–1906), then as president (1906-1908), could be seen in the wide range of plans presented to the national convention in San Francisco in 1905. Mrs. Moses had gained renown as an organizer and fund-raiser during her Kansas days as state secretary for CWBM. She was called to the Indianapolis office to raise the endowment for the Bible Chair at Ann Arbor while serving also as editor of *Missionary Tidings* and as corresponding secretary. Helen Moses had battled serious health problems to become one of the ablest speakers among the Disciples national leadership and one of the visionaries who was able to share her vision with an audience in such inspiring terms that it would become their own. Mrs. Moses prepared the report containing CWBM's plans for celebrating one hundred years of work, but she was unable to make the long trip to San Francisco for the 1905 convention and someone else, likely her coworker Effie Cunningham, made the report for her.

"We recommend that our Centennial offering rally cry shall be one hundred thousand dollars…over and beyond the regular offerings which must apply to the support of our regular work," the report stated. This would be increased to $200,000 in 1907. It indicated amounts and locations for six buildings totaling $70,000. Four stations in the United States would receive the remaining $30,000. The report also states, "a doubled membership for our Auxiliaries, to be obtained by enlarged efforts or organizers, by increasing the number of field workers, by personal work of auxiliary members, and by appeals from pastors." The report was enthusiastically adopted without change and without a dissenting vote.

Not one to be idle very long, Mrs. Moses spent time with a friend in Kentucky during the San Francisco assembly. Ida W. Harrison, likely "the friend" in Kentucky, reported several years after the event that while the two were talking about the Centennial aims, the friend suggested that one of the greatest needs was a missionary training school, a venture that could well be added to the 1909 goals. In her words:

> Mrs. Moses had that sweet reasonableness that ever made her open to new suggestions, and this appealed to her so strongly, that soon after the return of the Executive Committee of the Board from the West, she recommended that a Missionary Training School should be added to the list of Centennial Missions…The response to it surpassed that to all the others.[25]

Helen Moses did not live to see the women's achievements that were celebrated at the Centennial Convention. She spent her last days completing plans for the new missionary training school, and signed the final contract for the erection of the proposed building two weeks prior to her death on May 11, 1908. Her careful consideration of every aspect of the building program included preserving the stately elm trees that were an impressive part of the building site. Edith Eberle (Yocum) characterized Helen Moses' service with CWBM as "years of crowning leadership, marked by shining vision, intellectual power, and spiritual depth."[26]

For four years a Centennial Campaign Committee, made up of fifteen men and one woman from the numerous agencies that reported to the General Convention, and a few representing the church at large, planned and promoted the Centennial aims. This was the first time in the hundred years of recorded history that all the organized units of the Disciples of Christ had come together to work for a common purpose. It created a sense of unanimity all across the church generally, and women especially resonated to this attitude of working together to achieve specific goals, for this had been their style for more than thirty years. They were ready to broaden their participation in the church's celebration of its past by facing the future on a new level of commitment. Helen Moses represented them on the committee until her death in 1908, when she was followed by Anna R. Atwater, who also succeeded her in the presidency of CWBM.

During the nine days of the 1909 convention, each major board or society was in charge of some portion of the program, with the larger units having responsibility for morning, afternoon, and evening sessions on a given day. Tuesday, October 12, was designated as CWBM Day. Because of the very large crowds that had come to Pittsburgh for the celebration, it was necessary that three parallel sessions be held in three different locations. Without benefit of modern-day sound technology, it was necessary to use presiders and speakers for each simultaneous session. The three presiders selected were CWBM President Anna R. Atwater, Vice President Ida W. Harrison, and Nancy E. Atkinson, who was a past president. She was prevented from being present by illness, and was replaced by Mrs. A. E. Jennings, state president of Michigan; Mrs. John Gay, state president of Kentucky; and Mrs. Maud D. Ferris, who had made an annuity gift of $25,000 in memory of her mother for the Missionary Training School mentioned earlier.

It is interesting to note that on the days the other two missionary societies were in charge of the full day, no other programs were offered, but on CWBM Day the men were not willing to turn one full day over to the women. In the afternoon, the men held a session of The Brotherhood of the Disciples of Christ, a new undertaking aimed at involving laymen in the programs of the church. Robert A. Long, a prominent business executive from Kansas City, Missouri, was the active agent who spearheaded the afternoon and evening sessions of the newly formed Brotherhood. This laymen's group did not last very long; however, it provided a basis for the organization of men's groups that was to come some thirty years later.

At the women's sessions, brief but glowing reports were made concerning their work, especially the Centennial achievements, all of which were over and above the ongoing yearly work. It was reported that 545 new auxiliaries and mission circles had been formed the previous year alone, and total membership had risen to 73,608. While the goal of doubled membership was not fully attained, the increase of some thirty thousand new members greatly strengthened the work and provided for a substantial increase in financial support, as indicated by the surpassing of the $200,000 goal by $130,766.21. Small wonder that the prevailing attitude among the women at Pittsburgh was a glorious mixture of enthusiasm and consecration. They celebrated the achievements of their past history, but they were ready and eager to take on the future.

The final act of the evening session on CWBM Day was the recognition of the states that had attained one or both of the Centennial aims: doubled membership and $200,000 in special funds. Bronze medals had been designed bearing the likeness of Thomas Campbell circled by "Centennial Convention, 1909" on one side and the CWBM seal on the other. Iowa was the only state that reached both goals. Thirty-one states received recognition for having reached one goal and making considerable progress on the second. Ida W. Harrison, Centennial Secretary for CWBM, was also given one of these prized pins in appreciation for her outstanding service during this special project.

In general, women of the Disciples of Christ had made significant inroads toward being recognized as a force for good within church-related structures, and their abilities and commitment were slowly but surely coming to the forefront by the time of the 1909 convention. Prior to this, there were very, very few women in leadership positions at the annual conventions, except for CWBM sessions, but this convention marked a turning point. Here women delivered fifteen major addresses, or about 9 percent of the total, a rather impressive change. This was due in part to greater participation in the planning committees, which in turn provided a venue for women's leadership to be demonstrated and appreciated. Readiness on the part of CWBM leadership to be involved in a larger measure with the aims and goals of the total church also added incentive.

AFTER THE CENTENNIAL

The days following the Pittsburgh celebration were filled with added workloads for all the national agencies of the church. The programs and work already in place needed continuing direction and resources; and the numerous new enterprises required new energies, new creativity, and new staff to bring to reality those lofty goals. Certainly this was true for CWBM. In responding to all that had taken place at the convention in 1909, the remarks of Mrs. Persis L. Christian in *Missionary Tidings* helped to sharpen the focus. She wrote:

> The most impressive things were not those which came to the surface...(it was) the intuitive realization, shall we not say through the enlightenment of the Holy Spirit, of the *mighty energy* of the women...There is no alternative for God's servant. She must *go* or *send*.

There were many who offered themselves for service at one of the rapidly expanding enterprises' locations, and funds received during the Centennial Campaign were earmarked for a "Centennial monument" in the form of a new or renovated building on each of the fields where CWBM was present. On the home front, the Board already had mountain schools in Hazel Green and Morehead, Kentucky, both of which were flourishing by 1910. Two other schools were assured by Centennial monies: one in Beckley, West Virginia, in 1908, and the other in Livingston, Tennessee, the following year. Management of the Beckley school rested largely with the local board of education, while CWBM took responsibility for the property. This work was discontinued after ten years because the community had become able to support its own program.

Livingston Academy in Tennessee built the largest student body of any of the mountain schools. Its program continued to flourish as it met a real need in the southern mountain region. Social and civic developments in transportation and educational methods made conditions much different from the earlier days of CWBM's mountain ministries. Poverty and illiteracy, while not yet eliminated, were less powerful, and the schools were able to reach more students and impact whole communities. Livingston Academy continued to serve under the auspices of CWBM and its successor organization, the United Christian Missionary Society, well into the 1940s.

Other homeland projects were to: (1) open another Negro school, (2) purchase property for the Chinese mission in Portland, Oregon, (3) undertake evangelistic work in Utah, and (4) erect a missionary training school and CWBM headquarters building in Indianapolis. Added to these were building projects in Jamaica, India, Mexico, Puerto Rico, and Argentina. Also planned was the opening of a new work in South China. All this work was begun as special funds came in, much of it before the Centennial Campaign. All, that is, except the proposals for South China. The spirit of cooperation which was mounting among the mission boards prompted the women to delay the opening of new work in South China while it pondered more deliberately the work of FCMS in Central China.

Finally, CWBM decided that a girls' school in Luchowfu would be its initial project, and land was purchased with Centennial funds for this purpose. In 1915 two missionaries, Wenona Wilkinson and Lillian Collins, were sent to have charge of the new school. Both were college graduates and had received special training at CWBM's College of Missions, as the missionary training school was now called. The Board joined FCMS in its other points of mission work in China, and together they were able to provide a superior type of education that held great attraction for the Chinese. Both organizations shared equally in ownership of the property and administration of these mission stations. This was yet another step toward the union of national boards, which culminated in the formation of The United Christian Missionary Society in 1919–1920.

Christian Woman's Board of Missions also entered into interdenominational higher education, with four other churches, to provide the first college for women in Central China. Located in Nanking, Ginling College was destined to become one of the most influential schools for higher learning among women in China, and it played a prominent role in supplying the leaders needed in the emerging women's movement. With the coming of new political leadership and the establishment of a republic of sorts under American-educated Dr. Sun Yat-sen, hopes ran high for the improvement of life for the Chinese. Sadly, such hopes were never fully realized because of the continual military uprisings and periodic interventions from provincial and foreign forces. It was in the midst of this unrest that Christianity lived out its finest service on the Chinese mainland.

Ginling College was an excellent example of how Christians could work together for a common cause while maintaining their denominational identity. The mission boards of Baptist, Disciples, Presbyterian, and two Methodist denominations shared proportionately in the ownership and administration of the institution. Many of them, like the Disciples, found a ready supply of students in their own elementary and secondary schools. The majority of students came from Christian homes, and many who came as non-Christians left, after the completion of their studies, as Christians. Once again, the Centennial Campaign provided a strong resource for the realization of this aim to "open a new work in China."

College of Missions Building
222 South Downey Avenue
Indianapolis, Indiana

THE COLLEGE OF MISSIONS

Of all the plans projected as aims and goals of the Centennial celebration, the one that proved to be the most popular and at the same time the most important was "the establishment of the Missionary Training School." As soon as Maria Jameson had led the first executive committee of CWBM to raise enough money to send its first missionaries to Jamaica, she knew that specific training was necessary to achieve the greatest good. She watched Dr. and Mrs. W. H. Williams depart from their brief interview and orientation one chilly January afternoon in 1876 to catch the train to New York City, where their boat would sail the next day, and she knew full well that more preparation for their momentous task was needed. From that day forward she forged the dream of a training school, and she made sure that succeeding committees and officers would keep that dream alive until its time for fulfillment came. Helen Moses inherited the dream, and Ida Withers Harrison shared it, along with the impetus to make it part of the Centennial.

To fully appreciate the appropriate timing of the school's beginning, it is helpful to look briefly at developments in the larger church as well as in the secular world. The development of the Sunday school movement during the 1870s and beyond found great support among most Protestant groups, including Disciples, and quickly gained popularity because of its nonsectarian character. This was true also of Christian Endeavor, a program designed for young people. Disciples readily incorporated it into congregations, and many youth groups that were reported as mission bands to CWBM leaders were, in truth, Christian Endeavor-based. By the turn of the twentieth century, a number of delegate-assemblies of Protestant sects began to suggest that denominations seek ways to form a federation that might provide a means of better cooperation in action projects and evangelism. All of these required leadership that was trained as well as willing, and church officials began to look for ways to provide effective training for their members.

The federation movement found its official beginning in 1908 when the Federal Council of the Church of Christ in America was born. Within a brief span of two years, the Foreign Missions Conference of North America and the Home Missions Conference had been created. The Ecumenical World Missionary Conference had been held in 1900 in New York City, challenging the mission boards of the evangelical churches to find ways by which they might more effectively evangelize the world. To do this demanded a larger group of well-trained missionaries.

Industry, education, and the refinement of social services and ethics were changing rapidly as railroads and highways and the promise of air flight emerged at the beginning of the new century. America was the hub of mass immigration as persons from Europe, Asia, and Latin America poured into the country looking for better jobs and relief from poverty and oppressive governments. The need for trained leaders to serve at home and abroad was felt by observers on every continent.

Against such a background in 1906, the campaign for the College of Missions was launched. The swiftness with which the campaign was completed and the great enthusiasm for the project, alluded to earlier, were but two of the many indications that CWBM leaders had chosen wisely and well to embark on an enterprise of such magnitude and service. In addition to the $25,000 gift from Mrs. Maud D. Ferris, given in memory of her mother, Sarah Davis Deterding, Disciples women of Indiana pledged a matching gift and actually raised more than twice the amount pledged. Enough money was in hand in 1907 to purchase property adjoining the Indianapolis campus of Butler University on Downey Avenue, and on August 29 of that year, ground was broken for the main building. Anna R. Atwater was elected CWBM president at the end of that year and was present the following August to lead the cornerstone-laying ceremony.

A justification of the necessity of establishing such an institution is given by Ida Withers Harrison in her second history, *The Christian Woman's Board of Missions, 1874–1919*:

> These changes [in the world] had created new problems for the church. The work of missions, while not deviating from its primary aim of evangelization, had necessarily become complex in its methods and differentiated in its phases and departments. The task of instructing, organizing and developing the indigenous churches on the foreign field, of reaching the vast unoccupied areas, of creating a Christian vernacular literature, of lifting primitive peoples to the place of Christian civilization, of instilling Christian ideals into new systems of education and new forms of national consciousness— in short of Christianizing the impact of the West upon the East, all of this was a call for a missionary leadership at once expert in its abilities and varied in its activities.

Missionaries already on the field added to the great hue and cry for specially trained workers, and as they came home on furlough, many of them spent time at the new College of Missions.

From its beginning, the college provided a broad-based curriculum built on the recommendations of the World Missionary Conference completed at Edinburgh in 1910, a scant three weeks before the first classes were begun in September of that year. Foreign service was featured, of course, but training unique to home missions workers was also provided. The college was a graduate school, incorporated under the laws of the state of Indiana, and operating under its own board of trustees. Although it was founded by a board of the Disciples of Christ, it was, in reality, nonsectarian in spirit. It was open to approved missionary candidates, returned missionaries and students of all boards and denominations, and enjoyed a diverse student body throughout its history. Dr. Charles T. Paul, a Canadian and former missionary in China, was the first president, leading in the design of the highly specialized graduate program and promoting the school's effectiveness among Disciples and in interchurch circles alike.

In founding the College of Missions, CWBM provided an outstanding service to the whole missionary cause. From its halls, a long line of missionaries, specially equipped in mind and heart for the challenging tasks of Christian leadership in the entire world, went forth to pursue their life's work. Conducting the college as a nonsectarian institution was a deliberate stance taken by CWBM because of its complete commitment to the ideal of unity among

The Ivy Chain Ceremony of the College of Missions "World Call," July 1925

God's people, and the willingness to let the college's purpose be melded into a larger goal came because of that very commitment to unity.

From its beginning, and continually for several years after it became a secondary part of the 1920 formation of The United Christian Missionary Society, the college was very intentional in helping its students to feel united in the bonds of their mutual preparation and calling. As each commencement exercise took place, all students participated in a ritual commonly referred to as "the Ivy Chain Ceremony," in which they formed a circle, enclosed by an ivy vine. The ceremony included a brief welcome to friends and families who surrounded this outdoor event, a class poem and prophecy, and the traditional Last Will and Testament. Then, in a more solemn moment, President Paul cut the ivy vine, symbolically severing those students who were graduating from those who would remain for additional studies. Momentarily, the sense of separation was very acute, for each student was left holding a branch of the vine that symbolized the friendships and common tasks that had bound them together in the College of Missions. As one plant, the ivy vine, had been uprooted, there was now to be another planting in a new place. The procession of graduates moved ahead to the east side of the building, and the ivy was replanted where previous annual plantings had also occurred. As long as the College remained in Indianapolis, this ceremony was a very meaningful part of every commencement. It was frequently referred to in letters from the missionaries on the field as a constant reminder of their sense of unity with other Christians.

The College of Missions' enrollment grew every year until the early twenties, when developing world events made a major impact on the College and its future. First, the drift of graduate students toward larger university centers and the cost of carrying on overseas missionary work greatly increased during the post-World War I years, while contributions from congregations and individuals leveled off for several years in a row. At the same time, the college prepared additional workers and the new United Society sent them to replace retiring missionaries and, in some cases, to open new work. Another factor was the changing emphasis in locations where missionaries were now becoming associate workers *with* the native people instead of *for* them, and more and more mission stations were becoming self-directing and self-supporting. The trend was toward more and better-trained native leaders and stronger and better-equipped stations. Finally, China's government began forcing Americans out of its country, thus making available a sizable group of skilled and committed persons who could be assigned elsewhere.

In short, the move of qualified students toward larger graduate centers and the need for additional trained workers was so greatly reduced by 1926 that the board of trustees of the college took action to suspend its teaching function for the 1927–28 year. At the same time, the United Society was preparing a survey of the entire missionary enterprise and determining the number of candidates needed and the type of training required.

Those students in preparation for missionary service were transferred to the Kennedy School of Missions, Hartford, Connecticut. This proved to be a satisfactory arrangement, so the teaching functions of the College of Missions were more or less permanently affiliated with the Hartford school. The college maintained its legal identity and granted degrees for many years afterward. In 1956 the school's program of training missionaries of the Disciples of Christ was reactivated, and plans were developed for a summer session made possible by the gift of a spacious cottage at Crystal Beach Christian Assembly near Frankfort, Michigan. Today the functions of the college are administered by Global Ministries of the Christian Church (Disciples of Christ) and the United Church of Christ.

Sacred Traditions

Leaders of CWBM knew well the value of observing certain traditions that helped to establish and nurture bonds of friendship among like-minded Christians. From the beginning days of organized work, they observed the Hour of Prayer each Sunday afternoon beginning at five o'clock. At first the meetings were primarily a gathering of women to pray for the mission work being undertaken by the new board. It slowly evolved into a full hour in length and included hymns, scripture readings, and brief talks designed to inspire and encourage. Suggestions for the Hour of Prayer meetings were included in every issue of *Missionary Tidings* over its life of thirty-five years. This weekly event was recommended as an observance of the entire church during the General Convention of 1887, and afterward it had special prominence at national meetings, as well as in many localities in the United States, and at all CWBM mission stations abroad.

Another tradition of long standing had its roots in the early days of CWBM; namely, that of designating one Sunday in the year to be set aside as National CWBM Day. This practice began on July 6, 1890, the first Sunday in July, and gradually evolved to Woman's Missionary Day, then Woman's Day, and in recent years to Laity Sunday. The purpose was to impart information concerning the work of CWBM and to inspire churches to take more seriously their responsibilities for undergirding the mission work of the Disciples of Christ. The observance was changed to the first Sunday in December by CWBM at its twenty-fifth annual assembly in 1899. Years later, when the Woman's Board merged its work into The United Christian Missionary Society, the name of this special day was changed to Woman's Missionary Day, then almost immediately shortened to Woman's Day. With the emphasis on the laity movement in the 1960s, there came an agreement that Woman's Day be renamed Laity Sunday and that women and men might share the mission emphasis. However, the participation of women and men in total church life became the focus in most congregations. Program suggestions are available annually from Homeland Ministries in Indianapolis. The *1994 Year Book & Directory of the Christian Church (Disciples of Christ)* reported that "several hundred" of these packets were made available to congregations.

A third tradition, and one that has not undergone major changes since its inception, is the benediction used at meetings of women's groups since 1906. At that time, a member of the national CWBM executive committee, Helen L. Dungan, suggested that the opening verses of Psalm 67 be adopted as the official benediction of CWBM. With the addition of the last line, it was unanimously chosen:

> God, be merciful unto us and bless us;
> and cause your face to shine upon us;
> that your way may be known upon the earth,
> your saving health among all nations.
> Through Jesus Christ, our Lord. Amen.

For a brief time, the colors of lavender and silver were specified as "CWBM official colors." Reference is made to the use of these in announcing the publication of Ida Withers Harrison's book *The Christian Woman's Board of Missions, 1874–1919*, the cover featuring a lavender background and silver lettering. How official these were is debatable, for no record of action taken concerning this has been located by this writer.

Pins were an important item, and were worn proudly by the members of the auxiliaries of CWBM. The early pins featured a circular disk bearing on the outer margin the words "Christian Woman's

Board of Missions Seal" and in the center a representation of an open Bible. These pins were fashioned of solid gold or sterling silver. The June 1917 *Missionary Tidings* listed gold pins for two dollars and silver pins for fifty cents. When The United Christian Missionary Society was formed, the desire for a membership pin was still strong, so a pin was designed that duplicated the official logo of the Society, featuring a round model of the earth upon which lay an open Bible supported by the upper portion of the cross of Christ. Years later, this outline was simplified for the design of the emblem for the newly organized Christian Women's Fellowship, with the initials CWF encircled on a green field superimposed against a white cross. This pin was widely circulated soon after the official start of CWF on July 1, 1950. In recent years, however, its cost has increased and Fellowships more often give it as a token of appreciation for services rendered by retiring presidents than encourage its use by the membership in general.

As a means of developing the habit of systematic giving among the women, one of the first projects of CWBM involved the use of containers for special offerings and sacrificial giving. The earliest available records make reference to a Mite Box for use during Easter Week of Prayer and Self-denial. Later this term was changed to Thank Offering Box, and women were urged to spend the week in prayer and self-denial so that on Easter Sunday they would be rightfully prepared to bring offerings in response to their heightened awareness of Jesus' sacrifice on the cross and their thankfulness for his manifold gifts to them. The women continued this annual observance, as did their children's and youth auxiliaries, well into the twentieth century. The offerings were designated for the General Fund of CWBM until a few years prior to 1920, when a portion, if not all, of this special Easter offering was designated for the National Benevolent Association.

The requirement of membership dues is hardly ever practiced in church women's organizations at the present time, but this has not always been true for Disciples women. The very first Constitution of CWBM, adopted October 22, 1874, stated that "any woman may become a member of this Board, who contributes one dollar a year to its funds, or is a member of an Auxiliary Society. Anyone may become a life member by the contribution of twenty-five dollars in two years." In 1890, these requirements were raised to five dollars and twenty-five dollars annually. Meanwhile, Auxiliary Societies (state and local groups) stipulated that one must contribute "monthly a definite sum, not less than ten cents," for the missionary work of the states and the general offices in Indianapolis. Richard L. Harrison, Disciples historian and president of Lexington Theological Seminary, writes:

> Within ten years of its organization, the CWBM put more missionaries in place, in the United States and abroad, than the male-dominated ACMS (American Christian Missionary Society) had done in its entire history. The secret of the CWBM was the organization of state and congregational units to which the members showed great loyalty and financial commitment.[27]

These early traditions of the women's movement played a vital, though simple, role in its success. Records indicate that the early leaders found strength in setting lofty goals, some of which seemed impossible to attain, but often were surpassed. A casual study of the traditions and their effect indicates that for the time during which they were followed, they provided ties that bound members together in a sisterhood that was mutually beneficial and accomplished much for the mission set before them.

SPANNING BORDERS AND CULTURES

Transportation advances in the early years of the twentieth century helped greatly in the establishment of new congregations of the Disciples of Christ, especially in the eastern provinces of Canada. There had been members of the Campbell-Stone movement in that area for many years, possible dating to the 1830s, though not in significant numbers. Disciples congregations in Canada often evolved from established groups of Scottish Baptists and Scottish Presbyterians that had come under the influence of Campbell-Stone itinerant preachers. Especially was this true in the provinces of Ontario and Prince Edward Island. Prominent leaders from the United States made personal visits to some of the strong points of the Canadian Disciples church throughout the years prior to the first annual Convention of the Cooperation of Disciples of Christ in Ontario, held in 1887. In that same year, the Ontario Christian Woman's Board of Missions came into being, and Canadian Disciples rapidly made great strides in foreign missions work, particularly in the recruitment of missionaries.

Ontario alone produced the majority of the thirty-six Canadian women and men who went on to provide outstanding leadership to the missions movement. Among them was Dr. Susie Rijnhart-Moyes, the first Canadian woman to earn first-class honors in medicine, who served as a medical missionary in Tibet. Others included Jessie Mary Trout, a missionary to Japan before joining The United Christian Missionary Society staff and leading in the development of Christian Women's Fellowship; Mary Lediard Doan, also a missionary to Japan before serving as vice president of the United Christian Missionary Society from 1940 through 1949. Alice Porter is one of the more recent Canadian missionaries to serve under the United Christian Missionary Society, going to India as a nurse-educator and displaying her Christian depth and commitment through generous gifts to several areas of ministries of the Christian Church (Disciples of Christ). Prominent among evangelists and preachers in Canadian churches was Princess Clark Long, born in Van Wert, Ontario, in 1862, and married to Edward Clarence Long in 1887. Princess Long was often featured as a soloist for state assemblies and other large gatherings of Disciples, including the Pittsburgh Centennial Convention.

Mrs. R. V. Romig provided leadership in organizing the Western Canadian Board in 1908 after having visited all the churches and women's groups in western Canada over a period of eight years. Meanwhile in the East, the women's groups in Nova Scotia and New Brunswick joined in forming the Maritime CWBM. Fourteen years later, an all-Canada convention was held in Ontario to launch a new program to be known as the All-Canada Movement. Women were heavily involved in this new venture, which set its headquarters in Toronto. Mrs. Romig was sent on loan by the United Christian Missionary Society to be the field secretary for women's work for a brief time, and was followed by Marion Royce, who served until the National Women's Committee was formed in 1927.

The first woman elected chair of the All-Canada Committee was Mrs. George H. Stewart, whose husband had been one of the early leaders of the movement. In 1949 she was the first woman to hold such a position in any denomination or church group in Canada. While she was in office, the National Women's Committee became the Christian Women's Fellowship of Canada. Mrs. V. E. Lemon was elected president, and during her term about 80 percent of the Canadian women's groups adopted the CWF program and constitution.

CWBM had become international in 1913, with the cooperating provinces of Canada and the organized states of the United States serving equally following changes made in CWBM's constitution. A new spirit of cooperation was fostered by this action, a spirit that carried over in the formation of the International Christian Women's Fellowship in 1953, and a spirit that continues today.

The impact of African American women on the missionary efforts fostered by CWBM is seen throughout the history of black Disciples. It is shown in the development of many facilities that housed home mission programs and services, from child care to higher education, and from health clinics to places of worship. Brief sketches of several individuals will help describe both the nature and the scope of work done by black leaders. Sarah Lue Bostick's name is

Sarah Lue Bostick, National President and Organizer, Negro Christian Woman's Board of Missions

quickly on the lips of those who know black women's history among the Disciples, for she, more than any other, gave outstanding leadership, both organizational and spiritual, for more than forty years.

Born May 27, 1868, near Glasgow, Kentucky, Sarah Lue Howard was one of ten children, largely self-educated and fiercely independent. She moved to Arkansas in 1888, where she met and married Mancil Bostick, an ordained minister who also practiced medicine. This dual career enabled him to generously support struggling black pastors and small congregations, and also to provide extensively for Sarah's travels on behalf of women's work in Arkansas and surrounding states. Sarah Bostick helped organize the first CWBM auxiliary at Pea Ridge, Arkansas, in 1896. For three years this was the only women's society reporting to the state convention. In 1899 she organized two more, and the next year three more. She was appointed state organizer among the black congregations in Arkansas in 1902.

Mrs. Bostick's great vision for educational opportunities for her race led her to accept the invitation from Bertha Mason, CWBM field worker in Texas, to spend some time there among the black congregations, organizing missionary societies for the women and promoting the much-talked-of school for black young people in east Texas. Debra Hull's book, *Christian Church Women*, gives a detailed accounting of Bertha Mason's involvement in raising money for a college for black students, and of her invitation in 1904 to Sarah Lue Bostick to assist. Mrs. Bostick was national president of the Negro Christian Woman's Board of Missions, and her presence in Texas, to coordinate the efforts of both boards, helped greatly in realizing their mutual goal.

An article appeared in the September 1925 *World Call* that helps to better explain how the working together of both races achieved far more than could be done by either group alone. Under the sub-heading,"What Has Been Accomplished," it reads:

> The first thing to be noted is the handsome way in which the southern churches have lined up for the work. More prayerful thought is given to it than to any other missionary work. The workers have been given a dignified place in their work, contributions have been generously made, as for instance the $25,000 raised by the Texas white women for Jarvis, and a deep interest has been shown in the welfare of young Negro graduates.
>
> The Negro Disciples are finding themselves in all this in a gratifying way. They were so completely and so long segregated in the social and political realms of our land that they had come to the place where ambitious leaders among them were making the effort of segregating themselves a slogan, which was seen by those who studied the situation to be a most dangerous menace to religious ideals throughout the world. For unless the American people can demonstrate their ability to work together in the ideals of Christianity, our foreign missionary efforts must all end in disaster. Consequently it is a gratifying achievement that the Negro Disciples of Christ have been willing to patiently overlook any discriminations for the larger things that were coming farther on.
>
> We wish to mention here what we feel was one of those providentially fortunate things. In 1900 the work fell into the hands of the Christian Woman's Board of Missions and remained there until the forming of the United Christian Missionary Society. The women of the land could lay a foundation such as men could never have laid. Those who have heard Mrs. Ida W. Harrison and Mrs. Ida C. Jarvis tell of the devotion of the southern woman to the welfare of the slaves in the ante-bellum days, can readily see how fortunate it was that the southern white women were among the architects of this work.[28]

Bertha Mason received a promise in 1903 of several hundred acres of land from Ida Jarvis if the women of Texas would assume responsibility for raising the necessary funds to establish a school for blacks. It was at this point that Sarah Lue Bostick agreed to help, and during the next ten years these two women were deeply engrossed in efforts to convince women of the necessity of establishing such a school. Jarvis Christian Institute, as it was initially known, was officially established in 1911 and opened in January 1913. Bertha Mason Fuller (she had married J. J. Fuller in 1907) and Sarah Lue Bostick continued to work in the interest of black students at Jarvis for the rest of their active ministries though both moved away to Arkansas, where Bertha Mason Fuller was involved in pastoral ministry while serving as secretary for the Woman's Missionary Board from 1922 to 1942. Mrs. Bostick died in Arkansas in 1948, some ten years before Mrs. Fuller.

It is interesting to note that Jarvis Christian College is the only missionary institution established by CWBM for the training of African Americans that is still in existence. In 1991, President Sebetha Jenkins, the first female executive, was elected to administer Jarvis' program for a student body that continues to increase.

Mentioned earlier as a training school provided by CWBM long before its involvement with Jarvis, Southern Christian Institute (SCI) helped shape the lives of many African American women who became leaders in the Christian Church during the first half of the twentieth century. Three who were at SCI during the same period were Deetsy Blackburn (Gray), Rosa Brown (Bracy), and Rosa Page (Welch). Each was an outstanding student while on the Edwards, Mississippi, campus, and each distinguished herself in her chosen vocation afterward. Deetsy Blackburn's work among elementary students led to her selection as the first African American children's worker within the National Christian Missionary Convention, an organization called for and controlled by more than 600 black Disciples congregations in 1917.

Rosa Brown was twelve years old when she entered SCI, leaving her home in Port Gibson, Mississippi, where her father pastored the black congregation. Following her school years and graduation, she taught school for a brief period before being named the first Field Secretary for Negro Work by CWBM in 1917. She continued with the new organization, The United Christian Missionary Society, in 1920 in her dual role as a staff member of both UCMS and the National Christian Missionary Convention (NCMC). After her marriage, Mrs. Bracy continued to organize women's groups and to promote the missions enterprises of CWBM and UCMS until she retired in 1938. She continued her efforts for the Disciples of Christ until the time of her death, The November 1960 issue of July 17, 1960. *World Call* magazine, indicates she was president of the NCMC Christian Women's Fellowship at the time of her death.

In *Rosa's Song*, author Oma Lou Myers described Rosa Page Welch:

> The experiences, hardships, and mistreatment of her grand-parents during and following a devastating Civil War left their mark on her life. Her childhood memories lingered and enriched her character. It was during those years that a deep Christian faith was formed as she grew up in Port Gibson, Mississippi, under the influence of a deeply devoted Christian mother and under constant involvement in the life of the church. Rosa Page has been one of those persistent American Negroes who, in spite of many obstacles, grasped every opportunity to become and achieve what she believed to be God's will and purpose for her life.[29]

Born in 1900, Rosa Page grew up knowing Rosa Brown as a slightly older friend who opened many doors of opportunity for her to use her musical ability, and especially her singing, to the glory of God. It was Rosa Brown who presented Rosa Page's name for enrollment at SCI in the summer of 1917, making it possible for the young music student to meet and work with white teachers for the first time. Rosa Page had a long and distinguished life as an "ambassador of goodwill," traveling across the length and breadth of America and into many other countries as she spoke and sang her way into the hearts of those who heard her. Oma Lou Myers wrote, "She did more for bettering race relations and understanding than almost anyone I have known."

In recognition of her many contributions as an ecumenical witness, the Disciples Council on Christian Unity established a lectureship in her name that enables the International Christian Women's Fellowship to invite a world-renowned ecumenical leader to make a major address at the ICWF Quadrennial Assembly. Although Rosa Page Welch is no longer alive, her Christian witness continues to impact the lives of countless thousands throughout the world.

The story of Hispanic women in the Christian Church is one that has depended more on oral tradition than on the written word for its telling. One must read between the lines of records to discern the many ways that Spanish-speaking women have served the church.

Disciples historian Debra Hull states that there were relatively few Hispanic people in the United States before the twentieth century, and this may help explain the scarcity of Hispanic women's names in the early annals of the women's Christian movement.

CWBM was the first of the national Disciples boards to reach out to people of Spanish, Mexican, and Puerto Rican descent. At the turn of the century CWBM had established work in Mexico, Puerto Rico, and Argentina. Home missions stations serving the Hispanic community were begun in several locations along the Texas-Mexico border, but the one most notable and still in full operation at this writing is the Inman Christian Center in San Antonio, formerly known as Mexican Christian Institute. This center has evolved into a full-service social, educational, health and housing center, where medical and dental services are also provided for low-income families.

Leaders of CWBM saw fit to expand its witness to other areas of the United States where there were large Hispanic communities. In 1913 the Kansas City Mexican Mission was started in the back room of a grocery store, largely through the efforts of women in that area. In each case, local people, men and women, worked alongside the American leaders in equal or greater numbers. Most significantly, it was following the creation of Christian Women's Fellowship and its international and world organizations that discovering and preserving the stories of Spanish-speaking church women became a high priority. When *Christian Women Share Their Faith* was published in 1986 by the Department of Church Women in Indianapolis, it featured the first-person accounts of numerous modern-day women, including those of Latin American, African American, Asian American, and Native American heritage.

CHRISTIAN WOMAN'S BOARD OF MISSIONS AND MEN AND MILLIONS

The year was 1912. Woodrow Wilson had just been elected President of the United States, and New Mexico and Arizona became the forty-seventh and forty-eighth states. Congress was talking about a Constitutional amendment which, if ratified, would impose an income tax on all citizens. The ocean liner *Titanic*, on its maiden voyage, hit an iceberg, and more than 1,500 lives were lost. The world seemed to shrink a bit as people became more aware, and more quickly, of events happening around the world.

It was during this eventful year that the Foreign Christian Missionary Society, under the highly respected leadership of its president, Archibald McLean, decided to raise one million dollars to expand its overseas missionary enterprise. Before the program was launched, however, leaders of the other two missionary boards, CWBM and ACMS, along with the National Benevolent Association, the Board of Church Extension, and the Board of Ministerial Relief, decided to join in what developed into a major comprehensive stewardship project. The goal was more than doubled, and the newly reformed Board of Education, composed of Disciples colleges and universities, voted to participate. Robert A. Long, a wealthy Disciples layman from Kansas City, offered to give one million dollars provided that the Men and Millions Movement, the project's new title, would raise an additional $5,300,000. The campaign was launched officially in 1913, and was scheduled to be concluded in five years. Actually, it covered a decade, for World War I, the merger of the above-named boards in 1919–1920, and the overwhelming need to replace aging buildings and equipment in all the mission enterprises around the world caused the planners to extend the program and develop it so that the total church would benefit.

What had started as a financial drive for overseas mission stations blossomed into a united campaign to recruit 1,000 volunteers for missionary careers, to establish a systematic budget support plan in every congregation, and to secure $6,300,000 from individuals to adequately equip every home and overseas mission station and substantially increase the endowment of Disciples educational and benevolent institutions. By early 1919, more than eight million dollars had been given, and more than eight thousand Life Commitment cards had been signed. CWBM had been intimately involved in the Men and Millions Movement from its beginning and received $600,000 as its budgeted share. The president of CWBM, Anna R. Atwater, served on the planning committee throughout its tenure. In seeking a more equitable financial basis for the total work of the church beyond the congregation, this united churchwide campaign illustrated again that the various agencies of the Disciples of Christ could be very effective in their cooperative strategies. Once more a call for unifying the missionary and benevolent agencies of the church was heard throughout the church, only this time the call was stronger and the hearers more attentive.

A conversation between Anna Atwater and Archibald McLean in September 1912 reflected the pressure being brought to bear on the CWBM officers. Mrs. Atwater wrote:

> Mr. McLean was in my office in Indianapolis. We had a very
> long talk about the work of our societies and the relationships

between them. He remarked that our societies ought to be one. I replied that it was impossible because the Christian Woman's Board of Missions had been born independent and through the years our organization had been self-determining, and that we could not become auxiliary to another board and be directed by it. With characteristic brevity and promptness he said, "You ought not be. You do not need to be. We must have a society with equal representation of men and women in its conduct and management."[30]

This was but one of many conversations that took place regarding the matter of unification. As the Men and Millions Movement began to see successful results of its unified approach, all the societies and other boards began to talk more favorably of unifying. The nature of their work—missions, evangelism, and education—brought the three missions boards together frequently. Of these three, CWBM was the strongest in terms of assets and programs and, unlike the others, had a strong network of state workers and local auxiliaries. It was of vital importance that CWBM not lose the effectiveness of its multifaceted work or the control its administrative officers held over its accumulation of almost forty-five years of enviable and highly productive work. Mrs. Atwater was convinced that unification of the three boards would work only if women and men shared equally in the planning and administration.

A proposal to publish one magazine instead of the numerous papers and journals that each of the agencies had produced over the years came to the forefront once again as conversations continued to highlight the urgency of cooperation and unity. The Men and Millions Movement agreed to assume the sponsorship of such a publication, and the first issue of *World Call* was produced in January 1919. The editorial committee of CWBM, which had published *Missionary Tidings* since 1883, was opposed to the merger at first because of the impact of its magazine on the women's groups in congregations, and because its readership of 60,000 subscribers was the largest among the journals of the unifying boards. Their reluctance was lessened, however, when the concept of equal planning and administration was assured. The name for the new magazine was suggested by Daisy June Trout, a member of the CWBM executive group, who became the first circulation manager for the new publication. Mrs. Effie Cunningham moved from a CWBM position as editor of *Missionary Tidings* to become the first associate editor.

Over its fifty-plus years of publication, *World Call* had only one woman editor, Bess White Cochran, whose tenure ran from 1929 to 1932. The concept of equality was never realized fully.

FORMATION OF A DREAM: UNITED CHRISTIAN MISSIONARY SOCIETY

In her book *The Shape of Adam's Rib*, Lorraine Lollis suggests three great chronological themes that reveal the awesome story of women in the Christian Church (Disciples of Christ). They are (1) the worldwide missionary enterprise; (2) the plea for Christian unity, including sexual and cultural barriers and agencies of the denomination; (3) the search for woman's place in church and society.[31] For well over seventy-five years, their passion for missions held top priority. Seeds were planted from the earliest days of organized work toward the fulfillment of themes two and three, of course, but the all-consuming thrust of Disciples women was mandated by the great commission. Christian Woman's Board of Missions existed for twenty-five years before it came to be regarded by the male leaders of the church as a worthy partner in efforts toward unity within the general or national structures of the Disciples of Christ, and even then there were those who opposed.

By the time the 1918 International Convention was scheduled to meet in St. Louis, it had been well demonstrated and documented that women not only could but should be included in the planning and implementation of unifying the three major national societies of the church. Almost ten years earlier, after a successful Centennial Convention in 1909, officers of CWBM were credited with having played a major role in making it a high point in Disciples history. As a result, a Committee on Cooperation and Unification was formed; its purpose was to explore ways by which the mission boards might better coordinate their work to avoid overlapping and duplication. Over the next eight or nine years, this committee was enlarged and its purpose adjusted to include additional concerns such as calendarizing special days and promotional drives.

CWBM officials had been careful to avoid opening work where one of the other missions boards had already established a station, but on several occasions they accepted invitations to jointly open a new venture. India, China, Japan, and Latin America are glowing examples of cooperative work and shared personnel between CWBM and FCMS. Similar examples of cooperation with ACMS are to be found in work among ethnic groups, new church establishment, and evangelism projects in the United States.

Under the visionary leadership of Anna Atwater, CWBM planners moved steadfastly toward the culmination of the Unification Committee's projected goal of creating one umbrella agency that would streamline administration, coordinate program planning and implementation, and make better use of personnel. At the same time, such an organization would remove the sin of competition among the variety of agencies and would take advantage of the increasing use of annual budgeting by congregations, a practice introduced during the Men and Millions Movement.

In addition to Mrs. Atwater, CWBM representatives on the committee included Effie Cunningham, Ellie Payne, Josephine Stearns, and Daisy June Trout. They were well aware that of all the boards and societies planning for the united effort, CWBM had the most to lose, and they intended to proceed with all due caution even as they worked willingly to achieve the unity of the church, as this major step was designed to do. Mrs. Atwater trusted the process outlined to provide equal standing and authority of men and women, but not all of her staff were as willing as she was. On one occasion, one of the women took her to task for favoring the new agency. "Don't you see that you are sawing off the very limb on which you are standing?" After pacing the floor several minutes, she continued, "I believe you want to be the *last* president of the Christian Woman's Board of Missions!" Mrs. Atwater's smiling response was, "Yes, that is just it!"[32] She continued to believe the "work of such inclusive nature for men and women and children in our own land and throughout the world could be better planned and administered by men and women working together."[33]

Anna Robison Atwater had come, like Queen Esther of Old Testament stories, "to the kingdom for such a time as this." Sometimes called "Queen Ann" by her associates because of her regal demeanor, she also knew what hard, physical work was about. Orphaned along with her two brothers and two sisters, at age twelve, Anna Robison and her siblings chose to stay on the family farm in Ohio where they carried out most of their parents' plans and traditions. They all went to Hiram College, from which four of the five graduated. Anna taught school, married a minister in 1892, who died in 1900, and became vice president of CWBM in 1904 and president in 1908.

The next eighteen years were highlighted with events of major significance for Disciples of Christ, in each of which could be seen the unmistakable leadership of Anna Atwater: the Centennial Convention, the building of the College of Missions, the Men and Millions

Movement, the formation of the United Society, and the Golden Jubilee, which celebrated fifty years of organized work by and for
women in the church. Following her retirement in 1926, Anna
Atwater was lauded for her devotion to her work and the special
care she gave to colleagues and staff. Her poise and faculty of remaining unruffled in the most bothersome circumstances won the
admiration of countless persons who benefited from her compassion. The trust with which she led CWBM into the formation of The
United Christian Missionary Society in 1919–1920 grew out of her
firm conviction that the church must be unified in its mission, "that
they all may be one,"[34] and her vision of a united society spreading
the gospel to every part of the world was the motivation that sparked
her actions during the years of its formation. Unfortunately, the
promise of shared leadership did not materialize as CWBM officials
expected. No woman was elected to the presidency during the fifty
years of the United Society's active service. It was not until the election of a woman to be president of one of the two divisions of the
holding company, which UCMS had become in 1971, that the promise that "offices would be equally distributed between men and
women" was finally realized.

It is interesting to note that the 1918 St. Louis International
Convention, scheduled for October, was canceled at the very last
possible moment. Many delegates were already in St. Louis for
meetings prior to the convention. *Missionary Tidings* described it thus:

> The CWBM International Board would meet on the 8th in a
> closed session, to consider for adoption the Articles of
> Agreement. Joint sessions of CWBM and FCMS were planned
> for the 10th, with Mrs. Atwater and Mr. McLean alternately
> presiding. Similar joint sessions of CWBM, ACMS, and the
> Board of Church Extension were scheduled for all day on
> the 11th, with F. W. Burnham and Mrs. Atwater alternating
> the chair.
>
> The International Woman's Board met as planned with
> thirty-eight officers and eight members of the Executive
> Committee representing twenty-six states and western
> Canada. Mrs. Atwater asked Mrs. Cunningham, editor of
> *Missionary Tidings*, to read the Articles of Agreement, which
> were considered and adopted *ad seriatim*, including the
> following provisions: the name of the new organization
> would be United Christian Missionary Society; equal
> numbers of men and women would make up the Board of
> Managers and the Executive Committee; men and women

would both be eligible to any office of the United Society, and insofar as possible, offices would be equally distributed between men and women.

This historic business was scarcely finished when an unexpected announcement was made. Owing to the prevalence of influenza in St. Louis, all public meetings were ordered discontinued, the holding of the convention and all meetings pertaining thereto forbidden by the City authorities.[35]

Once again the women found themselves ahead of the male leaders of the other organizations, which were slated to consider the Articles of Agreement in their now canceled pre-convention sessions. The next International Convention was held in Cincinnati in October 1919, exactly forty-five years after CWBM's formation in the same city. Once again the women gave compelling leadership to the birthing of a new organization, and in so doing demonstrated their willingness to assume a lesser role of leadership and administration of the impressive mission work they had established and directed for almost half a century.

One observer, who had been present at the 1874 convention when CWBM was created, noted that the day in October 1919 when the United Society was approved was a momentous time, but not a happy one. The vote had carried only after much dissension and argument. Women gave up the autonomy they had enjoyed, though Russell Errett, editor of the *Christian Standard* and son of CWBM's staunch supporter Isaac Errett, charged that UCMS would surely be dominated by women. After all, CWBM was bringing assets in excess of 1.4 million dollars, amounting to 53 percent of the total assets of the new Society, plus a well-defined network of twenty-six states and more than 4,100 local auxiliary organizations, a mailing list of 60,000 subscribers of its magazines, and mission stations on four continents. In addition, they owned and managed the College of Missions, the first graduate-level training school for missionary personnel in the United States. Mr. Errett's charges were ill-founded, as history revealed. Conservatives generally felt that such a threat would further weaken the Disciples position on scriptural reform, and they vehemently opposed having women take positions of leadership ahead of or over men. Had it not been for the very persuasive and steady leadership of Anna Atwater during these days of attack and controversy, the Disciples of Christ might not have been acclaimed to be the first of the great communions to grant its women such generous representation.

Early Leaders

Mrs. Caroline Neville Pearre,
founder of Christian
Woman's Board
of Missions

Mrs. Maria Jameson,
1874–1880

CWBM
PRESIDENTS

Mrs. O. A. Burgess,
1880–1881

Mrs. Anna R. Atwater,
1908–1920

Mrs. Nancy E. Atkinson,
1902–1906

Mrs. Helen E. Moses,
1906–1908

THE *Unifying* Years
1920–1949

BEGINNING IN ST. LOUIS

The United Christian Missionary Society (UCMS) began its new life on June 22, 1920. By mandate of the 1919 International Convention action, the headquarters would be located in St. Louis, though most of the units involved in the new agency were located east of the Mississippi River, in Ohio and Indiana. Staff members and their families were involved that summer in packing and moving, locating schools for their children and adjusting to a new mailing address for their offices at the Missouri State Life Building at Fifteenth and Locust. Twenty-two months later, larger offices were occupied at 425 DeBaliviere Avenue. In 1928, the convention voted to move the headquarters to Indianapolis, to occupy the College of Missions building when that institution moved to Hartford, Connecticut. A study of the terms of the bequest under which construction funds were given indicated this building must be used for missionary purposes or revert to the estate of the donor, according to historian Lester G. McAllister, Jr.[1] The well-known address, 222 South Downey Avenue, was the location of UCMS and its restructured offices for the next sixty-seven years.

Independent and often competitive operation of the missionary societies and other national boards was essentially eliminated when the United Society was created by the 1919 convention. It included the following enterprises: American Christian Missionary Society, Board of Church Extension of the ACMS, Board of Ministerial Relief of the Church of Christ, Christian Woman's Board of Missions, Foreign Christian Missionary Society, National Benevolent Association.

"The high spirit of cooperation engendered in the nation by World War I may have aided this action," according to Disciples historian Alfred T. DeGroot.[2] Certainly a mood of optimism swept over the congregations that had long encouraged unification of the national boards. Many Disciples members saw this merger as a positive step toward achieving the unity that had long been regarded as the "polar star" of this Protestant movement. Excitement was mounting, to be sure, but beneath the optimistic aura lay obstacles that would delay ultimate success, if not prevent it altogether.

Not everyone among the Disciples of Christ congregations was thrilled about the formation of yet another organization on the national level. There remained harsh opposition among the more conservative leaders, especially those at the Standard Publishing Company in Cincinnati, who continued their outrage for almost a quarter of a century more. While those in opposition were a minority, they were, nevertheless, a very loud and insistent opposition.

The depression years following World War I—a decade before the Great Depression of the early 1930s—also made an impact on the new United Society before it could establish itself firmly among the congregations. Because of its historic stance as a free church, locally autonomous and free to choose the agencies it would "cooperate" with beyond its own doors, the Disciples of Christ still did not have complete unification with the coming of the United Society. Another fifty years would pass before such restructure would occur.

The original structure of the United Society included divisions for administration, promotion, education and service. Other boards, such as ACMS, found that their work would readily fit into such an organizational pattern, but such was not the case for CWBM. The promotional division included a department of auxiliary organizations, and much of the work of CWBM was moved into this office. However, there were at least two other pieces of CWBM's work to be located somewhere else in the Society structure. Overseas mission work was combined in the Division of Foreign Missions, with Archibald McLean as chairman for the first few months of its life, followed by Anna R. Atwater, who directed this work until her retirement in 1926.

Home missions projects of CWBM were turned over to the Division of Home Missions, under the leadership, from time to time, of Effie L. Cunningham and Daisy June Trout, among others. But there was a highly significant aspect of CWBM's makeup that was more difficult to place; namely, the strong network of local and state auxiliaries and their unique educational and organizational requirements.

After a brief trial period in the Development Department, it was felt that the Department of Auxiliary Organizations would be the logical locale for the women's groups. This was tried, but it soon became apparent again that some requirements were not being adequately addressed. Not until the Department of Missionary Organizations was formed on July 1, 1927, did there appear to be a workable structure to adequately service state and local missionary groups. The Department of Missionary Education, headed by Joy Taylor, had been set in place earlier.

Golden Jubilee of the CWBM

Prior to the formation of the United Society, CWBM leaders had launched a five-year plan leading up to its fiftieth anniversary in 1924. Anna Atwater and her CWBM staff, now scattered through several departments in the new structure, were encouraged, nonetheless, by their colleagues to continue with their strategies for the Golden Jubilee celebration. Their proposals included:

500 new societies
50,000 new members
$1,000,000 Jubilee Gift
5,000 *World Call* new subscriptions
5,000 *King's Builders* new subscriptions
50 new buildings

On October 22, 1924, the International Convention met in Cleveland, Ohio. There, amid colorful pageantry, CWBM's fiftieth anniversary was celebrated and the one-million-dollar goal was reached. An attractive, sixteen-page brochure was distributed, replete with photographs of CWBM leaders, a brief history of the board, pictures of the work at home and abroad, and these words by Affra B. Anderson, who had directed the Jubilee project:

> The Golden Jubilee has ended. Fifty years of woman's organized missionary work have become history. Now what? On to the still greater things ahead! The faith, the courage, the world vision of the original seventy-five women who saw new empires rise out of nothing, and adventured gloriously, must be the distinguishing characteristics of our women still; else we would not be worthy successors of theirs...Let us press forward to make more widespread the missionary passion in our churches...With a good, live missionary society in every church, there would be no report at end of year of churches that had disbanded...Look forward to the time when not a preacher will go out from our colleges without the missionary information that sets him on fire for the gospel.[3]

Affra Anderson was executive secretary of Missionary Organizations from 1920 until a few months before her death on September 5, 1927. She had served as secretary of women's work in California for seven years before moving to Indianapolis in 1919 and joining the CWBM staff with the assignment to direct the Golden Jubilee campaign. Shortly after her arrival, a conversation with Josephine M. Stearns, another CWBM staff member, took place. Mrs. Stearns began by saying, "When I was a young girl, I had a classmate named Affra." Mrs. Anderson responded, "Really? And where was that?" "In Switzerland County, Indiana." "I am your Affra!" was the delighted response. The two had separated at age twelve when Josephine's family moved, and had lost touch. Their friendship was quickly rekindled as they worked closely following the formation of the United Society. Josephine Stearns served chiefly in missionary educational work until 1928, when she assumed the position of general secretary of the newly created National Commission of Protestant Church Women.

In the midst of the Golden Jubilee campaign, Affra Anderson had major surgery and was not allowed by her physician to travel to Cleveland, Ohio, for the celebration. Her vigorous spirit brought her back to her position, but never with the fullness of her former energy and buoyancy.

As plans for the Golden Jubilee matured, a project was approved to set in motion the making of a thorough survey of all the cooperative tasks of the Disciples of Christ administered through the International Convention. Each society was asked to survey its own work, making it an accurate inventory and audit as well as a clear assessment of its mission. It was difficult, in every instance, to deal with the need for change when that appeared, and especially when such changes might result in the demise of a group or structure.

Originally it was thought that the surveys might be completed in two years, but this proved to be inadequate. No other denomination had attempted a project of this magnitude; there were no precedents to guide the first leaders. Under the general editorship of W. R. Warren, the completed report was published in 1928, five years after its beginning. The *Survey of Service* represents one of the most comprehensive publications of its kind in the history of American Protestantism.

FORDS, FLAPPERS, AND FINANCES

Perhaps no other invention has affected daily life and moral inhibitions of Americans in quite the same way as the advent of the automobile. From the earliest days of the Stanley Steamer to the introduction of Henry Ford's Model A in 1927, life on Main Street U.S.A. took on a different dimension when the automobile came to town. It became part of the American way as it changed our lives, our cities, our countryside. And our churches. Sunday driving became a national pastime, reducing the numbers of summertime church attendees dramatically, though church membership numbers grew.

The 1920s marked the nation's first youth culture in which a generation of Americans under the age of twenty-five cut loose as never before, launching a whole new set of styles, attitudes, and behaviors. The most visible representative came to be known as "the flapper." She loved to be seen, and to make certain of this, she dressed for shock value. Dress lengths shortened, materials thinned, waistlines dropped, and bobbed hair became the fashion. Churches felt the impact of the flapper fad as well, along with many other fads that made the rounds among most of the churches' young men and women. Movies were making their bid for the attention of all ages during this decade, which came to be known as "the Roaring Twenties," and for good reason: such rapid social change was taking place in every sector of American life. Women won the right to vote; Prohibition was put into effect; the Ku Klux Klan aimed attacks at Catholics, Jews, blacks, and immigrants; Charles Lindbergh made his daring solo flight across the Atlantic; and "Black Tuesday" signaled the start of the Great Depression.

The Great Depression actually began in early September of 1929. Stock market prices topped then and immediately started dropping. On Tuesday, October 29, 1929, sell orders poured in, and by day's end the damage was all too clear. Within a few weeks three million people were out of work, and many had lost everything they owned.

Such drastic changes were bound to reach into the very center of church life in America, and the resulting damage was felt for years to come. The annual net increase in church membership, for example, began to drop in 1924, and by 1927 had skidded to a "Loss" in the membership chart. What naturally followed was a noticeable decline in congregational giving to the United Society and other general agencies of the Disciples of Christ. It is interesting to note that although a decline in giving occurred among the congregations, the women's missionary groups continued to *increase* their giving for several years before the national economic decline had an impact.

An attempt to explain how the largest volume of contributions to UCMS came from women's missionary groups was made by W. R. Warren, editor of *World Call* magazine. After stating that women had given $541,733.64, some $20,000 more than congregations, for the year just completed, he asked, "Why do women give twice as much as men to missions?" His answer was direct: "There are just two reasons: first, they know the facts; second, they have a chance to give."[4] These two reasons were to play a very important role in the structure and function of the women's organization in the Disciples of Christ throughout its entire history.

The organizational pattern for women's missionary societies in congregations featured systematic studies of the many home and foreign areas of mission work, augmented by personal information about missionaries and their specific duties. Meetings were held monthly, sometimes more often, for the express purpose of learning more and thus being motivated to give more. This combination of constant exposure to missionary information and "the chance to give" has continued to be a critical force in the life of church women's groups, regardless of adjustments in format and function. Indeed, it has been "the secret of the success" of women's groups wherever there has been success. The original CWBM embodies this in its stated purpose: "to disseminate missionary intelligence, and to secure systematic contributions."

WOMEN'S COUNCIL PLAN GAINS MOMENTUM

One of those adjustments in format and function was made for Disciples women during the 1920s. From the day of the United Society's beginnings, there came a series of changes that affected the makeup of local organizations also. The emergence of an alternate pattern for local women's groups, known as the Women's Council plan, had sparked the imagination of women in Missouri and Kansas as early as 1913, and many other states experimented with this proposal for an organization designed to broaden and unify local women's activities. While it was intended to include the missionary society, it had the effect of competing instead, and many congregations suffered as a result.

The Women's Council was an attempt to offer something for all the women of the congregation, whether it be missionary society, ladies' aid, Bible study groups, prayer groups, or leadership development. For thirty-five years or more, state and national leaders of women's work struggled with the problem of finding a way to maintain the intent and effective network of the missionary society while broadening the scope of women's participation in congregational life.

In the 1928 Missionary Organizations Handbook, a new purpose statement was included:

> To develop a trained Christian womanhood; to unite them in worldwide service for Christ; to encourage systematic giving for missionary work through The United Christian Missionary Society.

This embodied much more than the CWBM statement, which had remained unchanged for some fifty years. Clearly it was an attempt to hold fast to the missionary spirit of earlier times while enlarging its sphere of activity.

The new purpose statement came as a result of the conference of ninety-eight persons held in November 1927, shortly after the establishment of the Missionary Organizations Department in the Division of Education of the United Society. Those in attendance represented thirty-five states and Canada, and included national and state staffs of the National Christian Missionary Convention (the black Disciples agency). The major product of this conference, under the leadership of Daisy June Trout, was a revised constitution and new handbook for local use in incorporating the Women's Council plan while retaining the missionary society. Almost 15,000 copies of this handbook were sold the first year of its availability, a strong indication that women were ready for clarification of the missionary society/Women's Council conflict.

This conference, featured in an article in the January 1928 *World Call*, was considered to be the impetus for the organization of state presidents and secretaries, together with the headquarters staff of related workers. Called "a workers' conference," it was the second such gathering of those who were responsible for women's work in states. The first, also directed by Daisy June Trout, had been conducted on a smaller scale in 1917. This group was the forerunner of the present-day Church Women Staff Fellowship and the International Christian Women's Fellowship Cabinet.

Daisy June Trout's penchant for clarifying snarled administrative practices and promoting a harmonious work environment, not to mention her leadership on the CWBM staff, made her an obvious choice to head up the newly formed Department of Missionary Organizations in 1927, though she was at the time in charge of the Home Missions section for the United Society. Miss Trout served on strategic committees and commissions within the total work of Disciples of Christ boards during her fourteen years of distinguished service to the church. Hers was the rare combination of a visionary yet practical approach to her assigned work, and her enthusiasm and commitment were major factors in the transition of the societies and boards that comprised the United Society.

A defining incident in May 1929 left its mark on Daisy June Trout, taking her away from the administrative life and bringing her ultimately to the "life of purpose" to which she often referred. On the eve of Memorial Day, she was sitting beside Alma Evelyn Moore, who was driving her new Essex, when the car plunged down a steep hill and crashed into the guardrail at the curve below. Miss Trout and two other passengers were not seriously hurt, but Miss Moore was fatally injured. Following this tragic accident, which took the life of her good friend and coworker, Daisy June Trout spent a long period of time contemplating her own life. Ultimately she determined to resign her position, which she did at the end of 1929, and return to school for advanced study. Following that, she spent most of her active life working in direct contact with young women through the YWCA. For health reasons, she was later forced to curtail her activities, and returned to administrative duties, this time with the United Council of Church Women.

Two events, both of which took place in the latter months of 1928, impacted the development of women's work as the decade drew nearer its close. Earlier in the year, the executive committee of the United Society received an offer from CWBM to move its headquarters to the Indianapolis building formerly used by the College of Missions. After careful deliberation, the offer was accepted, and the ivy-covered College of Missions facility became known as Missions Building. UCMS took up permanent residence September 1, 1928. Its eight years in St. Louis had been pioneering ones for the United Society, especially for the CWBM staff who had been housed in this same structure prior to the move to St. Louis. With the problems of adjustment behind them, the psychology of permanent and adequate headquarters, rich in traditions and spiritual history, imparted to the staff a new challenge for future effort.

The second event was the resignation of Josephine M. Stearns as UCMS second vice president and associate secretary for Missionary Education, to take effect December 31. It was said that no other woman in active service at that time rendered so important a part in the Disciples' missionary history. She had served as a missionary and as field staff and national CWBM staff before UCMS was structured in 1920. Her experience uniquely qualified her for leadership in the world missionary enterprise. Mrs. Stearns was called to be the executive general secretary of the newly created National Commission of Protestant Church Women, known at this writing in 1999 as Church Women United. The Disciples were honored as well, and felt that such recognition by a group that in its organization was interdenominational and in its concerns international was compatible with the Disciples' plea for unity.

Mrs. Stearns' move to interdenominational fields of endeavor marked the beginning of such moves by numerous women's leaders in years to come.

THOSE TURBULENT THIRTIES

In the spring of 1931, the Empire State Building was opened in New York City. Intended to be the very incarnation of American power and wealth, its 102 stories remained largely empty throughout the Depression. Men who had recently walked on Madison Avenue carrying briefcases now stood on street corners selling apples for five cents each. Many others left family at home while they rode the rails to find work in Midwestern towns and beyond. Breadlines formed all across America.

By 1933 UCMS, like every other headquarters of American Protestants, published news of the severe cuts being forced on its staff at home and abroad. Fifty-two missionaries had been withdrawn from overseas fields, and major cuts were made at home. UCMS personnel had their salaries cut by one third, and during one brief slump, staff went without paychecks for two months.

The Department of Missionary Organizations was headed by Mrs. Alda R. Teachout for two years beginning in 1930. She was succeeded by Ora Leigh Shepherd, who had joined the department staff earlier in 1930 as the successor to Alma Evelyn Moore. Mrs. Shepherd brought to her new position a kind of decisive acumen that was characterized by some coworkers as "stubbornness" and by others as "brilliance." She was known for her deep consecration and demonstrated courage. Lorraine Lollis, Disciples historian, credited Ora Leigh Shepherd with making a far greater contribution during those hard Depression years than is generally known. Her strong emphasis on the stewardship of resources led many women to move beyond giving specific amounts as "dues" to giving according to one's ability.

When Mrs. Shepherd resigned in June 1940, she left a legacy of administrative leadership that had greatly strengthened local women's organizations and had made a more comfortable place for women on state and national levels of church life. Under her administration, the Women's Council plan had flourished, and with it came a broader interest in and concern for social issues beyond the more traditional one of missions, which women's church groups had been passionately associated with for well over sixty years.

This broadening of women's concerns for the social issues of the 1930s was evidenced in their stated aims and goals for the sixtieth anniversary of the organized women's work, to be celebrated throughout 1934 and culminating at the Des Moines International Convention in October. Their theme: "Looking Upward, Reaching Outward, Moving Forward." Emphasis was placed on the three aims, but the middle one was lifted up as a broader outreach than only the missionary aspects heretofore practiced. It was defined this way:

> *Reaching outward* to claim areas of geography yet untaken for Him but also to reach unclaimed areas in our own hearts where He has not yet been welcomed, that we may manifest Him in every relationship; reaching out to those who live next door and at the same time to those on the other side of the world.

Four specific goals were promoted as "Gifts of Gratitude" for the sixtieth anniversary. They included the attainment of 6,000 local organizations; 60,000 new members; 3,000 mission study groups; and $600,000 in offerings. For the first time in its history, missionary organizations were unable to reach all the goals set for this specific celebration. The Great Depression had finally impacted the women's groups in devastating terms.

EMERGING AND WITHDRAWING AGENCIES

The Depression affected Disciples of Christ congregations in almost every aspect of their individual and collective ministries. Some congregations had assumed heavy mortgages in the belief that prosperity was an assured condition. Many found themselves unable to pay their ministers, and quite a few were forced to cut staff members and programs that had been added during the more prosperous days of the 1920s. State and national agencies likewise were experiencing diminishing offerings and other support. Many new programs were not resourced, and staff members were furloughed as parts of existing programs were eliminated or abandoned. The Depression continued into the middle of the decade without much sign of economic recovery.

UCMS was still in a period of adjustment and continual reorganization as it moved into the 1930s. Some of the agencies that had come into the United Society at the time of its formation had since determined that a missionary society was neither administratively designed nor psychologically geared for such agencies as the emerging Pension Fund, the National Benevolent Association, and the Board of Church Extension. The withdrawal of these three enterprises resulted in a major overhaul of the United Society structure.

Out of this came the proposal for a separate agency designed solely to coordinate promotional principles and distribution of receipts for those causes that comprised its membership. Loren E. Lair, longtime executive secretary of the Iowa Society of Christian Churches, declared that the organization of Unified Promotion, Incorporated, was the most forward step in promotion taken by the Disciples of Christ in all its history.[5] He augmented this claim with the record showing that receipts from the churches for the causes in Unified Promotion were less than one million dollars the first year of its existence. "Now [1962] they exceed seven million dollars annually." At the time of this writing in 1999, the successor agency, Church Finance Council, reports offerings in excess of twenty million dollars.

When Unified Promotion began on January 1, 1935, the offerings from all women's groups were specified for UCMS. This practice continued without interruption until 1957, when they were released to support all the causes in Unified Promotion. This will be treated more fully in the next chapter.

The 1930s were years of fear and bewilderment for most Americans. From the adversity and suffering brought about by the Depression, the fiber of Americans had toughened, the mentality of Americans had matured, and the heart of Americans had grown more compassionate. Certainly this was true for the members of Disciples congregations. The formation of the World Convention of Churches of Christ in 1930, the year in which Christians all around the globe celebrated the 1900th anniversary of Pentecost, made American Disciples more aware of their kinship to others in the Campbell-Stone tradition as well as to those in other countries and religious bodies. Also, the many programs fostered by the Roosevelt administration called attention to the plight of those in areas of this nation, such as the Dust Bowl of the Southwest, where millions of people were left destitute by the ravages of nature. The sense of social responsibility had a new awakening among church people as the decade continued.

Having survived the worst economic crisis in their history, Disciples, along with all Americans, emerged from the experience better equipped to endure the hardships demanded of them in World

War II. And they were better prepared to assume the enormous responsibility of world leadership in the postwar years.

CHOICES AND CHANGES

Nazi Germany, under the dictatorship of Adolf Hitler, began to make its move on other European nations in 1938. First Austria, then Czechoslovakia, Poland, Denmark, Norway, Holland, Belgium, and, finally, France fell. Alliances were formed with other dictator-led nations, and the threat of World War II became inescapable. The Disciples Peace Fellowship was formed in 1935 during the International Convention in San Antonio, its purpose being to educate persons, especially youth, in the issues involved in world peace. So great was the response to the aims of this group that many related concerns were added. These themes became part of the studies prepared for women's groups and helped in preparing the church for the inevitability of war.

Under the Women's Council plan, which more and more congregations were espousing, specialized groups formed to promote such war-related skills as first aid, food preparation and storage, and rolling bandages. When Thelma Marx came to the United Society in 1940 to head the Missionary Organizations Department, she found quite a variety of women's groups existing in congregations, for very specific purposes.

Ora Leigh Shepherd had resigned as head of the women's department on June 30, 1940, prompting the United Society president to express "deep regret at her decision." Dr. Hopkins spoke glowingly of the effectiveness of her work, and voiced the esteem and affection of her associates. A search for her successor centered on Thelma Marx of Colorado, who had served seven years as president of the Colorado Woman's Christian Missionary Society. The growth in the women's work of the state under her leadership had been remarkable, and her active participation in almost every aspect of the church's life had especially prepared her for this new work.

Mrs. Marx's husband had already entered the U.S. Army when she moved to Indianapolis in the fall of 1940. Shortly afterward, a special conference of the state secretaries of women's work was called for December 10–12. The first order of business was her formal installation, which followed by only one month her ordination in Graham Chapel of Missions Building. By this time, the practice of ordination was routinely followed for all persons elected to staff positions in the United Society, if they were not already ordained.

Mrs. Marx was an excellent speaker, and a very popular personality at state and national church gatherings. Highly respected for her knowledge of church life locally and throughout the world, she was sought out for participation in many areas beyond her assignment as head of the Missionary Organizations Department.

When the churchwide "Emergency Million" drive was launched under the auspices of Unified Promotion in July 1941, its purpose was to raise an over-and-above offering of one million dollars, over a two-year period, to meet some of the pressing needs and emergencies confronting the church. Thelma Marx was named one of the four associate directors for this drive. A second was Jessie M. Trout, who will be discussed later in this chapter. Mrs. Marx gave herself completely to the tasks to which she was called during her term of service with UCMS, and she left a legacy of leadership that greatly enhanced the role of church women during the dark days of World War II and following. She resigned her UCMS position when her husband came home from the war.

The Women's Council plan had spawned a number of splinter groups in congregational life in the early 1940s, not all of which enjoyed a long and purposeful existence. Those which were war-related, for example, did not last very long, most of them being discontinued even before the war ended in 1945. During this time the Missionary Organizations Department staff continued its efforts to keep alive the passion for missionary work at home and abroad. Political developments in those countries where Disciples' missions had been most successful had now turned against American church leaders in their lands, and in some instances had expelled missionaries even before World War II had begun. Once the war started, sixteen United Society missionaries were interned in enemy prison camps. Their names were posted in the chapel at Missions Building, where prayers were lifted daily on their behalf.

It was noted in the July–August 1943 *World Call* magazine that the popular "Women and World Highways" page would, in future issues, be directed to members of Women's Councils in local churches. This was in keeping with the staff's desire to expand its services to local councils. That same issue carried an article written by Genevieve Brown titled "Susan Doe Joins the Council."[6] Requests for reprints poured in and were widely distributed among the congregations. The article spoke of what a woman should expect of her Council experience: inspiration, study, fellowship, a boundlessness of spirit, thought and action, and missionary motivation. A

casual perusal of publications from the women's staff in the late 1930s
and early 1940s indicate that the national leaders were trying dili-
gently to support the Women's Council and give it every chance to
succeed, while hearing the plea from the more discerning local leaders that there were too many choices now available to church women,
often resulting in a weakened organization, described by some as
"too watered down." The competition of several local groups pulled
women in too many directions at once and repulsed those who were
looking for a cause that rose above such competition. It was this
dilemma that Thelma Marx and her staff struggled with throughout
her five-year tenure.

Two bright spots emerged during the dismal days of war, reduced programming, and diminishing leadership among churches
as men were called into the armed services. One was that women
were forced to take more responsibility for keeping the congregational machinery running. The other was the timely appearance of
church program planning manuals, the forerunner of the functional
church plan, which was being refined and sharpened to take a firm
hold on the way Disciples congregations reorganized themselves
following the publication in 1946 of O. L. Shelton's book *The Church
Functioning Effectively*. Once again, women in the church, as in society generally, were drawn into larger tasks of leadership while their
husbands, fathers, and sons were away. And once again, as had happened during previous wars, women proved themselves capable of
managing the family farm, the neighborhood store, and the church
board. They successfully filled civilian jobs and became a vital part
of the war-related work force in aircraft factories and ship-building
plants, even as they accepted local church duties usually handled
by males. They also brought a spiritual dimension to the church tasks
of financial officers, education workers, and property managers.

With the ending of the war and the new enthusiasm surrounding the functional church plan, returning servicemen were met with
many changes and more than a few choices as they reentered congregational life. The women, having discovered for themselves, as
did their mothers and grandmothers before them, that they were
capable of, and enjoyed, the challenges of increased leadership, were
reluctant to return to the men all the tasks previously regarded as
theirs exclusively. Their widespread hope was that, in the "new
world" they envisioned after the war, men and women might share
equally in the building of a new Christian order, both in and beyond
church life.

THREE TRAVELING WOMEN

During the 1930s and 1940s, the Disciples of Christ produced a large number of women who contributed outstanding leadership to the organized work of the church. These were years of unparalleled opportunities for women to develop and make use of their skills and creative capacities for the betterment of humankind, and many, many women among the Disciples of Christ gave themselves to this end. Neither space nor information permit the listing of all, but it is appropriate that three representative stories be included here to assist the reader in grasping the full impact that women of this time period made on their world.

Mary Lediard Doan assumed the vice presidency of the United Society on January 7, 1940, after a long and unusual service as a missionary to Japan. For fourteen years she taught in the Margaret K. Long School for Girls in Tokyo, while also serving as treasurer of that school. From Tokyo she was transferred to Akita, where she worked among the Japanese church women until her marriage to Robert A. Doan, a Disciples businessman-turned-Christian layman, working for the United Society full time and at his own expense. Together they worked on the Survey of Disciples boards and agencies mentioned earlier. "Reddi," as she was affectionately addressed by close friends, was born and educated in Owen Sound, Ontario, where her father was pastor for many years of a congregation that produced an unusually large number of pastors and missionaries.

One of Mrs. Doan's responsibilities while working in Tokyo was to serve as hostess at Fellowship House, where guests of Dr. Toyohiko Kagawa were made welcome. In time, this task was given to Mrs. Doan's lifetime friend, Jessie Trout, who was Dr. Kagawa's coworker for five years, from 1935 to 1940. After Mr. Doan's death in 1937, "Reddi" went back to Japan to serve at her own expense in the girls' school she loved so dearly. It was from this work that she was called in 1940 to take the reins of second-in-command at the United Society.

During the ten years of her service as vice president of UCMS, Mary Doan participated in numerous events and experiences that would not normally fall to that office but, because of her firsthand knowledge of the church in its worldwide expression, she was a willing and very capable participant. For example, one month after her installation, she went as one of three women, of the eighteen Disciples appointed, to The Philadelphia Study conference, convened by the Federal Council of Churches, to consider the relationship of the churches to the rapidly developing international situation. Again, when the International Council of Church Women was formed in 1941, Mrs. Doan was elected to its national board, a position she retained throughout the 1940s. A woman of genteel rearing, she exemplified the highest and noblest traits of Christian character, and she willingly gave of herself in response to the high calling of the church she loved.

Miss Carnella L. Jamison's selection as national field secretary of Negro Missionary Organizations during the Denver International Convention in 1938 was achieved so easily that it almost went unnoticed. A young woman of quiet elegance, she moved to Indianapolis in November and took up her new work in the offices of UCMS with the quiet efficiency of one who knew where she was headed and how she should get there. In a very impressive evening service held in Graham Chapel, Carnella was ordained to Christian ministry on July 25, 1939. She received her early education at Southern Christian Institute, a home missions training school of the Disciples of Christ, where both of her parents had been students. Young Carnella resolved to obtain a better-than-average education and worked steadily toward that end. She later joined the faculty at Southern Christian Institute, and after teaching for several years, she resigned to enter Talladega College, finishing the four-year course requirements in two years. Following graduation, she returned to teaching until her call to Indianapolis.

Because she worked with different age groups, Carnella was in demand in a rich mixture of training events for children, youth, and women. During her seven-year tenure with the national office, she traveled across the width and breadth of the United States, many times under less than pleasant circumstances when hotels and restaurants, for example, would not welcome her. She managed to handle discrimination without letting it thwart her intended goals, thereby gaining the high esteem of all who knew her. She was in the church's limelight at the very time racial intolerance was in the headlines of the nation's newspapers. By her presence and demeanor in troubling circumstances, she was able many times to prevent hostile encounters. She worked under the supervision of Thelma Marx most of her years in Indianapolis, and this proved to be a rewarding relationship for both women. Traveling in the company of Mrs. Marx often facilitated the journey for Miss Jamison and opened doors that might otherwise have remained closed. Mrs. Marx, in turn, found strength in Carnella's quiet steadiness and determination.

A pivotal time for both of them came in 1945 when Carnella, through Thelma's encouragement, resigned her position on February 7, 1945, to accept the directorship of the Community Christian Center of the Avalon Christian Church in Los Angeles. Later that same year, on October 15, Thelma resigned from her work with the United Society to move with her recently discharged husband to Muncie, Indiana. Both women were central to the successful completion of the national project initiated in the early 1940s that called for recruiting, training, equipping, and sending out 150 new foreign and home missionaries. Carnella married Anderson B. Barnes after her move to California, and mothered triplets. As years went by, her name appeared again and again in the chronicles of the 1950–1990 history of the Christian Church, especially in the story of organized women's work among Disciples of Christ. Mrs. Barnes died January 4, 1997.

A significant step in cooperative missionary work was taken by the United Society in 1935 when it made available the services of one of its missionaries, Jessie Mary Trout, as a coworker of Dr. Toyohiko Kagawa, upon her return to Japan. Dr. Kagawa was highly regarded among the religious leaders of the world at that time, and the opportunity to work with him was seen as a unique experience for a non-Japanese, especially for a woman. Because he worked as a Japanese national, independent of any mission board, this assignment was regarded as an exciting new adventure in missionary cooperation, with coworker status being the norm.

Jessie Trout's temperament and training uniquely equipped her for work among the Japanese. Born in Owen Sound, Ontario, Canada, she received her early education there, going on to the College of Missions, from which she graduated in 1921, before being sent by the United Society as a missionary to Japan. Her work with Dr. Kagawa was the crowning achievement of her nineteen years in Japan and served as a sterling opportunity for her to become intimately aware of the church's best hope for meeting the world's

Mary Doan and Jessie Trout visit with Dr. Kagawa at Fellowship House concerns, as seen through the eyes of a Christian statesman. Miss Trout was a visionary leader, and her active service in the missionary arena sharpened her intellect and helped shape her vision of a world fellowship among Christian women, a vision that she inspired into reality later in her career.

A message from home arrived one spring day in 1940 telling of the serious illness of her mother. Jessie booked passage on the Japanese steamship *Tatuta Maru*, arriving in San Francisco on May 19. Sadly, Catherine Trout died while her daughter was en route. Jessie joined her father and two sisters in Owen Sound, where she stayed for a year because her father became ill and passed away the following spring. The world situation had become so uncertain and so unsafe by mid-1941 that it was impossible for her to return to Japan. Instead, she was asked to become one of four associate directors of the Emergency Million drive, a churchwide effort to raise money for special needs facing the Disciples of Christ. She became acquainted with Thelma Marx, the other female associate director, and thus received, though unintended, a thorough orientation for becoming Mrs. Marx's successor a few years later.

In the two years of this assignment, Miss Trout gained new insights into the evolving nature of the American churches, seeing for the first time the inner workings of congregational life and the leadership roles women were and were not assuming. The Women's Council plan, with its intricate weaving of service, study, and assorted other emphases, was a great challenge to her sensibilities. Clutter was not part of her makeup, and she found it difficult to sort out the many parts of the puzzle that, from her perspective, the Council plan had accumulated.

Jessie Trout stepped from the Emergency Million's successful effort into the position of national secretary for *World Call* magazine. In her two years with this publication, she was successful in her efforts to raise its circulation to the highest figure in the twenty-seven years of its existence. George Walker Buckner, editor, wrote in the January 1946 issue: "Her associates on the *World Call* staff regard Miss Trout not simply for what she has accomplished, but even more, for the rare qualities of heart and mind she brought to her work." It was to this office that news came from the various national agencies as well as from congregations, and especially local women's organizations. As she read the letters, Jessie's interest in and concern for the women continued to grow. Like Caroline Neville Pearre before her, she went through a time of agonizing over the dilemma, long before she accepted the position of executive secretary of the Missionary Organizations Department. And like Caroline

Pearre, Jessie Trout carefully and prayerfully deliberated on the many options, the sharp controversies, and the pitfalls risked, and whether action or inaction was called for.

When Thelma Marx resigned on October 15, 1945, as executive secretary of the Missionary Organizations Department, there was little doubt about who her successor would be. The following month the board of trustees gave quick and enthusiastic approval to the appointment of Jessie Trout, and she began her new work the following January. When her friend "Reddi" Doan retired from the vice presidency of UCMS at the end of 1949, Jessie was given that assignment as well. Her knowledge of world conditions was wide and accurate, and the experiences of the 1940s previously mentioned uniquely prepared her to serve wisely and well in both positions.

Lorraine Lollis wrote concerning the Women's Council situation in *The Shape of Adam's Rib*:

> Women's organizations had reached a condition that could well be called anarchy or chaos. We were a bit like Humpty Dumpty after the fall, and leaders at state and local levels were pleading that the national office give leadership in putting us together again...Too much local autonomy had created a proliferation of ladies' aids, missionary societies, guilds, councils, and all sorts of independent circles with a variety of names. Often these organizations exhibited rivalry, jealousy, and pettiness that were not pretty. Women who moved their membership from one place to another often found strange patterns, had difficulty feeling at home, and did not know what, if anything, to "join." In practice, membership in some organizations was by invitation only...
>
> When Jessie Trout became the chief executive, professional, that is, she knew that women's council versus missionary society had become a sharp issue. She was called to many churches to reconcile the controversy...The last years of the Forties were a season of grass-roots demands and growing impatience.[7]

At the time, many thought the national staff was moving too slowly. In retrospect, however, it became obvious that Jessie Trout and her staff were moving with as much haste as humanly possible, given the seriousness of the upheaval.

A CRUSADE FOR A CHRISTIAN WORLD

"Missionary organizations closed the missionary year June, 1947, with approximately 4,500 organizations including Women's

Councils, Missionary Societies, Young Matron's Missionary Societies, Business and Professional Women's Guilds, Circles, Triangles, and Children's Missionary organizations. These groups have entered fully into plans and preparation for 'A Crusade for a Christian World,' and the Crusade call for new persons in a new church in a new world has been the foundation of a prayer program in many organizations."[8]

"A Crusade for a Christian World" was launched in 1946 by the Disciples of Christ, and women's organizations, as noted above, embraced its goals for new congregations, new members, new ministers, and new mission fields. A second major development during that year was the publication of Orman L. Shelton's book dealing with the functional church pattern, a new practice among Disciples congregations. Women especially liked this new way of organizing, for it clearly indicated there was room for, and indeed need for, women in the total life of the church. Jessie Trout's article "On the Crusade Road" appeared in *World Call*, using the imagery of several roads converging on one destination. She wrote:

> It is thrilling to travel with good companions all intent on reaching the same goal; and when the goal is nothing less than making a Christian world, the Crusade road fairly echoes with their marching songs. Sometimes the Crusaders march and sing with the evangelistic group; again, they join the stewardship band; or they may walk with those whose major contribution is Christian education.[9]

The article mentioned that for each year of the Crusade, from 1947 to 1950, women's organizations pledged to contribute $200,000, given through their local churches, but specified for certain projects dear to women's hearts. After describing many of these, the article concludes, "One dares to predict that many newcomers will join our great group of faithful women who already joyfully walk the Crusade road together."

Miss Trout and the members of her staff invested much of their time and energies in the Crusade, for its projects of evangelism, world missions, and Christian education were of special interest, and certainly they were compatible with the aims and achievements of organized women's work from the 1874 beginnings. Miss Trout was an officer of the Crusade administrative group, and several field staff secretaries and state presidents were included in the directory of volunteer workers. The women saw the Crusade, a churchwide program, as an effective means of working with lay leaders and ministers to achieve shared goals in the life of the church.

The Crusade's final year, 1950, ended with the achievement of most of its goals. More than 3, 000 young people were recruited to full-time Christian service, with one third committed to overseas mission fields. New congregations were organized at home and abroad, benevolent homes were increased, the rehabilitation and relief work necessitated by World War II had been substantially supported in Europe and Asia, and attention was given to areas of church life in America's rural and small town settings. The goal of $14 million had not been achieved by June 30, 1950, however, so it was determined that the ending date for the Crusade would be extended through 1951. Because of the Crusade efforts, the Disciples of Christ, in all its areas of programming, experienced a resurgence and vitality greater than ever before.

IN THE FULLNESS OF TIME: CHRISTIAN WOMEN'S FELLOWSHIP

The year was 1949. Bess Truman's husband, Harry, had just been elected in his own right to be President of the United States, while across the Pacific Ocean, Madame Chiang Kai-shek's husband was stepping down as President of China. Clergyman writer Lloyd C. Douglas had just released his newest novel, *The Big Fisherman*, and John Gunther's *Inside U.S.A.* was receiving rave notices.

On Broadway, the stage musical to see was *South Pacific*. People waited in long lines for $4.80 tickets to see Mary Martin "wash that man right out" of her hair. The golden age of television was about to be born, with Milton Berle becoming its first big star. The first North Atlantic Treaty Organization (NATO) treaty was signed in Washington, and the policy of apartheid became firmly established in South Africa. George Orwell's book *1984* projected the reader's attention to the way things could become during the next decades, and India adopted its first constitution as a newly formed federal republic.

Women leaders in the Christian Church responded to a clarion call from their constituencies to make a careful study of women's status in the church generally, and of women's organizations specifically. Normally the annual conference of presidents and executive secretaries of the state women's missionary boards met in April, but in 1949 this meeting was slated for January 8–17. Two months earlier, Jessie Trout had mailed notices of the meeting, along with a letter outlining the special task facing those who would attend. She also sent a request that all state women's board members be engaged in daily prayer, using a series of devotionals that she had personally prepared for the ten-day meeting. Each day's meditation included the prayer that God's will would be revealed to the women. Many,

many women shared in this great undergirding of spiritual power and strength. The participants were given preparatory assignments to complete before going to Turkey Run State Park at Marshall, Indiana, assignments that would help give a true picture of the super-abundance of organizational patterns and purposes currently in use in local settings.

Seventy-five women from all parts of the United States and Canada traveled by car, by bus, but mostly by train to meet during cold, crisp January days in Indiana. Expectations of changes and improvements ran high, and those who attended were not disappointed. It was pointed out that this meeting, coming exactly seventy-five years after the first organizational meeting took place in the basement of the Richmond Street Christian Church in Cincinnati, also had seventy-five women in attendance, an interesting coincidence. There were thirty-four state women's staff, thirty-one state presidents, a representative of Canadian women, two members of businesswomen's guilds, the women's staff member of the National Christian Missionary Convention, and six staff members from the Department of Missionary Organizations.

In addition, four guests were invited to make presentations in the early days of this event. Dr. H. B. McCormick, UCMS president, spoke on the work of the United Society, tracing briefly the history of CWBM and other boards that preceded the formation of the United Society in 1920. Mary L. Doan, who was completing a ten-year tenure as UCMS vice president, reviewed the development of women's missionary organizations, beginning in 1874. A third outsider, who went to Turkey Run to speak on "Women in the Church," was Mossie Allman Wyker, an ordained Disciples woman and president of the Ohio Council of Church Women. Much of what she said at Turkey Run was later included in her book *Church Women in the Scheme of Things*. Dr. Kathleen MacArthur, a YWCA executive and member of Park Avenue Christian Church in New York City, gave leadership to the daily Bible studies that the women shared.

The days were structured to begin with a period of worship led by Mary Pollard, a returned missionary who was then executive secretary for the northern part of California. Mrs. Pollard was a woman of quiet spiritual depth, eminently qualified to meet the worship needs of her peers. Several times, when discussion became heated and differences seemed insurmountable, it was Mary Pollard who stepped forward to offer a calming word or a quiet suggestion, "It's time to pray." She would follow with the announcement of an hour's break, during which the women would find a place, in their rooms or by the huge fireplaces in the lodge or on a walk through the woods surrounding Turkey Run Inn, where serenity and rational thinking might be restored.

Much of each day was devoted to small group discussion and planning, with time for relaxation and personal renewal as well. Following dinner each evening, Mrs. MacArthur's Bible studies climaxed the day.

In *The Shape of Adam's Rib*, Lorraine Lollis details the results of a study that compared women's councils and missionary societies over a ten-year period. This study was examined very closely at the Turkey Run Conference. It revealed, for example, that during the 1937–1947 time frame, the number of missionary societies had slipped from 2,321 to 1,744, while the number of councils had increased from 687 to 1,467. During the same period, membership in societies was reduced by 13,596, but council members increased by 61,154. The next set of data was most revealing. Offerings from missionary societies—fewer in number and size—*increased* from $225,857.82 to $272,504.48. Councils also increased their offerings from $117,341.77 to $417,230.88.[10]

As the days went on, the women moved into three smaller groups. Mabel Crown, representing the women's board of Illinois, recalled that enthusiasm and excitement pervaded those discussions. "We had to change our old organizations into one new one," she said, "keeping the basic principles that we had in each of the existing groups." It was much like the old adage, "Customs are many, principles few; customs change, principles never do." Slowly, painstakingly, with fear and great concern, the women worked their way through moments of anguish, turmoil, and seeming despair until they were able to see a new form of organization emerging that slowly took shape as a simple, workable design for worship, study, and service, usable in churches regardless of size.

The name decided on for the new organization, Christian Women's Fellowship, was chosen to follow the precedent set by the vote at the International Convention of 1938 adopting a new, inclusive program for young people to be known as Christian Youth Fellowship. The men of the church had also considered the adoption of a similar name for their organization, but they did not take official action until 1951. The new purpose for the women's organization was simple: "To develop all women in Christian living and Christian service." The scriptural basis, recommended by Jessie Trout, was taken from 1 John 1:3, which states, "That which we have seen and heard declare we unto you, that you may have fellowship with us:

for truly our fellowship is with the Father, and with His Son, Jesus Christ" (KJV).

The day before the seventy-five would be returning home was an exciting culmination to what turned out to be a great historic event in the annals of recorded women's work. Arrangements were made to take the group by bus to Indianapolis where they spent several hours at Missions Building. For many it was a first visit to the national headquarters, and especially valuable to state presidents and new field staff. A luncheon was served at Downey Avenue Christian Church, two blocks away, at which all national staff members were invited to join the women for conversations around the meal.

By the time good-byes were said the following day, the accomplishments achieved in this extended meeting were hailed as gigantic forward steps, rich in the new unity toward which they had moved, and promising in what greater good might now come from women united in one strong body. It is easy to imagine the direction taken by conversations between presidents and secretaries as they journeyed homeward. Strategies for explaining and interpreting the new organization had to be laid out, they thought, and motivation for state boards and local women's groups must be carefully, prayerfully handled. "Christian Women's Fellowship was not something dreamed up at the top and imposed on local churches," said Lorraine Lollis. "The demand rising from the grass roots had become a shout, so the plan was greeted almost everywhere among Disciples as 'just what we were waiting for.'"

Truly, Christian Women's Fellowship had come "in the fullness of time."

THE MISSIONARY ORGANIZATIONS ERA

Executive Secretaries

Daisy June Trout
1919–1924, 1927–1929

Mrs. Affra B. Anderson
1919–1927

Mrs. Alda R. Teachout
1930–1932

Mrs. Ora Leigh Shepherd
1932–1940

Mrs. H. B. Marx
1940–1945

Jessie M. Trout
1946–1951

THE $\mathcal{R}$esurgent Years
1950–1968

"...IN THE SCHEME OF THINGS"

Looking back from the vantage point of 1999, it hardly seems possible that *World Call* magazine could give such scant coverage of the Turkey Run event as that which appeared in the March 1949 issue. An item printed on the *World Call* "News Room" page consisted of only three sentences:

> Presidents and executive secretaries of the state women's missionary boards met in Turkey Run State Park, Indiana, in January to consider women's work and missionary organizations. All states or areas were represented with the exception of New England. The work was studied and recommendations were made which will form the basis for a long range program of women's work in the churches.[1]

Fortunately for local women, news of the proposed new organization for church women spread like wildfire immediately upon the return home of the group of seventy-five who were at Turkey Run. A timetable had been drawn up that called for local groups to officially launch their reorganization and name change on July 1, 1950. This would allow the international office time to produce new manuals and program resources and make necessary administrative adjustments. Local women, however, were eager to get on with making changes from the old structures, and many groups began right away to use the new name. *The Shape of Adam's Rib* states that three Ohio groups were the first to do this, but other states have records of similar early beginnings. *So Great a Cloud*, the history of Georgia women from 1882 to 1986, reports that a new congregation was formed in Marietta, an Atlanta suburb, in the spring of 1949, and on May 13 of that year a Christian Women's Fellowship was organized, "the first to be formed in the region." Similar claims have been reported from numerous regions in recent years. What is important to remember is that change was in the minds and hearts of women across the continent, and this enabled the process to move forward rapidly.

The timetable called for an editorial committee to meet as soon as arrangements could be made. It also mandated a dismantling of the Missionary Organizations Department, to be replaced by the Christian Women's Fellowship Department. This entailed moving the staff for children's and youth organizations into another UCMS department, a feat that could not be achieved quickly. This work was transferred by July 1, 1951, and the women's department name change was approved by the UCMS trustees to take effect in July, 1952. It also meant shifting several assignments between the Missionary Education Department and the women's department, and negotiations to accomplish this were not without their share of stress and displeasure.

The editorial committee included three state secretaries, Bessie Hart, Agnes Henderson, and Mary Pollard; two state presidents, Freda Putnam and Ann McGlothan; and one guild president,

Missionary Organizations Staff
January, 1951
Sitting (left to right): Velva Dreese, Associate Secretary; Jessie Trout, Executive Secretary.
First row, standing (left to right): Edith Eberle, Jacquie Stephenson, Florence Sly,
Carrie Dee Hancock, Alma Scott. Back row, standing (left to right): Elsie Cook Liverett,
Alice Rist, Katherine Schutze, Orpha June Holman, Charles Mills.

Margaret Edwards. The four national staff related to women's work, Jessie Trout, Velva Dreese, Katherine Schutze, and Alma Scott, completed the committee. This group met for a full week, January 29 to February 4, 1951, at McCormick's Creek State Park, Indiana.

Once the new resources were ready for use in local settings, state women's boards began adjusting their structures to be compatible, and a new word, "unification," was introduced into the vocabulary of state officials, men and women alike. The wildfire of women's organizations in local churches was snuffed out, but the sparks of unification on the state level were ignited. Jessie Trout and her staff faced this new challenge throughout the 1950s and into the 1960s.

At first, every woman of each congregation was automatically a member of Christian Women's Fellowship (CWF). Each one was assigned to a group and encouraged to participate in a variety of ways: to observe the nine o'clock prayer time, to share in the monthly study group, to be involved in the numerous service projects and activities, and to support the missions pledge. Years later it was deemed wise to give women the choice of active participation in CWF as they began to see many opportunities in the total life of the congregation. But in 1950 this was not yet a reality. Christian Women's Fellowship was the only place in the church for Disciples women to develop and use their leadership skills. Other Protestant church bodies were aware of this limitation in their own setting, and enough questions were raised by a worldwide study on the life and work of women in the church, conducted by the World Council of Churches in the late 1940s, to cause a *World Call* editorial to flatly state:

> The Christian church has failed to make use of the services of qualified women in its life and work. It has not kept pace with the secular world in granting recognition to women.[2]

The Commission on the Life and Work of Women in the Church was appointed by the Central Committee of the World Council of Churches in 1950 to study this problem, and Disciples of Christ were prominent in such deliberations. It is of interest to note that Bertha Park, the state CWF secretary in Ohio, went to Geneva, Switzerland, at her own expense to give a three-month period of service to the Commission. Mossie Wyker, the first woman ever to be elected as first vice president of the International Convention, was also deeply interested in this study. In 1948 she went to the first Assembly of the World Council as an official representative of the International Convention, and there she had heard, at a pre-Assembly conference/consultation, suggestions of further steps enabling member churches to open full privileges and responsibilities of church life to women. And it was Mossie who had presented a paper at the Turkey Run Conference in 1949 that dealt with women in the church, their obstacles and opportunities.

Mossie Wyker, Author
Church Women in the Scheme of Things
President, United Council of Church Women, 1950–1955

In late 1953 Mossie Wyker's book *Church Women in the Scheme of Things* was published. According to her, "This book was written to stir the church, and particularly its women members. Time is running out," she continued, "and no group should be required to keep proving its intellectual and spiritual assets…Church women are *essential* in the scheme of things."[3] Before the book was published, however, a request was sent to Jessie Trout and all national women's executives to convene denominational committees to make studies within the constituting communions of the National Council of Churches. This request was signed by Mrs. Wyker, who was president of the National Council's Department of United Church Women at that time. A committee of nine was appointed and completed its report in time for the annual CWF staff meeting in February 1953. There a major block of time was devoted to hearing the reports and discussing their implications for the work of Disciples women.

Those in attendance were state CWF presidents and staff, and state officers of business women's guilds, along with staff members of the CWF Department. This conference proved to be a most significant one in the development of CWF. Reflecting on the sessions, Miss Trout told a colleague that "the meeting had initiated a study of the service and status of women which promised to have far-reaching results." Elizabeth Landolt, serving then as Missouri's CWF president, was asked to bring a special report on the history of women's participation in the church. She prefaced her report by saying that when she had received the letter from Miss Trout asking for such a report, her husband matter-of-factly instructed her to write it and let him read it. He added, "When you give it at Clifty Falls, stay strictly to the script and don't palaver all over the place!"

Spurred on by what they had read and heard, those at the Clifty Falls State Park meeting reasoned that since through baptism all

people—male and female—are received into the church as full members, then women, as baptized members of the church, cannot be
barred from participation in all positions and activities within the
church. Therefore, these women declared their right to full membership, based on their baptism. Reports of this conference created
some intense questions and discussions within the Disciples of Christ
community. While the questions were never fully answered and the
discussions never fully completed, there were notable responses and
follow-up in many arenas. In Mrs. Wyker's book, "dedicated to
United Church Women of America, with complete faith in what they
may yet become," she spoke of the need for women to recognize
their potential as church members and emphasized the necessity for
women to become enablers of other women in church leadership. In
answer to an inquiry, she received a letter from Dr. Riley B. Montgomery, then president of The College of the Bible in Lexington,
Kentucky, in which he wrote on June 15, 1953:

> The College of the Bible accepts women for the Bachelor of
> Divinity degree because we believe that women should have
> the opportunity to share equally with men in Christian work
> and leadership…We would recommend women to the local
> churches for ordination as readily as we would men.[4]

Mossie Wyker concludes with a question: Can the women read
this statement and believe that it is *the men* who are holding us back?
What opportunities do church women really want? Such questions
were being voiced by a growing number of church leaders in North
America in 1953, prompted by the swiftness of World Council officials to set in motion its study on the service and status of women in
the churches. A full-length book, based on the study, was compiled
and interpreted by Kathleen Bliss.

One of the significant publications having a bearing on this entire study was provided by The College of the Bible (later Lexington
Theological Seminary). Roscoe M. Pierson compiled a sixty-eight-
page booklet in which a symposium of five Disciples presented some
of the thought of the Disciples on several aspects of the status and
service of women in the church. They were Elizabeth Hartsfield,
Mossie Wyker, Howard E. Short, Lewis Smythe, and Daniel Troxel.
All but Mrs. Wyker were staff members of the college. This material
continues to impact the church in the 1990s as newer congregations
give attention to the role of women in church life.

International Christian Women's Fellowship Beginnings

At the risk of sounding redundant, conversations at the Turkey Run Conference included mention of international and world organizations of church women. "International" was necessary because Canadian women had been in partnership since 1913 with the U.S.-based CWBM. "World" was inclusive of the twenty-plus countries voting to form a women's fellowship group related to the World Convention of Churches of Christ in 1955. For years, the Missionary Organizations staff had planned and presided over women's sessions at the annual International Conventions. There were no elected officers, no unified women's organization beyond the local congregation that women might participate in and select their own leadership during the thirty-year period between 1920 and 1950. It was felt that this brought on less confidence among women, less eager expectation of continued growth and expansion of their work. Certainly it added to the confusion that reigned during the controversy over women's councils and the excess of special interest groups in local settings.

Women left the Turkey Run meeting with the vision of an international expression of what Freda Putnam, Ohio women's president, had advocated while there. Freda was a coworker with Mossie Wyker, who had pointed out the disadvantage that Disciples women had in ecumenical settings because there was no elected person to represent them. Indeed, this was also a distinct disadvantage in our own denominational circles. It was generally agreed that major attention would be devoted first to the new organization locally, then internationally between the United States and Canada, and ultimately to the other world countries with Campbell-Stone ties.

More than two thousand women traveled to Portland, Oregon, in the summer of 1953, where they came together on July 4, the opening day of the International Convention, and launched the International Christian Women's Fellowship (ICWF). After thirty-four years, Disciples women once more had bona fide leadership as the election and installation of Freda Putnam as president, Hazel Rudduck as vice president, and Jessie Trout as secretary-treasurer took place. Gaines Cook, then executive secretary of the International Convention of Disciples of Christ, reported, "At Portland, the International CWF perfected their organization. This event will go down in history with the organization of the Christian Woman's Board of Missions in 1874." The purpose of ICWF was "to provide a channel by which all women of the churches of Disciples of Christ in Canada and the United States may be joined in fellowship and in making their contribution to the extension of the Kingdom of God."

In addition to the elected officers, the ICWF pattern called for a Commission made up of the executive secretary and president of each state, plus two others elected by each state, one of whom must be a businesswoman. The Advisory Council was composed of ten women from the Commission, two from CWF field staff, the program coordinator and one other woman on the Indianapolis staff, the chairperson of the ICWF nominating committee, the ICWF officers, and the retiring president, beginning one year after her retirement. This group of nineteen served for four years, planning general meeting programs for local CWF use, setting annual themes and projects, and providing for leadership for Quadrennial Assemblies and the annual women's sessions at the International Conventions. This new structure made it possible for local women to have a say in determining the issues that would be studied, the format of study and worship resources that were produced by the CWF Department, and the special projects recommended for a given period. Local and state groups of women felt greater ownership in every aspect of CWF, and it showed in the ways the organization flourished.

A third function of the ICWF, and perhaps the most important one, was the provision for a quadrennial assembly of women. Dubbed by many general church leaders throughout its history as "one of the best things that happen among Disciples of Christ," these assemblies have provided a means of showcasing the creative abilities of women, and have served as a training ground for preparing women for fuller participation in the total life of the church. The first Quadrennial Assembly featured women who were already in leadership positions in the general church. Freda Putnam and Hazel Rudduck were members of the UCMS board of trustees, as were ten others whose names are listed in the 1957 program book. Add to them the names of program personalities who were readily recognized for prior involvement in denominational and in ecumenical circles, and it becomes easy to characterize the 1957 event as one that was highly successful because of its proven leadership. The assemblies that followed found their success in introducing leadership who, for the most part, were unknown beyond local and state settings, yet possessed those skills and intellects that successfully validated their right to participate as leaders. It became an established fact that after each Quadrennial Assembly there appeared in other international arenas of the church some of those

Quadrennial leaders who now were being asked to take positions in total church life. Notable among these are Catherine Broadus, Eliza Cave, Lucille Cole, Fran Craddock, Brenda Etheridge, Claudia Grant, Delores Highbaugh, Mary Jacobs, Janet Long, Marilyn Moffett, Maureen Osuga, Odatta Redd, Mary Louise Rowand, Narka Ryan.

Janice Newborn, who served as executive for the Department of Church Women from 1988 until her retirement at the end of 1994, has said of the Quadrennial experience, "My first opportunity to go to an Assembly was in 1961. At a CWF meeting at my church, someone asked if I planned to go, and I said no, because of our two young children and limited finances. Later, one of the women said to me, 'Janice, I'm not going to be able to go, but I want to make it possible for you to go.' She handed me a check for the registration fee and said if I had trouble making arrangements for the children she could help with that, too. Just think, I went from being helped to go to the 1961 Assembly to coordinating the one in 1986!"

The initial ICWF officers were a creative trio. All three had extensive input into the creation of CWF, and all three shared the vision of an international fellowship. Freda Putnam went home from the Turkey Run meeting resolved to test the new organizational format in her home church, Euclid Avenue Christian Church in Cleveland. She and Hazel Rudduck worked together in beautiful harmony as they crisscrossed their way around America, explaining the new plan in countless state and local meetings. Miss Trout, a native of Canada, saw to it that Canadian women were actively involved from the beginning. Their selection by the ICWF nominating committee to serve as the first official leaders was indeed a wise one.

Freda Putnam was a stately presence, and her demeanor was that of a highly intelligent person who was widely read. She was a strong advocate of the ICWF Reading Plan. Freda possessed an uncommon flair for memorizing extensive portions of the Bible, and often recited the scriptures she had chosen for the basis of a devotional message she would deliver. Freda was quickly accepted in interdenominational circles as a respected leader, and the esteem of leaders in her own church was evident in the ways she was invited to represent the Disciples in many settings, even in overseas experiences. Her husband, Russell, accompanied her on several such trips, but his duties on the staff at the famed Case Institute kept him from joining her as often as he wished. Following her presidency, Freda continued to share in the growth and development of CWF locally and internationally until her sudden death on August 9, 1967.

Hazel Rudduck was uniquely qualified for her duties as the first of a long line of ICWF vice presidents. A longtime member of First Christian Church in South Bend, Indiana, she participated in district and state meetings of the Disciples of Christ after her two sons and her daughter were well along in school. Their father, a lumber company executive, had died in 1930, leaving Hazel with the challenge of raising her young children as a single parent. Following the year her oldest son went off to college, she married H. I. Rudduck and moved to Mishawaka where he owned a dairy. Hazel's knowledge of world conditions was wide and accurate; her interest in the newly forming United Nations in 1946 led to her becoming a volunteer interpreter of the UN purpose and programs, not only in the United States, but in twelve South American countries as well.

Hazel Rudduck's participation in Disciples of Christ international programs, especially her involvement as chairman of the United Society's board of managers in 1950–51 and her four-year term on its board of trustees in the early fifties, brought her to the attention of the ICWF nominating committee. Hazel and Freda were so nearly matched in their qualifications that the decision as to which would serve as president was made all the more difficult. They worked extremely well together and shared many tasks equally as their years in office proceeded. One of their first tasks was the creation of the ICWF Prayer, still used today in hundreds of CWF settings in Canada, the United States, and around the world. When plans for the first Quadrennial Assembly were begun, Hazel Rudduck was asked to be general chairman, the first and only time this heavy responsibility was given to a non-staff person. She tackled this with the same excitement and determination with which she has approached every other assignment in her life. In retirement she took up painting and has sold a number of her works. She was the leading force in a drive to establish a public library in her adopted hometown, Vinton, in the California mountains near the Nevada border. At this writing in 1999, Hazel Rudduck, at 103 years old, is a resident of a health-care facility, where she frequently plays the piano for the enjoyment of her "new family," as she calls them.

NEXT, THE WORLD CHRISTIAN WOMEN'S FELLOWSHIP

Jessie Trout's portfolio as executive secretary of the new Department of Christian Women's Fellowship and her expanding role as vice president of the United Society were enough to keep her busy, but the emerging International Christian Women's Fellowship brought additional responsibility. As secretary-treasurer she was expected to keep complete records and oversee the payment of all expenses. Generating funds was also her task. She took on the added administrative duties without a murmur; after all, it was her vision of a broader fellowship for Disciples women that resulted in additional work. Surprisingly, it appeared to energize her, for she wrote a book of devotions, *Like a Watered Garden*, which Bethany Press published in 1953, and took an extended world tour promoting her dream of a world CWF. On her way to the assembly of the World Convention of the Churches of Christ, meeting in 1952 in Melbourne, Australia, Jessie made a number of stops to meet with women, sharing with them her hopes for a fellowship that might provide encouragement and inspiration, especially for those in isolated parts of the world. The world organization would enable its members to know one another better and would help them feel a closer bond through prayer. Dr. Jesse Bader, executive for the World Convention, encouraged Miss Trout's efforts on behalf of an active women's group related to the World Convention, and, though he pushed for greater control by this group, he acquiesced to her firm insistence that a world CWF could not be administrative in any way. Further, she made it clear that the organization would be run by a committee of representative women from all the participating countries, and the Indianapolis office would handle details. When the World CWF was made official in 1955, Miss Trout, again by virtue of her position, was elected secretary-treasurer, but not before two honorary doctorate degrees were given to her, by Bethany College and by Butler University, in early June ceremonies.

August 20, 1955, marked the birth of the World CWF, which took place when women from twenty countries met in Maple Leaf Gardens in Toronto, Canada, to finalize the plans, that had been in formation for many months. On Tuesday, the opening day of the Silver Jubilee Assembly of the World Convention of Churches of Christ, the final promotion of the concept was presented at the week's largest luncheon, with 1,475 women present. This was followed by Saturday's session in the Gardens in which the election of officers took place, rules of procedure were adopted, and an offering of $1,004 was given for the new treasury. The stated purpose of the World CWF, as accepted that day, reads:

> The purpose of the World Christian Women's Fellowship shall be to provide a channel by which all women members of the Churches of Christ (Disciples of Christ) may be joined in fellowship and through which by prayer, study, and service

they may make a contribution to the extension of the Kingdom of God.

Changes in the World Convention constitution were enacted at
the Toronto Assembly, which provided that the World CWF president would automatically become a vice president of the World
Convention and that another woman member of the Convention's
executive committee would be named by the World CWF. In the
same business session, Charles K. Green, one of the outstanding laymen of the British Churches of Christ, was elected president of the
Convention. Only a few hours earlier his wife was elected as the
first president of the World CWF.

Hilda Green often said she was never sure whether she was British with American ties or American with British ties. During World
War II she brought her two young sons for an extended stay, first in
Canada and later in the United States. The Greens had been frater-
nal delegates to the International Convention on several occasions
and were well known in Disciples of Christ circles. While living in
the States, Hilda Green had visited many churches and was found
to be an excellent speaker and delightful program personality. She
served as president through the 1960 Edinburgh Assembly.

Elected to the vice presidency was Juliana Banda of Manila, Philippines, who was married to a young Filipino minister and active in
guiding the women of her congregation as they organized a CWF.
Mrs. Banda was instrumental in establishing the nine o'clock prayer
time among the women of the participating countries, and suggested
that each country take its turn in preparing monthly prayer topics.
This practice was quickly adopted, and the intercessory prayer topics that appeared in the annual CWF yearbook were those prepared
by women from many different countries. Another area in which
Juliana Banda gave leadership was the World CWF newsletter, to
which she contributed frequently.

Annual birthday celebrations were planned to be held around
the globe, lifting up prayers of gratitude for the worldwide fellowship
that the World CWF fosters, and receiving an offering for the service
projects that members support. Again, women around the world
have a part in providing the written service each year. The World
CWF meets in assembly every four years in conjunction with the
World Convention Assembly. Usually there is a meal function, in
addition to a women's session where issues of concern are the focus. Officers are elected, and members of the executive committee

share a pre-Assembly retreat. The World CWF has been of immense value to women in every nation that encourages participation.

GUILDS AND TOURS

Business and professional women's guilds had appeared in Disciples of Christ congregations during the late 1930s and early 1940s, but not in great numbers until the war years pulled more and more women into the business world. With this came the limitation on when women were available to attend meetings. Most church women's groups met during the day when children and menfolk were away from home and women had more freedom to arrange daytime schedules. As women filled jobs vacated by men going into the armed forces, however, this changed.

Evening groups increased in number as employed women began to push harder for a circle or group meeting at night, to address their special interests and concerns. In Kansas, as in Oklahoma, the state women's field secretary recognized the potential inherent in guilds and began promoting them widely. In Kansas, for example, the number of guilds more than doubled in two years. This phenomenal growth was as easy as making the suggestion, giving an invitation to organize, and a new business and professional women's guild was the result.

When the Turkey Run Conference was called, there were representatives of business women present who, according to Katherine Schutze, newly appointed national director for business women, were firmly set on keeping guilds out of any new organization for church women that might emerge from the conference. New at her job, Katherine was caught between standing for guild members' wishes for a separate organization versus being loyal to the urging of her new executive. In the end, a compromise of sorts was achieved. Guilds gradually became part of Christian Women's Fellowship, and Katherine's portfolio was expanded to include purposeful mission tours for businesswomen to home and overseas mission stations, many of which included a churchwide event such as an International Convention or a World Convention Assembly. In the nineteen years of conducting such tours, she personally led twenty-two, most of them designed especially for businesswomen.

In time, state retreats, often called house parties, were scheduled for guild members, particularly in those areas where guilds numbered substantially. In the latter part of the 1950s, especially following the first Quadrennial Assembly, business and professional women were becoming more integrated into the activities of CWF on all its levels and there was less emphasis placed on separate groups, events, and the like. The 1954 *Year Book & Directory of the Christian Church (Disciples of Christ)* was the last to report separate guilds.

UNIFIED PROMOTION AND CHRISTIAN WOMEN'S FELLOWSHIP

When CWBM became an integral part of the United Christian Missionary Society in 1920, its offerings were specified for UCMS. This was to be expected, for prior to that time all the funds that came to the CWBM office were expended for its mission enterprise at home and abroad. When Unified Promotion was set in place in 1935, it was intended to be the receptacle of all offerings to the international agencies of the Disciples of Christ. Again, the women's missionary organizations specified that their money be used solely by UCMS. This arrangement prevailed until July 1, 1957, when at the suggestion of Christian Women's Fellowship, both Unified Promotion and the United Society agreed that as of that date all regular offerings from CWF would no longer be specified but would directly support all the causes in Unified Promotion.

Spencer P. Austin, executive secretary–elect of Unified Promotion, wrote, "I believe this is a forward step for the women of our churches, equally as dramatic and significant as that in 1874 when the dream of a woman's board of missions was first conceived. Its comprehensiveness will commend itself to every thinking woman...I have confidence that the response of the women next year in the support of outreach causes will far exceed anything ever attempted before."[5]

To commemorate this new designation, state and international CWFs decided to adopt goals that would be worthy of this new, broader relationship to all the agencies in Unified Promotion. Their goals, totaling $1,943,235, were announced at the Quadrennial Assembly, but a suggestion from the floor to make it an even two million dollars was enthusiastically endorsed. However, that figure was not reached until 1962.

Related to the matter of offerings is the practice of using individual offerings boxes for special projects, a practice that had its roots in the days of CWBM when mite offerings were requested. In the early 1950s such offerings were called Love Gifts and were designated for scholarships to enable women overseas to receive leadership training and educational experiences. When CWF offerings were released to support all Unified Promotion causes, the over-

and-above Love Gift was changed to Blessing Box, still an over-and-above offering, but now designated for Unified Promotion. Scholarships for women overseas were handled through Unified Promotion's allocation to the Division of Foreign Missions.

The Blessing Box project was designed for the woman who was moved to give tangible evidence of her thanks for recognized blessings. Cardboard boxes were designed to hold quarters, dimes, and other coins, which a woman was encouraged to place in her box for large and small blessings. Women were urged to keep the boxes in convenient places—their desks and the breakfast table—as a reminder. Jessie Trout expressed her delight on more than one occasion after the annual reports began. "Blessing Box Offerings" appeared for the first time in CWF's statistical report in the 1959 Year Book, showing a grand total of $76,641.65. In the years following, it has averaged slightly more than 10 percent of CWF's regular offerings to Disciples outreach.

ICWF Quadrennial Assembly

From its beginning, the idea of a quadrennial assembly of Disciples women had captured the imagination of ICWF leaders. It was first introduced during the 1949 Turkey Run Conference. The "movers and shakers" at that event dreamed of a day when CWF would be firmly established locally, in states, and internationally. The next development, they reasoned, would be a major gathering when women—young and old, of many cultures and from many countries—might be called together to worship, study, serve, and fellowship. This dream was mentioned frequently whenever women leaders gathered until the World CWF organization was formalized in the summer of 1955. Once that took place, women were ready to begin planning what one observer described as "one of the major events of American Protestant Christianity."

This event was the first ICWF Quadrennial Assembly, scheduled for June 19–23, 1957, on the campus of Purdue University in West Lafayette, Indiana. Jessie Trout had heard from other

Quadrennial Assembly 1957

denominational executives, notably Presbyterians and American Baptists, reports of their church women's national assembly, and she had taken gleanings from such conversations to the ICWF Advisory Council where her recommendations were met with much excitement. She was invited to attend the Presbyterian assembly in 1954, and came away completely sold on the idea of holding a similar one for Disciples women. The machinery for such an event fell into place with relative ease, for CWF members were eager to spread their wings and venture into uncharted, (for them) territory. Hazel Rudduck, ICWF vice president, was chosen as general chairman and Mary M. Dale, a Dallas, Texas, laywoman, was appointed program chairman. Members of the CWF Department staff were all given major responsibilities in addition to their regular job portfolios. Velva Dreese worked on general arrangements, with several volunteers assisting. She continued this assignment through the 1966 Quadrennial Assembly. Martha Whitehead (who married Judson W. Faw one week after the Assembly) worked as program coordinator on the Hall of Music sessions. She served in a similar capacity for five additional assemblies.

Mary Mondy Dale was no stranger to Indianapolis. She had served for a brief time as national director of adult missionary education prior to her marriage to Jack B. Dale, a Dallas business leader. She was a participant in CWF's formation in Texas, and was elected as a member of the first ICWF Advisory Council. Mary's husband died suddenly in November 1956, but she continued with her responsibilities for the Assembly. Shortly afterward she became executive secretary of the Department of Institutional Missions, UCMS, and moved again to Indianapolis.

Program personalities at the first Quadrennial Assembly were of the highest caliber. Dr. Nels Ferre, the distinguished professor of Christian theology at Vanderbilt University and later at Andover Newton Theological School, gave four lectures on Romans. He requested that those attending prepare in advance by reading the New Testament book weekly, and by memorizing the King James Version of the twelfth chapter. Dr. Ferre's book *Making Religion Real* became a best-seller among the women because of his dynamic lectures. Mary Pollard, longtime missionary of India for the United Society, was another effective speaker for whom the audience held high esteem, for most had studied her work and knew of her service through the pages of *World Call* magazine.

Dr. Madeleine Barot was present from Geneva, Switzerland, to bring greetings from the women's office of the World Council of

Churches, and to lead a conversation group where she answered questions about her work and shared her vision of a church in which women and men work equally. Mossie Wyker, Rosa Page Welch, and Cynthia Wedel, president of Church Women United, rounded out the team of thirty ecumenical representatives from Protestant North American churches, Mossie and Rosa being Disciples of Christ women whose ministries at that time were largely in inter-church circles.

The size of the Edward C. Elliott Hall of Music was overwhelming and the latest in stage technology and design was breathtaking. Many women witnessed for the first time some of the special effects that can be obtained with a stage the size of a football field, parts of which could be set in motion with the flip of a switch. Unusual lighting blended with sound effects to produce an impressive pageant on opening night, and equally effective dramatizations of social concerns and missionary education. Seventeen young people were commissioned as missionaries of Disciples of Christ, with each one making a brief response. They went to India, Thailand, Paraguay, Mexico, and Africa.

On Sunday morning an impressive service of worship featured an ordained Disciples woman, Harriet-Louise H. Patterson, from Cleveland, Ohio; it was the first time many in the Assembly had heard a woman preach. The session concluded with an observance of communion, enhanced by music and lighting that gave added beauty to the setting.

The centerpiece of the assembly was the study and discussion of Samuel F. Pugh's manual, *Women's Place in the Total Church*, published by the CWF Department specifically for this use. Dr. Floy S. Hyde, staff member of United Church Women, met with 139 women in March of the assembly year to train them for leadership of the two-hour afternoon discussion groups. Because it was felt that women should know every phase of church life and prepare themselves to accept any responsibility made available, this study was mandated. It covered the eight functions of church planning as highlighted in Shelton's book, *The Church Functioning Effectively*, and emphasized in the local church program planning manuals widely used during this era in Disciples of Christ congregations. Dr. A. Dale Fiers, UCMS president, wrote, "This convocation will essentially be a great training institute for women so they can more adequately accept their responsibilities in the total functional life of the church."[6] Dr. Fiers was wholeheartedly in agreement with the assembly planners that women must be ready to make their full contribution to the Christian enterprise at all levels of its life. Because of this training at Purdue, 3,575 registrants returned home ready to make suggestions for change in their congregation's ways of doing things and prepared to accept their share of the workload.

It required more than a thousand volunteers to produce an assembly of such large magnitude. Needed were ushers, dormitory hostesses, press room assistants, bookstore and gift shop clerks, exhibits personnel, transportation (on campus) aides, and hostesses for program participants, overseas guests, missionaries, and the dining room. In addition, there were 168 choir members, 47 nurses, 14 post office workers, and 18 lost-and-found assistants. The registration fee was $37, which covered room and meals for four days, accident insurance, and the usual assembly costs. Interestingly, the CWF Department had no reserve funds, so Jessie Trout drew up a project proposal, which she presented to the UCMS president on behalf of the ICWF Advisory Council, requesting a loan of $10,000. After much questioning the loan was granted. Following the completion of the assembly, Miss Trout summoned her entire staff to accompany her to Dr. Fiers's office, where she presented a check repaying the loan in full. Surprised and delighted, Dr. Fiers said, "I must confess that when I gave you $10,000 months ago I kissed it goodbye. I really didn't think I would ever see that money again!" After ten additional assemblies, it has not been necessary for the leaders to borrow funds a single time.

THE BIG U WORD: UNIFICATION

When CWBM was formed in 1874, it became an autonomous organization with auxiliaries on the state and local church levels. The organization grew, as did its outstanding missionary service. When the United Society was proposed, one of the major concerns was safeguarding the work and place of the women leaders. When Unified Promotion was created in 1935, one of the issues was protecting the offerings from women's groups. The matter was further complicated as the Women's Council became the umbrella organization in congregations. Questions arose about how much mission study would be involved, and how much should be raised for missions.

The creation of CWF in 1949 solved many problems but created a few new ones for women, mostly revolving around the money question. Because the United Society still carried a budget item for assistance to those states with which it had long-standing agreements "to help provide for field staff and programs," the United Society found it necessary to negotiate with each state's administrative group to ensure that certain conditions were met. On the state level, unification meant that all boards, with their treasuries and programs, would unify in one total board with one total program. Women were uneasy about this until they had more than verbal assurances that the new unification would provide for adequate representation. When the women at the 1957 Quadrennial Assembly voted to apply their offerings to all Unified Promotion causes, not just UCMS, they provided an example for the whole church to follow, but it did create another dilemma in the unification process.

Unification status had been achieved in six states by 1958: Alabama, Nebraska, Iowa, Georgia, Illinois, and Missouri. It had been voted on in Indiana, Washington, Colorado, and Kentucky, to become effective July 1, 1959. This was a tedious process, especially in those states where equality of leadership was questioned. Jessie Trout and her associate, Velva Dreese, spent many, many days traveling to state meetings. Miss Trout included a comprehensive listing of the advantages of unification in the documents she provided for study, along with a similar list of disadvantages. The advantage list included unity of the state staff, more women and laymen serving on functional committees and the general board, more churchwide concern and responsibility for the outreach program, and better program coordination between the special interest groups and commissions.

So much was at stake concerning the women's program in each state. In areas where boards and other planning groups were mostly comprised of male pastors, it took longer to convince them of the advantages of adding women members to their respective planning groups. The training women received at the 1957 Quadrennial Assembly became a strong point for those arguing on the side of unification. Women's boards, on the other hand, had to make certain their programs and projects would retain the high quality of leadership and that their offerings would still help provide the types of training and leader development already set in place.

Unification provided another step toward the Disciples of Christ becoming "church" and being recognized as a structure through which the Campbell-Stone traditions might be sharpened and adapted for the second half of the twentieth century. To be sure, there were those among the international leadership who felt unification must be completed as rapidly as possible in order that restructure of the total church might move forward.

In the summer of 1957, under the auspices of the Council of Agencies, a consultative conference was held at the Disciples Divinity House in Chicago, the purpose of which was to raise two basic questions and examine possible answers. The questions were: (1) What are Disciples of Christ currently doing to discharge their full obligation as part of world Christendom? and (2) Are Disciples of Christ adequately organized for their task on all levels beginning at the local church? Out of this consultation, and other meetings that followed, came the statement by Willard M. Wickizer that set in motion the direction the church would take. It was said:

> At no time in our history, except in very recent days, has anyone dared to suggest that what the Disciples of Christ need to do is to look at its total organizational structure and attempt a major restructuring that would result in more effective operation.[7]

Restructure would take another decade to be accomplished.

MEANWHILE, BACK AT THE OFFICE

Throughout the 1950s, Christian Women's Fellowships participated actively in the Long Range Program of the Disciples of Christ. Initiated by the newly formed Council of Agencies in 1950, this program was supported by the women's organization through its four related goals of (1) deepened spiritual life, (2) doubled membership, (3) doubled giving, and (4) an annual school of missions in every church. These were emphasized in program materials and related resources such as *Guideposts for CWF*, a quarterly publication of the Department staff that provided information and suggestions primarily to local groups.

There were several staff changes during this period. Alice Rist Langford succeeded Florence M. Sly as program coordinator, and in 1955 she was succeeded by Martha Whitehead. Alma B. Scott, after a long service as departmental associate, retired on January 1, 1958, and was followed by Mildred Smith. Anna Bell Jackson, in 1951 the new director of Missionary Organizations-Education under the National Christian Missionary Convention, was invited to join the staff of the CWF Department. She served in this dual capacity until her resignation became effective in 1960, coinciding with the merger of program and services of the National Convention with the United Society. Anna Bell Jackson Jones was succeeded by Lois Mothershed. Lois, the youngest woman ever to be appointed a staff member in the women's department, went to her new position as director of Local Fellowship Services immediately following graduation from Phillips University. Lois joined the staff in June, only a few weeks prior to the beginning of the second Quadrennial Assembly on

July 19. She resigned two years later when her marriage took her to live in Holland. She was followed by Eunice B. Miller.

The ICWF elected officers changed at the conclusion of the first Quadrennial Assembly. Serving during the 1957–1961 quadrennium were Edith Evans and Elizabeth Landolt. As president, Mrs. Evans was called on to give leadership to the consultative conference in 1960, a conference that had been called for in the 1949 discussions at Turkey Run. Held January 25–29 at Indiana University, this ten-year review produced a general awareness of satisfaction with the status of CWF, choosing only to make an addition to the statement purpose. Now it would read "to develop all women in Christian living and Christian service as part of the witnessing church of Jesus Christ." Edith Evans proved her effectiveness as a speaker during this conference when she was assigned a series of lectures on "The Christian Woman." She had served as president in her local CWF and for five years as president of the Upper Midwest CWF, which included Iowa, Minnesota, and North and South Dakota. She was present at the Turkey Run Conference. She also was president of the Austin, Minnesota, Council of United Church Women, and completed a term on the board of managers of the United Society. Mrs. Evans continued to give generously of her gifts to the church for many years after her term as president. Ultimately her health failed, and she died in the summer of 1996.

Elizabeth Landolt was an excellent choice to serve as vice president. Her delightful sense of humor provided welcomed moments of respite in serious discussions of the Advisory Council and other CWF enterprises. She served in several capacities on the Missouri women's board, including that of president. Elizabeth was an entertaining, yet forceful speaker. An ordained minister, she served with her husband at Central Church in Moberly, Missouri, for a long ministry before and after her years as ICWF vice president. Mrs. Landolt continued to participate in church and civic causes until an extended illness ended her life on February 6, 1998.

The 1950s had seen the Korean conflict, the Russian space program's race past United States achievements, and the rush to suburbia, which made possible the American dream of marriage, home ownership, and parenthood for thousands of young people who longed for wholesome stability. The birth rate exploded by 1957 to an all-time high of 4.3 million, or one baby born every seven seconds, creating a boom that would echo across the land for decades to come. The church was challenged to help young couples cope with the pressures of middle-class conformity that had been portrayed in *The Man in the Gray Flannel Suit*, a best-selling novel of the day, and with the resurgence of religion. Reverend Billy Graham, Bishop Fulton J. Sheen, and Pope John XXIII were very popular on the world stage. Congress, in 1956, added the words "In God We Trust" to all U.S. currency. Only two years earlier, the phrase "under God" was added to the Pledge of Allegiance. Growing numbers flocked to the nation's churches. Polls showed that nine out of ten Americans believed in God. The introduction of the *Revised Standard Version of the Bible* resulted in the sale of 26.5 million copies its first year.

THE DECADE OF DECISION

The Disciples of Christ met these challenges head-on with a churchwide program it dubbed "The Decade of Decision." Beginning January 1, 1960, this program recognized that its predecessor, the Long Range Program, had made significant advances but there was much yet to do. For women, this involved new CWFs as new congregations were established. It meant providing creative programs of study, inspiration, and service; giving leadership and guidance and assistance in organization, spiritual growth, and personal enrichment; and increasing concern for witness, mission, and stewardship. Appropriate goals from other areas of program planning were also incorporated into program materials for women's groups, and the 1961 Quadrennial Assembly provided an excellent training ground for preparing local church women to assume places of leadership in their home congregations.

Quadrennial Assembly 1961

"Choose Ye This Day," the theme for the assembly, pointed to the Decade of Decision. Daily considerations in the Hall of Music, as well as in sixty "Let's Talk About It" groups, were designed to point women to greater involvement in the total life of their congregations. A study book, *Let's Talk About Decisions*, was prepared by Anne J. Beach, Pauline Thames, and Florence Sly to form the basis of the daily discussions. The Quadrennial Assembly committee also commissioned three dramas to be written and produced by Ralph Stone and The Texas Players. An interesting note concerning a member of this young group whom Ralph Stone had enlisted for the cast is that Susan Ferre, a niece of Dr. Nels Ferre, returned to the Quadrennial Assembly in 1978 and 1982 as organist. The dramas lifted up the basic choices that confronted women, especially in those areas under consideration by the 2,885 assembly-goers. The Bible lectures, given each day by Dr. A. Dale Fiers, UCMS president, related to the theme, as did major addresses by Dean James Robinson, Dr. Virgil A. Sly, and Dr. Perry Gresham, the latter two being well-known Disciples.

Many features of the first Quadrennial Assembly were offered again in 1961—the large choir, conversations with overseas guests, a bookstore, a large exhibit area, the international gift shop, and the commissioning of eighteen newly appointed missionaries for overseas service.

"That I, Too, Would Obtain"

Perhaps the most significant development in 1961 affecting the area of Disciples women's work was the resignation of Jessie Trout from her position of fifteen years as executive secretary of the CWF Department and its predecessor and eleven years as vice president of the United Society. At her own request, she was transferred to the World Mission Division, the successor group to the Division of Foreign Missions, which had launched her career as a missionary in 1921. Jessie devoted the last two years of her active ministry as executive secretary of Field Liaison, traveling to India, East Asia, Africa, and Latin America before concluding her service in her beloved Japan. She spent her retirement years in Owen Sound, Ontario, until her death on June 3, 1990, a few weeks short of her ninety-fifth birthday. In reporting her death, *The Broadcaster*, the Quadrennial Assembly newspaper, reported:

> She served as an impressive and outstanding leader for women of the Christian Church (Disciples of Christ). Her dedicated spirit will live on in the lives of women inspired by her strong sense of dedication of time and talent. Many have assumed leadership positions in the Christian Church (Disciples of Christ) because of her encouragement and support.[8]

In 1953, Jessie Trout wrote a book of devotional messages, *Like a Watered Garden*, which she dedicated to "the memory of my grandmother Jessie and my mother Catherine, in whom dwelt the sincere faith that I, too, would obtain." And indeed she did.

Jessie Trout's resignation opened the way for a former staff member to return to the United Society. Helen F. Spaulding, who had served as youth and children's director in the former Missionary Organizations Department, was called from the staff of the National Council of Churches of Christ to succeed Miss Trout, and began her new work on January 1, 1962. Velva Dreese was acting executive during the four-month interim. Helen Spaulding came during many transitions in the activities of CWF. New ICWF officers had been installed at the conclusion of the 1961 Quadrennial Assembly, as had new members of the ICWF Advisory Council. New relationships were evolving in the state CWF staffs, with seven retirements that year and all state staffs accepting the added assignment for service to all CWFs related to the National Christian Missionary Convention. It is of interest that CWF entered into plans for a major interdenominational emphasis on "Assignment: Race" during this year.

Helen Spaulding went into women's work in Illinois upon her graduation with honors in 1930 from the University of Illinois. For five years she discharged the duties of the women's state secretary, then moved to Indianapolis to take up her assignment with the United Society. In 1943 she moved to Chicago to work with the International Council of Religious Education. She also served with the National Council of Churches in New York before returning to Indianapolis, where she served with distinction until her retirement at the end of 1974. Miss Spaulding lives in Foxwood Springs, a National Benevolent Association retirement community.

An observer has suggested that the 1960s might well be characterized as "a dizzying decade of highs and lows," seeing some triumph but mostly tragedy in civil rights, John F. Kennedy's assassination, the ordeal of Vietnam and the Six-Day War in the Middle East. "The dizzying decade of highs and lows" was also descriptive of life among the Disciples of Christ, for restructure had kicked into high gear among the church's leaders, bringing with it heated discussion and polarization. Since the Council of Agencies meeting in 1958, with its report that at last someone "dared to suggest that what the Disciples of Christ need to do is to look at its total organizational structure and attempt a major restructure," this had been the subject of many conversations, committees, and conventions. It continued to be so until the Provisional Design was adopted by the Kansas City International Convention in 1968. The question was no longer "whether." Now it became "how."

Disciples women were greatly impacted by this major step, for many local congregations took action to disassociate themselves from the new "church" that the Design created, taking the local CWF with them. States, newly organized as Regions under the new plan, found themselves in various stages of progress toward the organizational pattern suggested by the Design. Those which had achieved unification were ready; but not all states were ready. The United Society was on the verge of separating itself into two major divisions of the church. Christian Women's Fellowship found it very difficult to adapt to this separation, for historically it was rooted in the cause of missions; but now it was to find its life in the Division of Homeland Ministries, which would care for the program and concerns of the Christian Church in the United States and Canada. There is little reason to doubt that restructure had an adverse effect on the outcome of the move toward a unified lay movement in the late 1960s.

The second ten-year review of the women's organization, agreed on at Turkey Run, was stepped up in light of the myriad of changes taking place in the church at all its levels. In 1968, the Consultation on Women in the Church was slated for February 28–March 3 in St. Louis. Lorraine Lollis wrote:

> The mood of 1968 was: CWF had fulfilled its purpose. If it has been effective as a training ground for leadership in the total church, let its members now prove themselves in this larger arena. Let them be, in name and in fact, a part of the "whole people of God." Let them think, plan, and work in terms of a lay movement, men and women together, in the church and in mission to the world.[9]

This will be treated more fully in Part II.

New Occasions, New Duties

The 1960s produced many new developments in church structures and programs, and along with these emerged many highly capable women leaders. As Jessie Trout prepared to transfer to another phase of ministry, she was concerned that the new ICWF officers taking charge at the end of the 1961 Assembly be fully capable. Lucille Cole, Helen Pearson, and Helen Spaulding brought to their tasks as president, vice president, and executive exactly those particular gifts needed to meet the challenges of their day.

Lucille Cole was a fourth-generation Disciple, educated at Hiram College, a Disciples school, and afterward employed as assistant pastor to Dr. Harry B. McCormick at Lakewood Christian Church in Cleveland. She served on several boards and committees of the Disciples in Ohio, including a term as state CWF president. Her experience as a member and later chairman of the board of directors of Unified Promotion, and her involvement on the board of the Council of Church Women in Cincinnati, stood her in great stead to be the president of an international church body.

QUADRENNIAL ASSEMBLY
International Christian Women's Fellowship
(DISCIPLES OF CHRIST)

ΙΧΘΥΣ

Courage To Be Christian

June 27 - July 1, 1966
Purdue University - Lafayette Indiana

Quadrennial Assembly 1966

Helen Pearson was an outstanding leader in Texas church circles. Like her mother before her, Helen taught an adult class and remained active in the local women's organization, even during the years of her service as ICWF vice president. She was a member of the boards of managers and trustees of the United Society, and was elected as second vice president of the International Convention. Like her coworker, Helen had served as state CWF president and brought to her new task administrative skills that she often needed.

For many years after her tenure as an ICWF officer, Helen Pearson continued to be in demand as a spokesperson for the Disciples of Christ. Declining health prevented her participation after the restructure of the early 1970s. She died December 9, 1990.

The World Convention of Churches of Christ was on a five-year schedule for its assembly, and the 1965 meeting was on the calendar for the same time as the third ICWF Quadrennial. The ICWF Advisory Council looked carefully at this conflict and decided that it would be wise to postpone the ICWF gathering for a year, given the fact that the world assembly would be in San Juan, Puerto Rico, and many Americans would take advantage of its closeness. This decision extended the terms of the ICWF officers and Advisory Council members. For one term in the fifty-year history of CWF, its quadrennium became a quintennium.

Staff changes during the 1960s included the following: Martha Whitehead Faw, director of program coordination, was succeeded by Jane Heaton in November 1961; Eunice Miller came in February

1965 to fill the vacancy left by Lois Mothershed; Essie Gandy began in 1965 as director of leadership development, replacing Leta Bradney, who had transferred to the World Outreach Education Department; Mildred Smith completed her service as departmental associate in 1962 and was followed by Olive Trinkle.

The retirement of Velva Dreese in 1967 marked the completion of a distinguished career that spanned thirty-seven years of official relationship with the United Society. She began as a missionary to the Philippines, then served on the Kansas state staff before joining the women's department just prior to the Turkey Run Conference. Velva served as associate executive secretary to Jessie Trout for nearly twenty years, a relationship described by one observer thus: "Jessie was the dreamer; Velva made the dreams come true." She had responsibility for the annual staff meeting, orientation and in-service training for all women staff, and the general chairmanship of the first three Quadrennial Assemblies. Miss Dreese died October 17, 1992.

Disciples women maintained a high level of involvement in local and state councils of United Church Women; the ecumenical organization in Canada was slightly different, but Disciples women there were equally as involved as were their sisters to the south. Christian Women's Fellowship staff and officers served on the national executive committee, board, and program committee of United Church Women. A unique expression of ecumenical solidarity came when Lucille Cole was selected as the American Protestant woman to be guest leader in the retreats of Protestant Women of the Chapel, related to U.S. armed forces abroad, in France and Germany in September, 1966. Mrs. Cole passed away September 29, 1998.

The high point in 1966 for Disciples women came in the form of the third ICWF Quadrennial Assembly. Between June 27 and July 1, 3,773 registered participants—more than were expected—filled their minds, hearts, and spirits with the theme's challenge: "Courage to Be Christian." Mae Yoho Ward, one of Discipledom's greatest speakers, gave the keynote address. During the assembly, other provocative and informative persons of faith were heard: Mossie Wyker, Congresswoman Edith Green, theologian Georgia Harkness, and Anna Arnold Hedgeman, an executive for the Commission on Religion and Race of the National Council of Churches. The main events of previous assemblies were again incorporated into the program activities, with one addition: Dormitory Chat Groups were planned for each afternoon. This assembly featured for the first time a "thread"—a monologue in which "The Woman" daily reflected on her experiences of the week—as a program piece. It was warmly received, and the dramatic use of such a piece has continued with each successive assembly: The Reporter, 1874–1974 women, Edith Ann, the Wizards of Oz, Grace and Eunice, Rocky McLean, and Grandma Bridges.

The 1966 Quadrennial Assembly ended with the installation of two new leaders as president and vice president. Betty K. Fiers was chosen to lead the women for the next four years, and Ann Burns was chosen to serve with her. Both brought a high enthusiasm for the roles women were assuming in the total church, demonstrating by their own involvement the high priority such roles filled in their lives. Both women were married to clergymen and yet found time to share volunteer service in state and general church settings. Betty and Ann chose to swap assignments for the 1970 assembly, thus giving responsibility for formal program to Ann and for general services to Betty. Mrs. Fiers continued to participate in church life until her death on June 28, 1998.

More to Come

Like the great church edifices of the world, any structural organization of a movement requires continued repair and, from time to time, perhaps remodeling, or at best, new construction. So it was with CWF. There was, and is, a sense of movement, life, and purpose in moving from one important stage in its growth to the next. Over the years, the purpose of the organization was to develop women in Christian living and service. The wording has been changed along the way, as have the methods and means when deemed appropriate, but the intent has remained the same. Whether individual, congregational, regional or international, CWF's intent is "to provide opportunities for spiritual growth, enrichment, education and creative ministries to enable women to develop a sense of personal responsibility for the whole mission of the church of Jesus Christ."[10]

ICWF PRESIDENTS AND VICE PRESIDENTS 1953–1978

1953–1957

ICWF President
Freda Putnam

Vice President
Hazel Rudduck

1957–1961

ICWF President
Edith Evans

Vice President
Elizabeth Landolt

1961–1966

ICWF President
Lucille Cole

Vice President
Helen Pearson

1966–1970

ICWF President
Betty Fiers

Vice President
Ann Burns

1970–1974

ICWF President
Mary Louise Rowand

Vice President
Fran Craddock

1974–1978

ICWF President
Carnella Barnes

Vice President
Virginia Bell

ICWF PRESIDENTS AND VICE PRESIDENTS 1978–2002

1978–1982

ICWF President
Betty Mohney

Vice President
Sybel Thomas

1982–1986

ICWF President
Marilyn Moffett

Vice President
Catherine Broadus

1986–1990

ICWF President
Martha Faw

Vice President
Odatta Reed

1990–1994

ICWF President
Bonnie Frazier

Vice President
Maureen Osuga

1994–1998

ICWF President
Lenita "Jackie" Bunch

Vice President
Peggy Gray

1998–2002

ICWF President
Josephine "Jo" Elkins

Vice President
Kathy Jeffries

$Part$ II
1968 TO THE PRESENT AND BEYOND

$Nancy$ $Heimer$

$\mathcal{I}$ntroduction to Part II

The year 1968 marked one of those pivotal moments in history when both achievement and notoriety explode onto the scene, sometimes without distinguishing which is which, when both magical and horrific events collide in a mad cultural war. It was the year of the assassinations of Martin Luther King, Jr., and Senator Robert F. Kennedy and the deadly city strife that followed. *Time* magazine called it the year of disillusion. There were the riots at the Democratic national convention in Chicago, the North Vietnamese Tet offensive that spelled the beginning of the end for the United States in Vietnam. It was the year of television's *Laugh-In* and the expression "Sock it to me." *Hair* opened on Broadway, with its total cast nude scene. "Here's to You, Mrs. Robinson" was number one on the pop music charts. Tiny Tim sang "Tiptoe Through the Tulips" and Janis Joplin, "Me and Bobby McGee," and the Beatles released their White Album. The ground was laid for the rock-fest known as Woodstock and the first human landing on the moon.

Women participated fully in the ferment and friction of the 1960s that stirred up society by challenging many roles, agencies, and activities. New visions and interpretations of who should do what were emerging in all areas of life—government, education, community, and family. Women were noticing where they were not: in business, in government, on boards and committees, and in the pulpit. They had the vote but they were not voting for other women—because no women were running. Some became outspoken in demanding their rights, however. While a significant portion could not understand what the fuss was all about, there was no question that, by 1968, the feminist movement was well under way. There were going to be some changes made—for women were on the march.

It was the year in which the women of the church held one of their most important consultations ever. As in the beginning of women's organized work in 1874, this conference was centered on mission. The participants defined both the mission and ministry of women in relation to new issues of racism, sexism, and classism. From the Consultation, processes ensued that brought women into boards, pulpits, community service, and advocacy. Issues related to structure were inevitably raised because of the massive restructuring within the Christian Church (Disciples of Christ) and also because of comparisons with women's and laity structures within other denominations. The Consultation resulted in a recommendation for a laity department. This move reflected—and was the prelude to— women's struggle over their structure and identity within the church. Would they unite the laity and more fully integrate their program and structure with the men, fitting into the new denominational direction? Or, would they follow society's direction and seek their own liberation, self-realization, advocacy, and solidarity? This dilemma led to intensive work over the next two years. Even now, it continues to feed a smoldering, unhelpful debate.

New directions became apparent for the Christian Church (Disciples of Christ) when they approved an unprecedented restructuring that promised to make this large institution more cohesive and integrated. Disciples reconstituted themselves as an international "church," as opposed to the collection of congregations, agencies, and individuals that for 120 years stressed their autonomies and competed with one another for the Disciples' hearts and funding. For at least twenty years there had been a strong movement to regularize the relationships of Disciples beyond the local congregation without treading on autonomies. The Disciples called the process "Restructure." Under Restructure, there was a representative (as opposed to mass) assembly, a General Board, and voluntary divisions and councils of the church, where once there had been independent agencies. The Disciples' more centralized structure was approved at the very time most structures in North American society—particularly big ones—were under attack. Decentralization was the rage. Individualism was the focus in what some called "the me generation." Yet, in Restructure, Disciples were integrating and fashioning themselves a more cohesive umbrella institution, centralizing, and basing it all on community and covenant.

While certain women—notably Mae Yoho Ward, former vice president of United Christian Missionary Society; Helen Spaulding, executive for the Department of Christian Women's Fellowship;

Dorothy Richeson from Minnesota and Sybel Thomas from Illinois were fundamental to the Restructure process, most women of the church were ambivalent or indifferent. If they were going to realize their potential as women, they would have to think about how they could enhance and advance one another. It would not do to simply acquiesce to the predominantly male status quo. They would have to build on their history as well as the momentum of women's organizations. They would claim their identity and full partnership in the church, and it would come at their own initiative. And yet, feeling they were the very heart of the church and the movement to restructure, they were supportive of the process, with all its integration and coalescence and all its attempts to downplay group distinctions. As we shall discover in another section, it would lead to a short-term attempt to merge the laymen's and laywomen's departments into a Department of the Laity.

No longer would the movement that coalesced in Lexington, Kentucky, in 1832 be called a "brotherhood," a euphemism for the dreaded word "denomination." "Denomination" was dreaded because the Disciples of Christ originated as a movement to promote Christian unity. The Disciples could hardly bear the thought that they had become another denomination. Not surprisingly, however, some women of the church believed that the word "brotherhood" was unacceptable. The news bureau of the Disciples demonstrated how absurd the word was to identify a religious body that included both men and women. On the news letterhead that went out to media outlets in the 1960s was the identification: "a brotherhood" of churches with "relations with sister churches" around the world. Most women were delighted to get rid of the "brotherhood" they had known, in favor of a "church."

LANGUAGE IS IMPORTANT

When one is dealing with an identity and liberation movement, language can be more critical than it would at first seem. Before the restructure of the Christian Church (Disciples of Christ), it is fair to say that the use of "man" as the generic for everybody didn't seem to be a big issue in the church. That was evident in the 1966 mission studies theme: "Christ and the Faiths of Men." As late as 1974, women in the program book of the Quadrennial Assembly were identified as "Mrs. John Doe" or occasionally "Doe, Mrs. John Q. (Jane)." Generic use of male imagery and language dominated the program materials and liturgies. Not because of the Restructure, of course, but commensurate with it, inclusive language became extremely important.

Disciples women activists were adamant about changing the male generic and set about to do so. They contended that if pulpit committees, for instance, wanted the "best man for the job," they might not get the best, but they would always get a man. Use of the male generic had become almost an absurdity within the church and society at large. A New York state assemblyman was quoted as saying: "When we get the abortion law repealed, everyone will be able to decide for himself whether or not to have an abortion." The place to start appeared to be in educating the church constituency in how language affects response and triggers sexist habit.

Women objected, for example, to the common term "chairman" to denote either a woman or man. Most frequently the term "chairperson" was a common replacement, but the struggle to determine a more appropriate term led to more accuracy with such designations as "moderator," "enabler," "convener," etc. While some women strongly objected to this change, others applauded it. Both women and men began to notice that language did have a way of shutting out or embracing people. As the president of the Council on Christian Unity, Robert Welsh, put it, "Once I heard the difference [between gender specific and inclusive language], I could not stop hearing it. Now it really bothers me when people use male terms to indicate all people."

It is so difficult to free our minds from identifying male as the norm. For example, as women began to serve more frequently as elders or as pastors, they were referred to as "women elders" or "lady pastors." Yet to refer to "men elders" or "gentlemen pastors" would be considered humorously redundant. It was assumed that, without a modifying word, the elder or pastor would be male.

One of the male general staff members of the Disciples of Christ provided a good illustration of what exclusive language does to one subconsciously. He said he had been attending an ecumenical women's meeting dealing with his expertise—stewardship—when he suddenly realized he was drifting off into other thoughts, and not participating, even though it was the subject he loved. Suddenly it hit him. Each time the women said "she" or "her," he felt excluded from the conversation. And so he opted out, subconsciously, even though he carried perhaps the most important information available on the subject and was expected to be a major participant.

In the 1970s, while serving as director of leader development in the women's department, I realized the importance of inclusive language efforts to the church. Therefore, I brought the issue to the attention of General Minister and President Kenneth L. Teegarden. The preponderance of male language and imagery used generically in the foundation document of the Christian Church (Disciples of Christ), the (Provisional) Design for the Christian Church, was a problem that had to be addressed. Both Dr. Teegarden and Dr. Ronald Osborn, a framer of the design, grasped the importance of this request and promised to take immediate action. As is often the case, these changes not only made the document more inclusive but also strengthened it.

Speaking of language, there may need to be some clarification of terms and their organizational manifestations in the restructured church. First of all, there is no "national" Office of Church Women. There is no national staff. Since Canadian women are involved equally—even though their numbers are small—the reference is to "international" office or staff, or to "general" offices and staff. The International Christian Women's Fellowship (ICWF) is the organization of women in the United States and Canada. They work through the Division of Homeland Ministries,the "general" unit of the church responsible for laity work, Christian education, social action, ministry, evangelism, and worship. On the other hand, the World Christian Women's Fellowship is the result of requests from around the world for a world organization. It meets in conjunction with the World Convention of the Churches of Christ, a meeting held every four years of the three religious bodies with origins in the Alexander Campbell-Barton Stone movements, with representatives from churches in countries throughout the world.

Memberships of local CWF groups totaled 21 percent of the membership of the entire church at that time. Women's giving to mission through those organizations amounted to $2.3 million, or more than 14 percent of the basic outreach dollar. Women were formidable in numbers and finance, even before they made their political impact.

Unification: A Threat to Women's Power

One thing women did not want out of Restructure was an updated version of what happened in 1920. Then, women accepted the idea of a unified mission program at the international level and merged their Christian Woman's Board of Missions with the American and Foreign missionary societies to form the United Christian Missionary Society (UCMS). This new organization represented the bulk of the national and world ministries of the Disciples. The women's board brought into the merger 53 percent of the total assets and most of the energy for mission. While the new board was built on equal numbers of men and women, the top leadership represented a perpetual second-class status for women. A provision stated that the two top officers of the newly constituted UCMS would be a man and a woman. In practice, that meant a male president and a female vice president, whereas previously women had headed the most powerful and effective of the three incorporated missionary societies for forty-six years and had done much of the missionary planting overseas. There was a small exception to the unbroken line of men. Jesse M. Trout, leader of the group that founded Christian Women's Fellowship (CWF), filled an interim presidency for two months in 1951. While there was a loss of power for women in 1920 with the emergence of the UCMS, the Restructure in the 1960s and 1970s was perceived as a possible threat to women's identity. And in the mid-1990s, there would be a new threat, both to power and identity.

THE 1968 WOMEN'S CONSULTATION

During the late 1960s several denominations, including the Methodists and Presbyterians, held consultations for women to identify how they perceived their future and the impact of this future on the church. Therefore, in 1968, Disciples women held a pivotal meeting to set new directions for women in the restructured church. About 150 women and men, lay and clergy, from throughout the church gathered in St. Louis from February 28 to March 3 at the Gateway Hotel to chart a new course. This meeting was planned by Betty Fiers, ICWF President, and Helen Spaulding, executive secretary to the Department of Christian Women's Fellowship. In her introductory report to the consultation, Spaulding said the effort would require a process of "feed forward." That, she said, is a process that anticipates, prepares for, a potential outcome. Feed forward is a "needed prescription" for a feedback—which the feedback may or may not confirm, she said. "For a successful feed-forward, we need to examine objectives or ideas from various viewpoints."[1]

President of the UCMS Virgil A. Sly was a key speaker at the meeting and another important figure in Restructure. "It is [the church's] responsibility to see that in the new structure churchwomen are accorded a place of leadership comparable to that which they have experienced and enjoyed in the United Society," he told the group. "This will not be easy. How do you carry a fifty-fifty representation throughout the structure of the church?" And he added: "One of the things you women are going to have to decide is whether you want a fixed representation or a representation based on merit alone."[2]

Already Sly was anticipating the resistance to an increased visibility of women in the total life of the church. And he raised an even more prophetic issue. "We have tried to fit women into men's molds and tried to measure their integrity and ability against men's objectives. There is no question in my mind that she can manage the role but, if this becomes her objective, she loses something of her integrity." He said further: "Any analysis of a woman's role starts with the fact that a woman is a person of equal integrity and ability with men, who are also persons. A woman's role, even as a person, is not the role of a man and, whenever women forget this, their whole cause is in danger. A woman is a woman. We must always face the fact that although women and men are identified as equals, we are men and women. I have a feeling it is in this area of the respective roles of the two sexes that we have do our hardest thinking."

The UCMS president offered the women's consultation several recommendations:

Involve women "deeply into a study of their role in the life of the church and try to see this role as fully integrated into and not apart from the totality of the church's mission to the world."

Reevaluate women's organizational structure "in order that it may fit in the totality of the Christian Church as a solid section of the concern of the church in carrying forward that mission."

Study "the special concerns of women as related to the gospel and its ministry and mission to the world in order that women can feel a significant responsibility for great areas of mission concern."

"I would alert women of their responsibility in pressing the issue of adequate representation. I would certainly see that they enlist the leadership of the church to do this, and not become specialized advocates for women's rights and/or positions (a stance with which I would disagree!), but to see to it that the representation is cared for with the understanding that women will assume the responsibility when the church provides them a place to do so."

"As we face the future," said Sly, "the issues are going to be far more subtle, far more difficult to achieve. Women in their new freedom are being used by the secular interests of society to gain ends that are not for the development of women or that contribute to their integrity as persons. The greatest role of woman is being a woman. We are facing an era of great unfaith and moral casualness. Where are the standards that we are going to maintain, stand for and fight for? In a day when religious faith is being questioned, what do we believe?"

Out of the gathering came seven principles: (1) In Christ all are equal. (2) Participation by laity is critical. (3) Competence for the task should be the criterion for leadership. (4) Action in reconciling ministries is critical. (5) An ecumenical approach is required. (6) Flexibility and openness to change are essential. (7) Structures should be simplified and duplications eliminated. In principle 3, Disciples women made it clear they did not want parity simply because they are women. An approach through work with other denominations and groups was, and is, essential. The last two seemingly resulted in some headaches for the Disciples women, an action and a pullback, in the middle 1990s.

While the women of the church may have had special issues that drew their collective attention, they were by no means monolithic in their concerns. There were those women who had their histories in the organized CWF. There were the laywomen of the church who, while fully committed to the church and its ministries, were not attracted to CWF. Then, there were the clergywomen, soon to explode in numbers. African American women, together with their Anglo sisters, were seeking equality within the life of the church, with special emphasis on the Convocation of Black Churches (the biannual meeting for information and fellowship among black Disciples churches). Hispanic women were just in the process of organizing beyond the congregation. Asian women, few in numbers, were just discovering themselves as a group within the congregation.

In this book the thirty-plus years since Restructure have been divided into five basic periods along with a projection into the coming century:

> *The Self–realization Years, 1968–1973.* During those years, the issue was promoting awareness among the women themselves about their need to be involved in the leadership and power structures of the church. Participation was the focus, often resulting in only token numbers on boards, committees, and commissions.
>
> *The Advocacy Years, 1974–1982.* During those years women moved beyond their promised one third of the membership of boards and committees by pressing for fifty-fifty representation. The period also was marked by new developments

in recruiting women as clergy, plus some opportunities for congregations to appreciate women in the pulpit. There was strong advocacy for the Equal Rights Amendment and other women's concerns. Through programs and projects, women advocated in powerful ways on behalf of themselves and on social issues.

The Empowerment Years, 1983–1987. This era increased the intensity another degree. The period marked transitions in the women's organization itself, from more centralized to more dispersed decision making. Women were empowered through a revitalized structure.

The Solidarity Years, 1988–1992. There was a growing understanding that women around the world shared hopes and dreams as well as oppressions. Disciples women initiated woman-to-woman programs that took them around the world in solidarity with other women the world over. Women in the United States also acted in solidarity to ensure a strong, identifiable presence within the restructured Homeland Ministries.

The Reassessment Years, 1993–1998. After the Restructure, the tension had passed. It was time to reflect on and evaluate both the organization and the division. At the end of the century, Disciples women discovered new ways of working together.

The Horizon Years, 1999 and Beyond. Where are Disciples women going? In this section, we explore the possibilities and the problems that women face as they move into the twenty-first century.

THE *Self-realization Years*
1968–1973

In every American war since the Revolution, women functioned in nontraditional roles as men went away to fight. World War II was no different, and this time the process helped prompt lasting social change. Women assumed many of the essential tasks in industry, agriculture, merchandising, medicine, and law. From Rosie the Riveter to Elsie the Executive, women worked to keep the home front active and productive. Once peace was declared, the men returned home and the women were sent to their homes. There were not sufficient jobs to go around and the men, fresh from their experiences on the battlegrounds, needed tender loving care as well as employment.

This time women remembered their important role in the war effort and when the opportunities came they were ready. The economy grew rapidly after World War II and lifestyles in North America changed, apparently forever. More and more people had second homes and vacation places and multiple cars and boats and color televisions. With new lifestyles to support, and with the increasing freedom of women because of safer, more dependable birth control and a growing understanding of their right to self-realization, the numbers of women in jobs outside the home soon proliferated. And, with the struggle to find "quality time" for family out of that milieu, the changes could not help but affect numbers of women available to participate in CWF. So those numbers declined even faster than the total denominational membership, which dropped (as did that of other mainstream denominations) because of the increasing freedoms and entertainment options. Institutions—even, or especially, churches—declined in people's esteem. Society was changing and time was short. Church was not always a priority.

At the beginning of the Restructure Era in 1968, there were 4,070 local CWF groups that reported 214,912 members.[1] By the end of the period, CWF recorded 183,299 participating members in 3,343 CWF's,[2] declining in numbers as the denomination's own numbers declined and as more women slipped into the workforce and fewer had discretionary time. Some women did choose to devote their time to the church but, nevertheless, found themselves inspired by the changing society. The decade following the early years of the post-war period saw the rise of the Self-Realization Years as women realized they could become full partners with men. During this time women were searching for more appropriate ways of defining their identity and exploring what that meant in their participation within church and society. Continuing to covenant together in a community of women, they affirmed one another and challenged the church to recognize the significant leadership they were already providing and to expand the opportunities for exercising that leadership.

A New Laity: Merging the Work of Women and Men

Early on in Restructure, the desire to bring into harmony the radical autonomies of the past led to a move to combine men's and women's departments into a single Department of the Laity. For some, it made sense. If men and women were equal in the church, then a department that demonstrated the equality and combined the programming for men and women seemed appropriate. Besides, the effort in Restructure was to consolidate, eliminate overlapping, and demonstrate wholeness. And, there was the little matter of inflation, which was eating up the value of the dollar.

At the 1968 Consultation on Women, Mary Ellen LaRue of Iowa's regional staff told of how her state had restructured to include both women and men in one department. A keynote speaker, Violet Lineback, a guest representing the United Church of Christ (UCC), spoke enthusiastically about the five-year-old Council of Lay, Life and Work, which also pointed to efforts toward a new inclusiveness for the work of women and men. That denomination's new council, however, also marked the dissolution of a national office for their women's organization. "And, it took us twenty years to get it back," observed Marilyn Breitling, retired national UCC executive.[3] By then all connection with the women's organizations had been lost.

The Consultation brought together strong Disciples leaders such as Nellie Kratz, CWF regional staffperson from Northern California. Committed clergywoman Kratz and others became articulate advocates for a laity department within the newly formed Homeland Ministries. Within a few years, Kratz admitted, "I was wrong. We needed to empower women first." She went on to become a strong role model for young female ministers in the church.

Staff leaders had reservations about unifying the laity. Much earlier, Jessie Trout issued a warning: "It is premature to think that women have equality in the church and immature to think that men and women could not have separate groups." Helen F. Spaulding, who followed Trout as the executive secretary of the Department of CWF, worried that the laity department would result in the elimination of women's leadership, the men "simply running it again." Foreseeing that costs might force an eventual formation of a Laity Department, she held out hope that attitudes one day would change.[4]

After great debate, the Consultation made a recommendation to Homeland Ministries that a Department of Laity be established. The hope was that women would not lose ground—that such a department could maintain the strength and connections that would increase their leadership and participation. The time was not right, however, for either the men or the women. There was no will for such a radical move. Women were more drawn to self-realization, a trend in secular society, rather than consolidation. Subsequently, in 1972 Homeland Ministries formed a Lay Advisory Council, which united some of the work of the existing men's and women's departments. This compromise also helped to illustrate the willingness of both women and men to be responsible to the goals of the church's Restructure.

This new situation brought challenges as the women and men learned to work together. There was no animosity in the joint meetings that went on for years, but the two groups struggled for common ground. Simply stated, men's and women's histories were different. At this point in history, men, in my judgment, primarily were looking for spiritual development. Women sought full participation in the life of the church. Women who were exciting and dynamic together often became quiet when the two groups met. Their objectives—and perhaps the men's as well—were being arrested by the conflicted objectives of the mix. Imagine a church that rejects the leadership of women in dialogue with another church that already has women ministers. The communications go past each other. They simply are at a different place and on a different pace.

The Best Yet: Quadrennial Assembly

Few Disciples would deny that the women of the church have a unique vehicle for growth and development in the Quadrennial Assembly of the International Christian Women's Fellowship (ICWF). By 1970, when the fourth one was held, the Quadrennials had a churchwide reputation for excellence in programming and leadership development. They not only provided guidance and direction for Disciples women in church and society but they also were sources for education and information sharing to and from all the other agencies and organizations within the church. As the meetings empowered women, they empowered the church. The most frequently heard comment at the conclusion of every Quadrennial was and continues to be: "It was the best Quadrennial yet." Every four years the ICWF Quadrennial Committee seeks to rise to this challenge. Their success is evident. If you want to know what is happening in the lives of Disciples women, just review the program for the most recent Quadrennial.

Quadrennial Assembly 1970

"Quadrennial is an affirming experience of community, enabling us to speak the truth in confidence and challenging us to move on from where we are," said Jean Munro Gordon, past president of Women's Inter-Church Council of Canada. "The whole event provided a profound impact upon my spiritual being making it one of the highlights of my faith journey."[5] While the church's General Assembly is twice as large in numbers, about eight thousand, its focus is diffused on a variety of church business. At the spiritual setting of Quadrennial, the focus is more narrowly drawn on women's and Disciples' outreach to the world. At the 1970 Quadrennial at Purdue University in West Lafayette, Indiana, women assembled under the banner of "We Act in Faith...and Miracles Occur." There, women looked to the ever-present, all-powerful God and the strength of their faith to provide guidance and stability through the "uncharted, turbulent waters" of an unknown future.[6]

The interest groups at the 1970 event were called "Express-o" groups that time being the era of coffeehouses. Such adaptations that reveal the tenor of the times are a Quadrennial hallmark. "POW-WOW," or "Power of Women Where or When," was the name of the interest groups in 1974, just as Disciples women were striving to cope with the idea that they had power. At the 1970 Quadrennial, as in the previous three, most of the speakers and interest group leaders were men. The women still believed men were the experts, and they felt that learning was paramount and that providing women an opportunity to showcase their skills was secondary. This is a defining difference between the periods I have chosen to call the Self-realization Years and the Advocacy Years, bumping together in 1973 and 1974. Also common at the time of the 1970 Quadrennial was a generic use of male imagery and language that dominated the program materials and liturgies. Except for Georgia Harkness in 1966, all the Bible lecturers at Quadrennial until 1978 were men.[7] In 1978, a Bible dialogue between Philip Potter, executive director of the World Council of Churches, and Beatriz Melano Couch, a theologian from Argentina, marked a turning point. The next Quadrennial, in 1982, included a Bible panel of three Disciples clergywomen and a male moderator.[8]

Except for the leadership, only a few men participate in Quadrennial and most of them are spouses of women attending. Yet there was a workshop at the 1970 Quadrennial called "Laymen, wake up, it's later than you think" conducted by Owen Hungerford of Columbus, Indiana.[9] Not a bad topic for the laywomen as well!

After the 1970 Quadrennial Assembly, some members of the Church Women staff thought that the time had come to redirect their energies, to end the Quadrennial Assemblies and discover other methods for addressing the demands of changing times. Mary Louise Rowand, newly elected ICWF President, said that there must be a Quadrennial Assembly in 1974 to celebrate the 100th anniversary year for CWBM. Fran Craddock, then ICWF vice president, recalled that Kenneth Kuntz, president of Homeland Ministries; Robert Thomas, president of Overseas Ministries; A. Dale Fiers, General Minister and President of the Disciples; and T. J. Liggett, president of UCMS, all raised their powerful voices in strong support of the Quadrennial. The decision was made to have an assembly in 1974.

PREPARING FOR THE PRESENT: LEADERSHIP EVENTS

Leader training, information sharing, and action projects have always been paramount among Disciples women, but in the 1970s, these emphases were especially important. In 1973, the women of the church held 337 leader training events, with 13,700 women participating.[10] Regional CWF workshops brought congregational CWF leaders together annually to inform and train them to lead the upcoming study material. "These are so helpful," I overheard one study director say at a regional workshop in Paducah, Kentucky. "The ideas we get here are really clever and yet simple enough for us to use back home. I didn't know anyone in our church who could do the one idea of a fake telephone call (Bob Newhart style), so we just made it into a skit." Women took information and ideas and adapted them to their own situation. Such creative partnership builds leadership.

In 1973 the first interregional training events were held. Just as the CWF spring workshops brought leaders from congregations together, the interregional events allowed regional leaders to meet and share ideas, concerns, and methods. Instead of one general staff-person resourcing them, as was the custom for regional workshops, three or more general staff would be available. They provided new ideas, the latest churchwide programming information, and other specialized expertise as requested by the regional leadership.

While sponsored by the CWF, regional retreats for women increasingly attracted all women of the church. These events centered on spiritual development, worship, and personal enrichment. Often built on the annual CWF theme, they spoke to the individual Christian woman and her faith journey. Women were on the verge of discovering a new approach to Bible study. After centuries of male-centered theology, clergywomen started producing their own writings. Realization dawned that there was a biblical message for women and there was a woman's perspective to theology. Little by little, individuals realized that their experiences and insights brought a new dimension to the biblical message. Later, this idea spread throughout the church.

In the later part of this decade, retreats centered on Bible study and theological understanding as feminist biblical writing proliferated and women saw the need to integrate their emerging self-realization into their personal theology. As more women entered the workforce and lacked time for monthly CWF meetings, these retreats also served to provide "crash courses" in the CWF study material for that year. These retreats reflected the growing consciousness that women were diverse with a variety of needs. In 1973, a total of seventy-five retreats drew 6,114 women.[11]

SOCIAL ACTION IN THE ECUMENICAL ARENA

During the Self-Realization Years, women sought to understand themselves and their place in the world, but they were not so preoccupied that they ignored the call to help those in need around the world. Many of the social action foci were determined ecumenically. In 1969, the CWF took on as a project providing school and hospital supplies for Haiti, the poorest country in the Western Hemisphere. They also undertook a project to train unemployable women. Several women involved themselves in the Church Women United "Causeway" visits to the Republic of South Africa, the Dominican

Republic, and Venezuela. Across the years women were the back-bone of the church's world relief effort.

They exhibited a strong commitment to the quality of life, both physical and spiritual, for themselves, their communities, and communities elsewhere. In 1971, women's concerns included migrants, school dropouts, retardation and mental facilities, Head Start, day care, Native Americans, prisoners, veterans, and the aging. Haiti continued to be a focus, and another twelve thousand pounds of clothing and school supplies were delivered there. In 1972, while retaining the ecumenical emphasis, Disciples women turned to ministries of reconciliation, including domestic hunger, camping for inner city children, and youth centers.

Within the church, education, mission work, and other humanitarian services have usually been the responsibility of women. So, it was and still is with one of the most relentless of social problems: poverty. In the 1960s a program began that sought to face that problem and ease the burdens one person at a time.

MOTHER TO MOTHER: FRIENDS ACROSS ECONOMIC BARRIERS

Three women from Douglass Boulevard Christian Church in Louisville, Kentucky, went downtown to pick up Margaret, a "welfare mother" who had become their friend through the Mother-to-Mother Ministry. After taking Margaret to purchase new shoes for her three children and picking up a quick lunch at a nearby fast food spot, they were surprised to hear their new friend remark, "Well, don't you get extra for these shopping trips?" Apparently, Margaret thought they received payment for helping her. In a way they did, but not the way Margaret imagined. She certainly did not realize how much she helped them in their own journeys. Self-realization arises from challenges: through leaving home, or crossing town, and looking back to where you were; through talking and listening to someone outside your sphere, and learning how similar she is.

The Mother-to-Mother Ministry, which was part of the larger foundation-funded Change Through Involvement effort, was birthed by a man, Norman Ellington, a black staff member of the Missouri State Employment Security Division. Ellington, together with Dolores Holt, also of St. Louis, gave the early guidance to make it one of the most effective church programs, one that has continued to this day. At its peak, some thirty-six cities and more than thirteen hundred women were involved. Its premise was that if middle-class suburban women could get to know welfare mothers on a first-name basis, they not only would be educated about their counterparts' special needs but also might be able to help them work through the predominantly white power structures to receive services to which they were entitled, but lacked the background or experience to demand.

Ellington matched three fairly affluent churchwomen with one woman in need of assistance. Although there was a risk the churchwomen might dominate, Ellington hoped the poorer woman could develop an intimate friendship with at least one of her new acquaintances. Volunteers soon came to realize that child care and housing were among the crucial needs of poor urban mothers. On many instances when poor African Americans went to obtain loans or to rent apartments, they were turned away—except when accompanied by their white friend. It was an opportunity for sheltered whites to see racial oppression and to feel an empathy with other mothers. It was an enormous education as well as a significant service. And its purpose was to change suburban women's attitudes toward inner-city mothers through direct involvement.

Time after time, the churchwomen saw the unfair treatment of welfare mothers and their children. One instance occurred when several women made some clothes for an urban mother's children. After seeing the children, a schoolteacher promptly called the welfare office, which stopped sending checks. Officials assumed she was a welfare cheat because her children had such nice clothing.

Stirring women to action, many participants fought for legislative changes regarding government assistance. Others took action more directly. One good example of how change through involvement took place is in the story of Lynn Hood, a New Orleans Westside Christian Church elder. Agitated about how welfare mothers were treated when they applied for community services, and how little they knew that such services were available, Hood investigated failed welfare contacts by calling the power people in city administration and asking what happened. Eventually, under the auspices of Change Through Involvement, Hood operated out of a New Orleans office where she handled community problems for inner-city residents.[12]

RESOLUTIONS: WOMEN HAVING THEIR SAY

As the Self-Realization Years ended in favor of the Advocacy Years women exhibited a newfound political acumen, as they brought a flood of concerns to the General Assembly that gave a new impetus, if not direction. The 1973 General Assembly in Cincinnati was significant for several reasons. Disciples elected Kenneth L. Teegarden, General Minister and President, to succeed the "George Washington" figure of restructure, A. Dale Fiers. Teegarden had been a deputy of Fiers, a regional minister, a local pastor, and a community leader. At the Cincinnati Assembly, Disciples were led by their first ethnic minority moderator, Walter Bingham, an African American pastor from Louisville, who the previous year led a delegation of twenty-four Disciples leaders on a church-to-church visit to Asia—Japan, Hong Kong, Thailand, and India. Women's leaders such as Fran Craddock, Virginia Liggett, and vice-moderator Margaret Wilkes were included on that unique visit.

Resolutions directly related to the interests and concerns of women began to appear more regularly. Between 1971 and 1991 at least two or three were on the docket of each General Assembly, with six resolutions in 1973. That year marked the departure from self-realization and entry into all-out advocacy. Also at the Assembly, there was a forum on the ministry of the laity, plus three workshops on Christian Women's Fellowship (CWF), one on the future, another on voluntary services. That same year the new Lay Advisory Council came into being.

Among the resolutions was one which, while not supporting abortion on demand, did call for support of women in their decisions regarding abortion.[13] Another resolution presaged the upcoming Advocacy period by calling for equal consideration of women in pulpits and equal pay for their efforts. Others affirmed expanding roles for women, supporting the Equal Rights Amendment, merging deacons and deaconesses into a single diaconate, urging boards and staffs to first call competent women to volunteer and paid positions in the church, and celebrating the 100th anniversary of the first Disciples women's organization, the Christian Woman's Board of Missions. Those resolutions symbolized the beginning of a new era for women with a new intensity. No longer was it a simple matter of women's presence in the leadership of the church. No longer was the objective pressing women to participate and men to let them participate. Now, it made sense that women, representing more than half the constituency of the church, were entitled to significant representation, not just token positions. This was a new approach, fraught with anxieties and threats.

FROM RESOLUTIONS COME POLITICAL ACTION

Several of the resolutions were more than just words of affirmation. While the Self-realization Years meant growing awareness and recognition for many women in the church, for others it was already time for political action both inside and outside the church. The federal Equal Rights Amendment drew women strongly into political and social advocacy. The amendment, which eventually passed Congress and was signed by the President before faltering in the states, called for an addition to the United States Constitution that equality would "not be denied or abridged by the United States or a state on account of sex."[14] It came close before its abandonment. In addition to being favored by the President, it was approved by a vote of 354 to 23 in the House of Representatives, and 84 to 8 in the Senate. Luz Bacerra, Director of Social Action for Disciples Women, led the church's campaign. That effort peaked in 1979, during the Advocacy Years, with all-out support of the amendment during a three-year extension of the process for ratification by state legislatures. Although Congress overwhelmingly supported an equal rights amendment, and more than thirty states did as well, the measure died because of the absence of ratification by the necessary three fourths of the states.

While society redefined women's place outside the church, women's life inside the church faced similar challenges. Women had begun to make inroads as elders, but a diaconate was another matter. Since modern translations of the Bible identified deacons and deaconesses in the church, it usually happened that men would serve at the communion table, and that women would prepare it and clean up. The original Greek of the Bible did not make the male-female distinction. Instead, the earliest manuscripts use the same Greek word for "helper" for Phoebe as it does for male deacons. Separate deacons and deaconesses "reflects a devaluation of the serving ministry of women," the women wrote, in a section of a resolution adopted by the Disciples' General Assembly in 1973.[15] A passage in the measure observed that the church has not "adequately exercised its prophetic function in affirming the full humanity and consequent rights and responsibilities of women." The Assembly said amen to that and urged congregations to eliminate separate boards on behalf of a single diaconate. The change was handled easily by many congregations, with some difficulty by a number, and completely ignored by some. But that's the way Disciples are.

Neither had the church adequately exercised its prophetic functions with respect to the clergywomen of the church. Giving the church the benefit of the doubt, the women commented in a resolution that "unintentional discrimination against women in the ministry has been allowed to persist, depriving the church of valuable resources in leadership."[16] A resolution called for affirming women pastors, giving them equal consideration and making scholarships available to them. It was noted that Disciples have ordained women throughout much of their history. A plethora of significant women dot the New Testament chronicle—Mary Magdalene, Joanna, Phoebe, Mary, Martha, the woman of Samaria, Dorcas, Priscilla, Lydia, Lois, and Eunice. Others are identified only by their relationships to men: the widow of Nain, the mother of James and John, and the daughters of Philip. The General Assembly resolved to encourage women's commitment to professional ministry, congregations' commitments to the filling of pulpits with women, equal remuneration with men, as well as equity on church boards, committees, and commissions for all women.

CONSIDERING THE PAST, WELCOMING THE FUTURE

By 1970, women were already preparing for the approaching celebration of the 100th birthday of the Disciples women's organization. In anticipation of the 1974 anniversary year, they commissioned Lorraine Lollis to write their history. A new history of the women's organization, *The Shape of Adam's Rib*, was published by Bethany Press. This short period, specifically 1973, was one full of changes as Disciples learned from the past and looked to the future. In 1973, the women reported 183,299 participating CWF members in 3,343 congregations, which was actually more groups than the church had reporting congregations in some years.[17] This renewed interest followed some big changes. On January 1, 1973, the Division of Homeland Ministries changed the name of the Department of Christian Women's Fellowship to the Department of Church Women. It was more than a semantic change. Recognizing that not all women of the church responded to women's initiatives through Christian Women's Fellowship, the department at the general level prepared to develop programming with women not reached by that organization, hopefully without diminishing its work with the organized women's groups.

At the 1973 Assembly, women celebrated the 100th anniversary of the Christian Woman's Board of Missions (CWBM) founded during the Cincinnati General Assembly in 1874, with leadership from a minister's wife, Caroline Neville Pearre of Iowa City, Iowa. The women's board grew partially out of frustration that the American Christian Missionary Society, founded twenty-five years earlier, had sent out only three short-lived missionary plantings overseas. Under the auspices of the CWBM and the strong push of committed women, Disciples exploded in mission to Asia, Africa, and Latin America during the next twenty-five years.

Mission was not the only thing to explode out of this time. Decisions, intentions, training, resolutions, name changes, and anniversaries, the last year of the Self-Realization period saw a flurry of activity, and it was just the beginning. For now that many women realized their potential and their power, they were ready for the next step on the road to fulfillment within the church.

They were ready to advocate for change.

THE dvocacy Years
1974–1982

Once Disciples women began to realize for themselves who God had called them to be and where God had called them to be, the next question was "How do we get there from here?"

The resolutions of 1973 provided a road map. There were clues not only to how the church needed to advocate for women but to how women needed to advocate for each other and for themselves. As Pope John XXIII had opened the windows for a new age within the church, the time had come for Disciples to open new doors to women.

From the mid-1970s, partnership became a word that defined the way women sought to work with and relate to one another. Programs and projects administered through the Department of Church Women were always done *with* women in the regions and congregations, seldom *for* them. Now, women identified and developed programs, projects, and studies that affected their lives. Often, basic concepts for new endeavors came from congregational women, who knew well what they needed, but were not aware of the most effective means of achieving their goals. General and regional staff could bring ideas gleaned from other congregations and other denominations. Together they discovered programs uniquely appropriate to each situation yet linked to the efforts of their sisters in other churches.

Regional staff working with CWF and women's concerns were increasingly required to be generalists. It became important, therefore, that the general staff be experts, who could provide the specialized knowledge and service so often required by their partners in regions and congregations. Such expertise was defined in their job descriptions and in their titles: Director of Stewardship and Worship, Director of Social Action, Director of Education, and so on. When a partner in the congregation wished to identify a consultant in a specific area, she had only to call and ask. Within Homeland Ministries the five departments—Education, Ministry and Worship,

Evangelism, Church Men, and Church Women—carried names linked to the functional committees within congregations. Partnership flourished. Staff members worked closely on task forces and interdepartmental groups but also consulted with each other individually. Of course, because there was one budget, the department executives would struggle for funding of their programs and projects. Then, as now, however, there were conscientious efforts to enable a healthy give-and-take while distributing the available resources with wisdom and equity. Once an amount was agreed on for each department, the department had the autonomy to determine how those funds would be allocated. Until the mid-1980s, records of CWF giving and Department of Church Women budgeting were kept by Margie Richardson and later by her successor, Alice Langford. Special funding was provided from the Homeland Ministries budget for programs compatible with their identified priorities.

RESOLUTIONS AND SOCIAL ACTION

The years immediately following passage of their six resolutions in 1973 marked a turn among Disciples women to a stronger approach to women's issues—more of direct advocacy than the simple participation involvement. The women asked the General Board for "proportional representation on all program and policy bodies."[1] That meant that the old one-third rule no longer worked for the women. At Restructure, this rule dictated that the members of the general church boards and committees would be one third laywomen, one third laymen and one third clergy, both women and men. The rule was interpreted to mean one third laymen, one third clergymen, and one third women total, though few organizations even aspired to that inequitable proportion.

The time was a whirlwind of actions and concerns. Women wanted equal consideration for staff positions, plus equal compensation for equal work. They urged congregations to increase their involvement of women in church leadership positions and suggested churches consider women when they chose new ministers. There was a conference at Tougaloo College in Mississippi for black women to lift up their special concerns. Following the United Nations' designation, the church endorsed 1975 as International Women's Year. In addition, Kenneth Kuntz, president of Homeland Ministries, announced a priority for the quadrennium 1975–1979 aimed at implementing self-awareness through advocacy, especially for women. In the resolution in support of this priority before the church's General Assembly, the Disciples women were called to examine local conditions to the end of helping eliminate injustices, "first in the church structures, then in the community."[2]

Further action by the General Assembly in 1977 spoke specifically to the condition of women ministers.[3] In the church structures, the women deplored the idea of women pastors' getting paid less than their male counterparts for the same work. The women suggested a salary support system for women just as the church had supported in principle the idea of salary support for ethnic minority pastors. It was observed that women generally are called to the small congregations that cannot adequately pay them and that, of the twenty female solo pastors out of about four thousand congregations in the denomination, only two served congregations of more than one hundred members. The Assembly affirmed the hiring of clergy couples by single congregations, but insisted it not be done to get two staff for the price of one, and that clergy couples should be engaged in two staff positions with separate salaries.[4] A resolution said that women earned $2,300 less than men in the same church positions.[5] The number of women in seminaries was identified as 21 percent of the student bodies, a tripling of the percentage in five years.[6] The seminary makeup was to become more than 50 percent women in the late-1990s. In 1991 the salary gap was still there. Women earned only $21,215 in salary and housing benefits, 77 percent of what men were paid.[7]

AFTER THE RESOLUTIONS

Actions taken in assemblies, committees, and commissions, like the passage of the six resolutions at the 1973 General Assembly, challenged and reflected advocacy within the church. They laid the groundwork for and gave impetus to programs and projects that reached out to communities, churches, families, and individuals to do and enable effective advocacy. It is easy to pass a resolution, but to put that resolution into action for change requires specific action. While it was important for women to bring such resolutions to the Assembly and for the Assembly to accept them, adopting resolutions was only the first step.

Change and growth within the church comes only with the growth and understanding of its people. Advocacy requires equipping the people, especially those most directly involved—in this case, women. Throughout the Advocacy Years, programs were designed through which women could claim their own power, identify their potential, and discover appropriate ways of being employed within the church. In the mid-1970s, assertiveness seminars were all the rage, but none were being held in a church setting. In 1975, I suggested that the two-year-old Department of Church Women develop such an opportunity with a biblical and theological dimension. Consequently, "Created to be..." awareness/assertiveness seminars for churchwomen was one of the earlier programs toward effective advocacy.

These events brought together all women of the church, lay and clergy, young and old, those in CWF and those not. Equally diverse was the planning team: a Roman Catholic sister from Denver, a Presbyterian clergywoman from New York, a St. Louis University professor and author of a book on assertiveness, and regional CWF staff member Raye Feltner from North Carolina. Each had a specific area of expertise that served to create an effective experience for Disciples women all across the United States.

Inevitably, response and results varied. Not everyone was happy with the assertiveness seminars. In fact, at one event, one woman announced, "Well, this is certainly not what I thought it would be!" and left. Fortunately, this was the exception as most participants, while somewhat skeptical at first, became enthusiastic by the conclusion two days later. During the partner practice sessions, one woman was overheard to say, "I'm going to an interview for a job I think I can do, but don't believe they think I can. I have a tough time interviewing anyway, so help me use these techniques to succeed this time." She got that job, we heard weeks later. "It feels so good to be able to say what I want to say in a Board meeting without the fear of being put down or putting down someone else, " another woman said. In an evaluation, one participant in an assertiveness training seminar in 1978 wrote, "The seminar has been the most meaningful experience I have had. I am discovering the joys each day of being assertive and finding new ways to function. This helps me to find satisfaction."

INCLUDING ALL WOMEN: MINORITIES AND LEADERSHIP

Unfortunately, few African Americans attended the assertiveness seminars. Even fewer Hispanic women came, though the many written resources used were all translated into Spanish. In 1975, as Luz Bacerra, general staffperson for Church Women, traveled around the country and visited among the African American Disciples, she received requests for some leadership training for the women. In keeping with the practice of partnership in planning, Luz gathered a group of black women leaders together in 1976 to determine what such a training event would look like.[8] What did they want and need? Once the purpose and goals for the event were determined and designed, three training sessions were held tri-annually, including leaders from regions and congregations across the country. Within less than a year, similar events were held for Hispanic women church leaders.

As with their white sisters, African American women were active in the leadership of their congregation through the women's organization and Christian education. However, because the authority of the black male pastor was so pronounced, resistance to women's entering the pastorate and other key leadership positions prevailed more strongly than in white churches.

While the forceful presence of black women has always been a part of the Disciples, it was not until the late 1970s that they were present in force. The church program on Reconciliation and the struggles for racial equality in both church and society began to produce results. African American women were represented on the ICWF Cabinet, participated on the Church Women Coordinating Council and told their stories in the herstory book, *Christian Women Share Their Faith,* a collection of mini-autobiographies of Disciples women.

To encourage more leader development, in 1981 the Cross-Cultural Program was initiated. Black, Hispanic, and Asian women leaders were enabled to share cultural experiences in regions and to develop an understanding of a variety of structures under which programs for women were planned and implemented. For instance, Texan Irma Delgado, under the auspices of this program, attended the women's retreat in North Carolina. Anxious about the reception awaiting her, she boarded the plane with great trepidation. However, the open acceptance and warm hospitality that she received soon encouraged her to teach her new friends some Spanish songs and to respond freely to their questions about her life as an elder and church leader in southern Texas.

In Kentucky, as in several other regions, the black women had their own CWF spring workshops. However, the president of the black CWF was a member of the regional cabinet, which planned the spring workshops. One year the Cabinet decided that at each workshop they would secure volunteers to preside and serve communion. Why not? Women were capable of doing it themselves.

While many women were reluctant to accept, the necessary two volunteers were secured at the workshop for the black women. At this event, held in Lexington, Kentucky, two male pastors observed the closing worship from an anteroom of the sanctuary. When offered the elements, these men refused to receive communion from women.[9] Of course, there are many African American congregations today in which women are elders and deacons, and most male ministers are supportive of women colleagues in the ministry. Courageous women had to break that prejudicial barrier.

The barriers that separate God's people, even within the church, are slowly disappearing. Like many African American people, Rosa Page Welch, the outstanding singer and leader, often found herself within a primarily white congregation. She and others were included because of the gifts they could bring, but without any of their African American sisters and brothers. However, by the mid-1980s, Rosa Page attended the CWF retreat in Mississippi, not because she would "entertain" but because she was a resident and went with other African American women to share in the experience together with their white sisters. She commented to Marilyn Moffett, who was the guest retreat leader, "I have prayed for this, and isn't it wonderful that it has come to pass that black women and white women are in retreat together in Mississippi!"

It is wonderful, but more must be done. Janis Brown, staff member in the Office of Disciples Women, has said that "Many members of the Christian Church (Disciples of Christ) are unaware of each other. There are lots of African American Disciples churches who don't know that there are white Disciples churches."[10] The opposite is also true, as many Caucasian church members do not realize that there are African American churches within the denomination. Yet there have been African American churches within the Disciples tradition right from the beginning. It is a shared yet separate history and one of which both heritages are not very knowledgeable.[11]

COMING TO POWER: WOMEN IN THE MINISTRY

During the height of the women's movement outside the church, women inside struggled to be allowed to serve God. Slowly women were employed as pastors, often of small congregations or as associates or assistants in larger congregations. Slowly attitudes changed. Mae Yoho Ward, a pioneer in Disciples' women's leadership, recalled that before World War II she went to New Haven, Connecticut, so that her husband could attend Yale Divinity School. Expressing interest in attending class herself, she was told she could, but must not speak and could receive no class credit. Three decades later, Mae, who was to become vice president of the United Christian Missionary Society, would be called back to Yale as the speaker in a noted lecture series. Ward once refuted the comment that women have no place in the professional life of the church because Christ called only men to be his apostles. "He didn't call any Gentiles either," snapped Mae.

Some regional ministers courageously insisted that congregations interview or at least consider a woman candidate. A few would not even suggest a woman for the post. Congregations, with no experience of a woman pastor and well-versed in the popular objections, would refuse to consider a woman. Education and counseling were needed and some regional ministers provided it. As more women were employed, more congregations could testify to their competence and the objections were put to rest. But, when a woman did not achieve the expected standards, the comment was often made, "We had a woman, and she did not do well. We don't want another." Every woman hired had to be the model for all the others. One was tempted to ask if all the men were successful. The quintessential compliment was, "She is as good as a man." There were some women who were even better!

After her retirement from the women's department staff, Katherine Schutze became a temporary, part-time consultant in the Department of Ministry and Worship. In that capacity, she made a study on women in ministry in 1973. "The contemporary church's view of women is that she is an aesthetically-minded, child-centered individual who has no talent for, or interest in, ordained ministry, administration or policy-making positions," she reported to Homeland Ministries the next year.[12] The church, functioning on this assumption, she concluded, was reluctant to seek women candidates for employment or to encourage the entry of women into seminary education. Her study showed that of women listed with ministerial standing among the Disciples, 88 percent had at least a bachelor's degree and 63 percent had earned graduate degrees. It also found that 76 percent were ordained, 64 percent were directors of Christian education, 5 percent were pastors, and 12 percent were on general or regional staff; the average salary was $6,500.[13] According to the study, the women interviewed felt that they were not taken seriously, and were overlooked and underpaid. Ministry is a man's work, they were told, so they should get a husband, or, at best, find a way to "prove themselves." The interviewed young women believed "an effort should be made to make successful women more visible in the churches."[14]

Subsequently, the Department of Ministry and Worship employed Deborah Casey for three years as a full-time consultant on women in ministry. The units, regions, and congregations of the church also looked closely at the number of women in their employ and participating on their boards. As Director of Leader Development in the Department of Church Women, I worked closely with the consultant in the Department of Ministry, and published regular statistical information on units, regions, and seminaries. We then sent this information out with a letter urging consideration for more participation of women. The statistics revealed that all the manifestations of the church took this matter very seriously. For example, the Pension Fund, the Board of Church Extension, and the Council on Christian Unity, all of which had very few women on their boards, immediately took steps to submit women's names for election at the next Assembly. Within a few years, all three of these boards included at least one third women.

Some women attending seminary had no intention of entering the pastoral ministry. Anna Jarvis Parker wrote, "There appeared to be three groups of women attending seminary—younger women, 25 to 35 years old, who were training for the pastoral ministry, younger women training for the professional ministry but not necessarily the pastorate, and older women, 35 to 55, most of whom were not working toward a degree but who wished to increase their biblical and theological knowledge."[15] By the mid-1990s, most of the latter group was no longer present. This may have been because "women doing theology" groups had sprung up across the country and more books were available on theology from a woman's perspective, or, perhaps, because seminary courses had become available to the following generations at a younger age.

WOMEN IN INTERIM MINISTRY

In 1977, as a result of the need to have congregations begin to accept women in their pulpits, the Women in Interim Ministry program was instituted. Women in seminaries in the master of divinity program numbered 8 percent in 1979, but the number was to grow to 33.5 percent by 1984 and 43 percent by 1991, and to more than 50 percent by the end of the century. With women gradually reaching equality in education for the ministry, how were Disciples going to convince congregations to hire them? The Women in Interim Ministry program began in 1977 with the idea that in interim situations congregations would be willing to "take a chance" on a woman senior pastor. Thus, they would discover what some people already knew, that women were at least the equal of men, but offered different qualities.

Growing numbers of women entered seminaries with the intention of becoming ordained ministers serving congregations. People in the congregations, however, were unwilling to accept a woman as their pastor. In the experience of most congregations, clergy meant clergyman. Even small congregations who offered themselves as training grounds for students would not consider a woman. Therefore, few, if any, congregations could testify to the ability of women as pastors. "If you've never experienced one, how can you say that you do not want one?" was a question often put before search committees.

When the Women in Interim Ministry Program was initiated, congregations without pastors could experience a woman as their interim pastor with little or no risk. This could be a win-win situation as women seeking pastorates needed opportunities for varied pastoral experiences and the congregation would have a chance to witness a woman pastor in action.

Interim ministries were limited to six months each and the person participating in the program was recruited for a period of two years. The first women selected were Barbara Graves, who ministered with churches on the West Coast; Winifred Smith, who served in Indiana; and Joyce Coalson, who went to Kansas, Oklahoma, and Texas. The Homeland Ministries Department of the Ministry contacted Coalson, who recalls that she was the first to be recruited for this program, while she was serving as pastor of Windmill Point Christian Church in Ontario, Canada.[16] Coalson later became vice president of Homeland Ministries, where she was responsible for the center that included leadership and ministry, and for the Office of Disciples Women.

Certain conditions were agreed to before a minister was sent to a region. The Ministry Department paid for the interim minister's health insurance and travel costs (from one appointment to another) and the congregation provided the salary and housing. It was also an understanding between the region and the general office that the region would seek to provide a healthy congregation. On at least one occasion, a minister's preparation included attending a conflict management seminar arranged by Thomas E. Wood, executive of the Department of Ministry. While a conflict situation was not anticipated, the very fact of a woman's presence as minister might create some conflict. Thus a less-than-healthy situation would make accurate evaluation difficult.

The program confronted traditional ideas about women and men. Not only were the attitudes of the congregation toward a woman in the pulpit confronted, but church people also struggled with the change in the male/female role in marriage: What will the husband do? What can we find for the husband to do? In the late 1970s few congregations would have asked similar questions about a minister's wife. The role reversal and the peripatetic nature of this program demanded understanding and support from a woman's spouse. One husband took these two years as a personal sabbatical to pursue his interest in painting and sculpture.

As with many such innovative programs sponsored through Homeland Ministries, there were some surprising results. Several months after she concluded her ministry in Coffeyville, Kansas, Coalson happened to meet a young laywoman leader from that church. The young woman said she was unsure whether to thank the minister or not. "I didn't realize while you were here how inclusive you made the worship service, and it didn't dawn on me until you left and our new pastor came and went back to the masculine language, how included I had felt [during your ministry]." Thus, this program also provided mentoring to laywomen, helping them to become part of the congregation in deed and word. "Eventually," Joyce continued, "this woman grew in her church leadership and was elected to the [Disciples] General Board. I was happy to have had that opportunity to encourage her leadership and help her to see the opportunities which the church offers."[17]

Winifred Smith, a retired missionary who with her husband Joe experienced internment in a Japanese prison camp in the Philippines in World War II, was one of the first women interim ministers. "I enjoyed my three interims," she recalled in 1998. "I enjoyed preaching and I enjoyed being concerned for all people. The distressing thing was that we couldn't get churches to accept women. All three of the churches said they would accept a woman minister if I would just stay. But they were not so sure about anybody else. Women were hesitant to accept women."[18]

After Win Smith's first service at her first church, a woman came up to her and said, "I am so sorry. I was the only one on the committee who voted against having you, because I didn't think a woman could do it." But Win Smith was put to the test by circumstances as well. With one of the worries about women ministers being their body strength while immersing people, Smith's first baptism was a large young man who had a broken leg in a heavy cast. The baptism proceeded without a hitch. In her second interim, another woman who had a dim view of women in ministry became Smith's best friend. At her friend's funeral many years later, Win Smith was asked to deliver the eulogy. Similar experiences followed in her third interim. She visited a hospitalized woman daily, and in three months was told by the woman, "If I don't make it, will you have my funeral service? I have been wrong about women doing ministry." Win Smith pronounced her experience in interim ministry "wonderful."

Due to lack of funds and the difficulty that the regional ministers had in securing willing, available congregations for Women in Interim Ministries, the program was terminated after four years. Nevertheless, it continues to provide a model for regional ministers to introduce the ministry of women to congregations. "I do think," Coalson says, looking back from her vice presidency at Homeland Ministries, "that it has been a way both for women who have had trouble getting a call to have an effective ministry and also for congregations to experience the ministry of women during an interim period."

Laywomen and Laymen Join in Ministry: The Diaconate

While in the past women's participation had been mostly behind the scenes, now there were some laywomen who, like clergywomen, believed that they were being called to be *in* the scene. They were ready to share the responsibilities of the eldership and the diaconate.

During the Self-realization Years, a resolution passed urging churches to form a common diaconate that included both men and women, rather than the separate deacons and deaconesses. Now women called for action on the resolution. They made the point that the original Greek of the New Testament used a nonsexist word most frequently translated "servant" or "minister" for Phoebe, and it was only in the twentieth-century translations that she was referred to as a deaconess. The cultural use of the term deaconess generally relegated women to the clean-up role in the process of the Lord's supper. And despite the apostle Paul's bow to his own culture in saying women should be quiet in church, he also said that there is neither male nor female in Christ. Additionally, when he fulfilled his role of taking the gospel beyond Asia, making it a world religion rather than a sect of Judaism, his first convert in Europe was Lydia, not only a woman but a businesswoman—a seller of purple goods. She brought her whole household into the church, certainly not the work of a woman who kept her mouth shut. In Paul's mind, the wife-and-husband team of Priscilla and Aquilla was a partnership of equals who shared the work of ministry.

The women were convinced that the move to a single diaconate had a strong theological basis, one that was substantive, while the separation was artificial. For some congregations it was hardly a leap to unite the diaconate. For others more resistant to change, it was a struggle. The well-respected matriarch of one congregation represented many others when voicing her strong objection, "If that ever happens here, I won't take communion." A few congregations ignored the issue.

Using the 1976 guide *One Diaconate,* Peter Morgan, Homeland Ministries staff member, together with an interdepartmental team, visited regions leading workshops to help congregations understand what diaconate was and how it could work in their home setting. In the discussion groups women struggled with their fears: "Those trays are too heavy for me." (And this from the very women who regularly hauled overladen grocery bags from store to car to house!) "The men will think we are taking over." They also shared "horror" stories such as the incident involving a matriarch and "saint," teacher and leader, who, had agreed to serve if she were elected as an elder. She was not elected. She was devastated; and felt that not only she but all that she had done for her church had been rejected. These fears of rejection, of the unknown, of not being understood—all were valid. It is to the credit of both women and men that so many congregations have embraced the eldership and diaconate with such equanimity.

LAYWOMEN-CLERGYWOMEN CONVERSATIONS

More clergywomen enrolled at seminaries and more laywomen entered decision-making bodies. Despite the struggles, it appeared to be a good time for women, but unexpected obstacles appeared within the ranks. Comments overheard betrayed distrust between clergywomen and powerful laywomen. "When my name was presented as a candidate for that church, it was a woman who blocked my interview," was an oft-heard comment, or "There is a problem between our new associate minister and our minister's wife. She seems threatened to have a woman minister assuming what she considered her place as the key woman of the congregation." Noting the possible rift between the clergywoman and laywoman, both the Department of Church Women and the Department of Ministry suggested a program to encourage dialogue between them. Eventually, Susan Robinson, director of Women in Ministry, was assigned the responsibility for "Clergywomen-Laywomen Conversations." These two-day events brought clergywomen and laywomen together to explore their common backgrounds, their journeys in the church, and to identify what each group needed from the other and what each group had to offer the other. Held in regional settings, these conversations led to greater mutual acceptance, appreciation, and affirmation.

Supporting Ministers' Wives: Rachel Events

As the participation of laywomen increased in key leadership and decision-making positions within the total church and as more and more congregations employed clergywomen as their ministers, the role of the wife of a minister became less clear. Previously, when national or regional boards and committees were seeking a woman for membership, they nominated wives of prominent ministers, just as similar bodies of congregations would often nominate their ministers' wives. With the advent of other female leaders, the supremacy of the minister's wife was no longer assumed. Many challenges remained for these women, and with the changing social climate many more came their way. For some women, who no longer were called to such roles, this caused a major identity crisis; others who had established themselves in a career were not as much affected. By 1981, the Church Women were sponsoring "Rachel Events" for wives of clergymen. While resourcing an event in Illinois, Fran Craddock was approached and asked, "Why don't you have something for those of us who are ministers' wives?" Consequently, the initial planning team was a small group of ministers' wives, none of whom would claim expertise in the field, but who were experts by experience. Once the purpose and goals had been determined, the planners asked Beth Glick-Rieman, a Church of the Brethren clergywoman, to work out the detailed design.

These two-day gatherings encouraged women to share their own faith journeys, to explore their identities, and to discuss in a safe environment the frustrations and the joys of being married to a minister. Regardless of the ever-increasing diversity within this sisterhood, the women discovered that by sharing their ideas and concerns they experienced a sense of unity that strengthened their faith and their lives.

Long-term friendships emerged. Bonds were forged between older and younger women as the more experienced gave ideas for coping or solving to the younger women. "It is so good to know that I am not the first one to be faced with this situation," one young wife said.

Similar local events were spawned as women went home and shared them with wives of ministers in their own communities. In some regions, these were so successful that they have been conducted annually and, as in Ohio, later events were redefined for ministers' *spouses* and so included the husbands of ministers as well.

WORLD CWF CELEBRATES TWENTY-FIVE YEARS

The world was in transition, but some things stayed the same. One of the organizations that continues to function without much change is the World CWF. Meeting in conjunction with the World Convention of Churches of Christ, this loosely knit group of Christian sisters from sixteen countries around the world share a breakfast meeting during the Convention. In addition, a World CWF Retreat is held immediately prior to the Convention at which members of the WCWF Executive Committee and two elected delegates from each of the sixteen participating organizations attend. There is often a theme for this retreat, plus opportunities for Bible study, worship, fellowship and the selection of an action project for the coming quadrennium. The president is almost always a resident of the host country and the secretary-treasurer is always the executive of the women's department.

Of special note was the celebration luncheon for the twenty-fifth birthday of the World CWF held July 1980 in Honolulu, Hawaii, during the World Convention of Churches of Christ. Canadian Marge Black, World CWF president, commented, "It was one of the largest retreats and World CWF breakfasts we have ever had, probably because of location. Everybody wanted to go to Honolulu. It was won-

Quadrennial Assembly 1974

derful." Because she and her husband frequently traveled around the world on freighters, she has been able to maintain World CWF friendships. Membership in the World CWF is of particular value to women in such countries as Vanuatu, Fiji, India, and the Philippines, women who feel isolated but who, through this network, are linked in a special Christian sisterhood.

Twenty-eight women representing thirteen countries attended the World CWF retreat held, as always, prior to the Convention. The resource leaders were Shanti Solomon from India and Gloria Santos of the Philippines.

At all the retreats, special action projects were identified for the upcoming quadrennium. They pointed to world needs of the time, especially those related to women.

Quadrennials: More Reasons to Celebrate

The Advocacy Years saw some of the most exciting Quadrennials ever. The 1974 meeting celebrated the 100th anniversary of the found-

Celebrating Communion at the close of the 1974 ICWF Quadrennial Assembly

ing of the Christian Woman's Board of Missions. It was a spectacular event. Many women remember the fireworks that greeted them as they left the opening birthday celebration and the huge fountain bubbling in the center of the stage during the closing communion service. Highly visible were the clergywomen, scattered around the stage at that final session to guide and direct the women as they filed onto the stage, received communion from a keepsake cup, and left to be greeted by the outgoing and incoming officers.

This was an assembly directed toward the future, even as it reviewed the past. One of the interest groups was "The Personhood of Women." Included under the heading was a report on the Berlin Conference on Sexism, given by Jean Woolfolk, president of the Church Finance Council. She was the first woman to head a general administrative unit of the Christian Church and would continue to

Jean Woolfolk
First woman to be elected Moderator of the Christian Church (Disciples of Christ) 1973–1975
First woman to serve as the President of a General Unit: Church Finance Council 1976–1983

be the only one for another decade. Woolfolk, a laywoman, was the attorney and senior vice president and financial officer of a major insurance company in Arkansas when she accepted the Church Finance Council position. Candace Adams, associate minister at First Christian Church, Knoxville, Tennessee, led a workshop on "Women in Ministry." Song leaders Avery and Marsh, who gave the assembly a new repertoire of songs of faith and celebration, provided memorable program moments.

Four years later, the new order was apparent at the 1978 Quadrennial Assembly. With few exceptions, all the speakers, musicians, and interest group leaders were women. While some were pleasantly surprised to discover the existence of so many qualified women, others expressed their dismay that there were so few men in leadership—even if it *was* a women's assembly!

Presiding at this quadrennial were Carnella Jamison Barnes, the first ICWF African American President, and Vice President Virginia Bell. The sixth Quadrennial Assembly of the International Christian Women's Fellowship proved to be the apogee in attendance. Registration grew to a record 4,914 in 1978, having reached 4,156 the previous assembly. The participants would top four thousand twice more before the attendance settled in at the mid-3,000s in the 1990s. Among the features of the 1978 Quadrennial were the Bible studies of Philip Potter, general secretary of the World Council of Churches, based in Switzerland, and Beatriz Melano Couch, an Argentinean theologian. The pairing fit perfectly with the World Council of Churches study, "The Community of Women and Men in the Church." Couch's power and knowledge matched Potter's so well that doors were opened to a new day of search for leading women to speak. Through her controversial dramatization of the biblical story of Sarah and Hagar, Suzanne Benton, an actress and sculptor, encouraged women to open their minds and hearts and consider the biblical message from a woman's perspective.

The 1978 theme, "Behold the New Day," seems, in retrospect, a perfect one for that time. After a long day of struggle to determine a theme that would reveal their message, the planning committee, unable to reach agreement, decided to "sleep on it." The next morning during opening devotions led by Luz Bacerra, the group sang "Morning Has Broken," and they had their theme! "Behold the New Day!" emerged spontaneously and received unanimous acceptance. Disciples women were claiming their power to initiate change as they eagerly moved into the new day.

At the luncheon meeting of the ICWF Commission held during the 1978 Quadrennial, Fran Craddock, executive of the Department of Church Women, said:

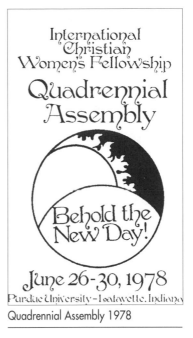

International Christian Women's Fellowship

Quadrennial Assembly

Behold the New Day!

June 26-30, 1978

Purdue University - Lafayette, Indiana

Quadrennial Assembly 1978

With the emergence of the women's movement, there has developed a new appreciation for the gifts of women and the importance of a woman's organization. However, as this quadrennium comes to a close there is one concern: due to budget reductions general and regional staff positions which carry responsibility for resourcing CWF have been reduced [from six to five professionals, and in the 1990s to four and then three in the general office]. From the early beginning, employed and volunteer staff members have worked together in building an organization, which at the present involves 3,322 local autonomous groups of women. If CWF is to maintain its vitality and strength, the network of communication and support needs to be nurtured, resources promoted and interpreted, leaders trained, and structures evaluated and made relevant to the changing concerns and needs of its members.[19]

Women celebrated twenty-five years of Quadrennial Assemblies at the next event in 1982. Coupled with celebration was the realization, stated in the theme "Hope for the Journey," that Disciples women had embarked on a long, yet hope-filled journey, a

International Christian Women's Fellowship
QUADRENNIAL ASSEMBLY

Purdue University
West Lafayette, Indiana
June 21-25, 1982
Christian Church (Disciples of Christ)

Quadrennial Assembly 1982

journey to be risked with courage as they traveled together with a global community of women. Certainly members of the Assembly program committee wished that someone had traveled with *one* woman from the global community. Mama Entombojei, a matriarch of the church in Zaire, was far from a world traveler when she confidently set out from Africa for Lafayette with only a plane ticket, her invitation, and faith in God. She believed this would be sufficient and she was right! Changing planes and crossing international borders proved a bit tricky, however, with no passport, very little money (and that from Zaire) and no ability to speak English. Yet, full of enthusiasm and confidence, she arrived a few days late announcing to her worn and worried hostess that the Lord was with her and that good people helped her along the way.

That assembly gave new visibility to lay, clergy, black and Hispanic, ecumenical and overseas partners. The Quadrennial programs by then revealed the ever-increasing sensitivity to the diverse needs of a diverse people. Even the program book was selected in order to provide space for larger, more accessible print for the elderly and visually impaired. This was a major change from the past.

A song written for the 1982 Quadrennial continues to be used in congregations today. Jim Strathdee, a song leader of the Quadrennial along with his wife, Jean, was inspired by the way I always concluded my letters, "In loving partnership," and wrote a song with that title.

THE UNITED NATIONS DECADE: A TIME FOR WOMEN

The sense of partnership prevailed in ecumenical circles as well. Women were all struggling within their own expression of the church to secure justice and freedom and to have their gifts recognized and utilized. Through Church Women United and similar organizations, they identified common ground and found solutions. Women discovered in one another both strength and hope as they shared a common vision and challenged the church with one voice.

One woman in the church could make a difference for all. Luz Bacerra, who fought against racism, classism, and sexism, demonstrated how. Luz, originally from the Philippines, wielded a style that was confronting without being alienating, softened by a bit of an accent. She had a selflessness, a total commitment to the cause, and a genuine love of people that carried the integrity of the message. At the same time, she was administratively astute, which enabled her to work with church bureaucrats and politicians so that she received respect and power. Luz could get the women to say yes. Committed to social action, Luz edited the two editions of *The Social Action Newsletter* that focused on women. These newsletters, sent to all Disciples congregations, reported on "Women Mid-point in the Decade (1975–85)" in fall 1979 and "Women, Change and the Church" in 1981. The first women's edition referred to the United Nation's proclaimed Decade for Women and its progress.

While most women in Disciples congregations were unaware of the UN Year of the Woman (1975), which initiated the UN Decade for Women, they were part of a worldwide network of women as they participated in programs and projects of the decade. Luz attended the opening conference in Mexico City and so became the network link for the Disciples as they began to work together in advocacy. One such project was the Nestle boycott, an issue that eventually grabbed the attention of the whole church. Women in developing countries alerted their sisters in the United States that the Nestle Company was not only providing but promoting the use of baby formula to replace breast feeding in their countries. Young mothers, because the formula was free and because they wished to emulate lifestyles in the Western world, ceased nursing only to discover that subsequent cans of formula were costly. By that time, their breasts had dried up and there was no money for such purchases. Through this and other projects, powerful partnerships were developed among women worldwide.

As the Nestle incident illustrated, women's and children's issues were often linked. As women gained self-awareness and power, they did not forget the lives they touched. Between 1977 and 1979, Disciples women prepared for the International Year of the Child. Brochures on service gifts and action projects were distributed for use in workshops and meetings. The CWF *Guideposts*, then edited by Lois Clark for the Department of Church Women, included bibliographies and other resources focusing on the child. Many CWF workshops, retreats, and leader retreats followed ICWF themes and concerns.

In addition to the UN conference in Mexico City, another major meeting in which women were prominent was held in 1975: the Assembly of the World Council of Churches held in Nairobi, Kenya. Among the Disciples attending were Walter Bingham, the first black moderator for the Disciples; Margaret Wilkes, vice-moderator; and Fran Craddock, the new executive of the Department of Church Women. Under the leadership of Letty Russell, Presbyterian professor of theology at Yale Divinity School, the women held a pre-Assembly caucus that produced documents challenging the Assembly to be aware that very few women were official delegates and to remedy this inequality at future Assemblies. Following their return to the United States, Craddock and Bingham were interviewed on CBS. Such visible representation showed the Disciples were serious about being inclusive.

As part of their advocacy efforts in response to actions taken by the women in conjunction with the Nairobi Assembly, the World Council of Churches sponsored a process of study and dialogue, "The Community of Women and Men in the Church," which included the exploration of problematic biblical passages. American theologian Constance F. Parvey guided this process for groups of women and men in local ecumenical settings worldwide. The four-year process culminated in a consultation held in Sheffield, England, in 1981 at which Disciples women were represented by Peggy Owen Clark, then regional staff in the Northeast Region with responsibility for CWF and women's concerns. At the Consultation, churches were urged to continue to pursue the process so "that insights might be realized in the day to day life of the churches, so that the Church may be transformed into an authentic community of women and men."[20]

During this extraordinary decade, women did their part to create that community. Two conferences on women in church government, sponsored by Church Women United, spanned the gap between the Self-realization and Advocacy Years. Those events trained women board members to participate fully in making policy decisions. Remembering her experience at one of these conferences held in Michigan, a Disciples woman related the poignancy of the moment when Catherine Gunsalus Gonzalez, then a professor of theology at Louisville Presbyterian Seminary, asked, "Have you ever been in a meeting with both women and men and made what you thought to be a significant contribution, only to have it fall with a THUD?" "You know," said the Disciples leader, "that had just happened to me the week before! I was so relieved to discover that it was the situation and not just me." These conferences began to alert women to define differences between meetings of all women and those with both women and men and to discover a means to become more comfortable in their contributions. Church Women United had been working on this for more than two decades—ever since the presidency of Mossie Wyker (1950–1955), a term that culminated in her book *Church Women in the Scheme of Things*.

SOCIAL ADVOCACY AROUND THE WORLD

Under the auspices of Church Women United, "Water without walking" was a program in 1977 through which women in congregations and regions purchased wells for women of developing countries who spent large amounts of their time walking miles to fetch water for their families. Through this widespread action of advocacy, Christian women reached out to their sisters, strengthening a worldwide partnership. In 1979 ICWF focused on China as the overseas mission object, a controversial move that was misread by many to mean the group supported a communist regime.

Social concerns at home were not ignored. During the late 1970s, women of the church worked in many diverse areas of domestic social action: Meals-on-Wheels, the Mother-to-Mother program, and foster parenting, and addressed such issues as justice for women, literacy, prison visits, abused children, TV violence, and ministries to the aging.

SOCIAL CONSCIENCE AND HUMAN SEXUALITY

As their work on the ERA and other issues demonstrates, many Disciples women owned a social conscience at pace with the times at the very least. In the mid-1970s, women were prominent in the work of a new Task Force on Human Sexuality, based in the Division of Homeland Ministries. Initially intended to address the issues of sexuality that were arising because of the growing advocacy for women, the group soon discovered that a greater concern loomed before the church: homosexuality. Advocates for one disenfranchised, marginalized segment of society often join forces to advocate for another. Yet, homosexuality was never quite the concern for women that it seemed to be for men. That task force labored for eighteen months, finally delivering to the church's 1977 General Assembly in Kansas City a study report that was extremely controversial. While the report neither approved nor condemned homosexuality, it encouraged a stance of openness to the issues.[21] It cited "questionable use of scripture" in developing conclusions on the subject. "Condemnations of homosexual persons sometimes do not consider the context and make a selective application of scriptures in doing so." Further, said the study, "there is no evidence that persons whose sexual orientation is to those of the same sex constitute a greater danger or threat to society than any other persons." And: "Jesus never stresses the seriousness of sexual sins above others."

In a highly emotional moment at the assembly, Carol Blakley of Boise, Idaho, rose and tearfully read a letter from her son, announcing that he was gay and asking for his family's understanding. The Assembly, deeply moved, voted in a closely divided ballot for protection of the civil liberties of gays. Beyond that, the Homeland Ministries document was simply offered for study. There was an outcry even at that, and General Minister and President Kenneth L. Teegarden found himself moving down into the assembly during sessions to reconcile persons of strong opinions and ward off a few congregations actually threatening to withdraw from the Disciples over the issue. Not long after the assembly, Blakley and others founded a new permanent organization called GLAD—Gay, Lesbian and Affirming Disciples.

Modeling, Mentoring, and Monitoring

Throughout these years women not only supported but mentored one another. They guided one another through the difficult changes and tedious times. All women needed this support, whether they were breaking new ground or fulfilling the more traditional female tasks. Housewives became "homemakers" and were honored for the diverse talents necessary in running a home amid the turmoil. "Just a housewife" became an obsolete phrase as women realized that they had never worked so hard as when they worked *inside* the home. Women entering the workplace in positions where women had not been before or participating on boards where few, if any, women had served, while they modeled new possibilities for other women, needed mentoring for survival. Support groups in many settings began to spring up so that the token woman would not be the isolated woman. As more and more clergywomen became visible in pulpits, they, too, experienced this loneliness and formed support groups.

In every congregation, there are unsung mentors who have the ability to see the potential for leadership in younger women and who encourage them to use their gifts. "I lift up the name of Lydan Range," said Lenita "Jackie" Bunch, ICWF president-elect, in an interview during the 1994 Quadrennial.[22] "She was very instrumental in my getting active on the state level with CWF." Jackie continued, "One day after a meeting, she said, 'By the way, Jackie, I have submitted your name for the state CWF Commission.'And I said, 'Mrs. Range, I don't even know what that is.' And she said, 'Don't worry. You can do it.' And it was from her looking at me and identifying some things in me that I became active."

Then there are the mentors who are highly visible. It was important for the Department of Church Women to be both model and mentor even as it monitored the growing participation of women. Building on the rich and firm foundation of her predecessor, Fran Craddock stated that, "It was of paramount importance to me that the decision-making process for women be as wide and as inclusive as possible."[23] Within the department no decisions were made unilaterally. Even Craddock as executive discussed her decisions with the rest of the staff.

Fran's philosophy of leadership style is further clarified with a comment made to Marilyn Moffett in 1997: "I always felt that the more experiences the staff could have, the richer the whole staff would be and the more contributions they could make to leadership and program development." Similarly, to strengthen any one part of the church enriches the whole when that part is a fully participating member of the whole. As Craddock encouraged growth of individuals in her department, the women's leadership wished to encourage such growth throughout the membership for the good of women and the good of the church. Mentoring, modeling, and monitoring could benefit all Disciples on many levels.

The staff focused on self-realization and ecumenical planning. They also worked to affirm the Christian Women's Fellowship, to communicate the church to women, and to maintain a regional network. These were all related to enabling effective communication, a form of mentoring. Following Craddock's policy, the underlying purpose of the department was to share knowledge.

SELF-STUDY: THE ACTION RESEARCH PROJECT

The time had come to look at the decision-making structures for women and determine how they could be more widely representative. Total church restructure was complete. Women's lives were in transition. Did Christian Women's Fellowship need to change also? The time had arrived for a careful study to evaluate the women's organization. Therefore, in 1978, a committee was selected to engage in the Action Research Project (ARP), which would be funded through the Department of Church Women. This committee (the ICWF officers, Betty Mohney and Sybel Thomas; and three regional staff with responsibility for CWF: Hazel McAfee, Jo Hill Snyder, and Kathryn Williams, and the DCW staff) engaged a team affiliated with the Alban Institute in Washington, D.C., which included consultants Mary Sharer Johnson and Vance Johnson from "Women in Transition," an ecumenically based research group.

Regional staff urged that everything needed to be "up for change." This included name, connections, structures, and goals. This attitude provided an openness, even an eagerness, to discover what women in congregations, regions, and in the general structures were seeking from their church.

Mary Sharer Johnson and Alice Langford conducted a survey to determine what women wanted and what type of organizations were needed to meet their needs. Questionnaires were sent to a random sample throughout North America, and some interviews were conducted. More in-depth studies were held in Ohio and Northern California, the selected sample regions. It was interesting to note that there was wide interest throughout the church in this project. The returned surveys revealed that within the previous two years all church women had significant change in their lives, most of which related to the family, and that family relationships were of primary importance in the lives of most women.[24] They also found the following results:

- Not all women were members of the CWF.
- "Eighty to 95 percent of the CWF members were satisfied that CWF was meeting their needs through spiritual enrichment, programs enabling growth, opportunities in service to others and contacts with other women."
- CWF members tended to be above the average age of women in the congregation; fewer were employed, and had lower incomes; few had ever been divorced. They were single, married or widowed. They had less mobility, had been members of the church longer, and found their friends in the congregation/CWF. They ranked attendance at CWF second only to worship.
- Women not in CWF tended to be younger, employed, mothers with children at home, more mobile, with higher incomes. These women were single, married, or divorced. Few were widowed.
- CWF resources, especially *Guideposts* and leadership materials, the regional staff working with CWF and women's concerns, and the effective networking through the CWF were strongly affirmed.
- All women were significantly active in Sunday worship, fellowship, children and youth activities.

- Some women believed the Lay Advisory Council was problematic—that it was not practical to combine the programs and work of the men and women.

Dr. James Anderson, a member of the Alban Institute team working with the committee, observed, "The women who were the founders of women's work in your denomination had a vision which worked very well for them. It was that vision which gave strength to the organization as it began the missionary work of your church and carried it on with great zeal." Following a brief pause he continued, "Perhaps you don't have a vision today and that may be a weakness." Apparently, our God's mission for us was unclear.

These observations were before the women as the Task Group, the ICWF Commission, and the Church Women's Staff Fellowship examined the results. One of the findings indicated that while there was no will to change the name of the organization, there was a need for structural alterations. Suggestions for adapting the congregational CWF were already available through the recently revised CWF Manual. In this, there was clearly encouragement to design the local CWF to meet the structural situation within each congregation while leaving the basic structure and terminology unchanged, in order to maintain links with the ICWF network. It was a time for creative flexibility, but also a time for retaining the unique interconnectedness that kept the CWF strong and enabled it to serve as a denominational system of communication, not only for the Department of Church Women, but for all the other departments and units throughout the church.

The study revealed a weakness in the method of decision making for women. The ICWF Commission was the existing decision-making body but met only once every other year for a luncheon. With such inadequate time for preparation, understanding, or debate, it was almost impossible for them to make responsible decisions. Inevitably, it fell to the Church Women staff, together with the ICWF officers and occasionally a few other interested people, to determine policies, plans, and programs for the organization.

If, reasoned the ICWF leaders, we want greater participation of women in the whole life and decision making of the church, then we need to look at ourselves and ways CWF women can more adequately assume responsibility for their life together. Also, if ICWF is to continue as the one clear, organized voice speaking to women and for women in the church, then it is important that their voice be representative and accurate.

After the results of the questionnaire were tabulated, a Task Force on Structure and Function was appointed. The diverse group included Betty Mohney (Kansas), Sybel Thomas (Illinois), Margaret McNeil (Canada), Bess Terry (New York), Eula Woodall (Tennessee), and chair Jo Hill Snyder (Oklahoma). Fran Craddock and Alice Langford were the staff members. The following outline came out of their many months of work. They recommended:

I. That the Church Women Staff Fellowship continue to be an organization of regional Disciples staff.

II. That the ICWF be continued with the following structural modifications:

  1. Membership: All members of CWF and other Disciples women who are in sympathy with the purpose and spirit of ICWF.

  2. Officers to be the president and vice president elected at each Quadrennial Assembly for a four-year term.

  3. That an ICWF Cabinet be established to carry out the purpose of ICWF.

     • Members to be regional CWF presidents, regional staff responsible for CWF/women's concerns, representatives from CWF constituency groups, ICWF executive committee members, chairperson of the CWF nominating committee, and Department of Church Women staff.

     • Functions: to develop objectives for women in CWF in harmony with goals for women in the Christian Church (Disciples of Christ); to develop programs and organizational resources to support congregational and regional CWFs, including the annual theme and areas for group study; to develop models for service/ action, resources and experiences in worship; to develop guidelines for selecting officers and members of the ICWF executive committee; to sponsor an assembly for women at least every four years and to provide direction and a method for planning it; to provide for motivation and information for the promotion of stewardship and CWF giving to outreach, opportunities in worship for spiritual development, and enable ecumenical contacts; to evaluate programming for CWF, Quadrennial Assembly, general and regional CWF structures; and to undertake any other tasks as deemed necessary for the ongoing of CWF.

- This Cabinet to meet biannually for approximately four days.

4. That an ICWF Executive Committee be established that would act on behalf of the Cabinet.

- The membership to be the ICWF president and vice president, a regional CWF president, one regional staff person, two members at large, Department of Church Women staff (ex officio with one Department of Church Women staff carrying administrative responsibilities).

- Members to be elected at Quadrennial Assembly for a four-year term.

- Functions: to implement decisions of the Cabinet within limits of budget and personnel; to plan for Cabinet meetings; to organize structures for Quadrennial Assembly; to use the resources of the Christian Church (Disciples of Christ) in planning; to strategize for implementing goals for Disciples women as developed by CWCC.

- Meets annually or as called by the ICWF president.

- Funding for the ICWF Cabinet and the ICWF Executive Committee shall be through income from the Quadrennial Assembly Revolving Program Fund, a travel pool for regional CWF presidents, the Department of Church Women, and the regional Christian Women's Fellowships.

III. That a Church Women Coordinating Council be established.
  1. The purpose of which shall be to provide an organizational structure that is representative of all women in the Christian Church (Diciples of Church).
  2. The function shall be to assist in integrating and correlating the program emphases and priorities of the Christian Church (Disciples of Christ) and its units with goals and programs for church women; to develop four-year goals and two-year objectives for women in the Christian Church (Disciples of Christ); to plan ways to implement goals for women in the Christian Church (Disciples of Christ); to recommend women for participation and representation on denominational and ecumenical boards and committees; to provide a channel to receive input and to express concern on important matters in the Christian Church (Disciples of Christ); to be an advocate regarding issues affecting women and for participation of

women in church and society; to identify, encourage, and develop women for positions of leadership in the Christian Church (Disciples of Christ); to advise and counsel the Department of Church Women regarding programming for women in the Christian Church (Disciples of Christ).

3. Membership: four women whose leadership is not in CWF, the ICWF president and vice president, two CWF representatives, one woman representative from the National Convocation, one woman from the National Hispanic Fellowship, one woman from the American Asian Caucus, two regional CWF staff persons, Department of Church Women staff—at least one of the members shall be a Canadian. A term shall be two years, and a member can serve two successive terms. Members to be elected at the General Assembly of the Christian Church (Disciples of Christ).

4. Nominating Committee to be three members: one woman member of the Division of Homeland Ministries Board of Directors, one a regional CWF staff person, and the chair of the CWF nominating committee, Department of Church Women executive (ex officio).

IV. That the Lay Advisory Council be discontinued.

The International Christian Women's Fellowship and the board of Homeland Ministries adopted these recommendations in 1982.

THE *Empowerment Years*
1983–1987

As the Advocacy Years were an era for programs and events, the Empowerment years saw the rise of structures. The Action Research Project had a major effect for years to come and prompted the formation of the ICWF Cabinet, the ICWF Executive Committee, the Church Women Coordinating Council, and ACE. Organizational structures, as unexciting as they may appear on the surface, can be an effective force for empowering people. Take, for instance, the American government and its interaction with the American people. Through government, people can take actions that affect their lives.

The challenge was to revitalize the decision-making processes within the organization so that women in congregations and regions would be able to take a greater part in making decisions for their own future within the organization and within the total church. Ever since the establishment of the Christian Woman's Board of Missions in 1874, women have been empowered to do that work through which they believed they had been called. Christian theology teaches that the Holy Spirit works in community and the Christian experience is that community happens not only in worship and fellowship but also in board and committee meetings.

The idea behind the new structures was, as always, to help women assume new roles in a new society. Understanding of what a community of women and men might be like surfaced both within the church as a whole and among the women themselves. Readiness to share in all areas of leadership grew. Training opportunities for more effective leaders continued to increase. Women were ready and some of the church was now open to their presence. It was time to go beyond acceptance of women's leadership to encouragement, for encouragement leads to empowerment.

CROSSING OVER THE BRIDGE: THE BIRTH OF THE ICWF CABINET

Through the Action Research Project, women in the congregations had determined that the CWF would remain but that some changes were necessary. Far from a mere bureaucratic change, the birth of the new ICWF Cabinet allowed women to provide even greater effective leadership to the church. In February 1983, seventy-five CWF leaders from across the United States and Canada met in Indianapolis for the opening ceremony of the first ICWF Cabinet Meeting, "Cross over the Bridge," a title referring to the change from Commission to Cabinet. Linking past, present, and future, the women held their celebration in the chapel of Missions Building, where missionaries, trained and ready to go to the mission field, had been commissioned under the auspices of the Christian Woman's Board of Missions.

The participants looked with confidence to the future amid the powerful presence of the past. In a small ceremony to emphasize the strong links between past and present and the hopefulness for the future, Jane Parker, cabinet member from North Carolina, was introduced along with her mother and infant daughter. The child was given a lifetime membership in the CWF.

Then the hard work began. "That first meeting was a struggle to keep moving as strong leaders kept challenging every step of the process," observed Marilyn Moffett, ICWF president at the time. "Yet we had built the process carefully in order to inform as completely as possible about what was happening in society and gave time for them to hear from leaders of the church of their ideas for the next quadrennium."[1] In addition, the Cabinet members had brought not only their own thoughts and concepts but also those of their organizations back home. It seemed a miracle that after four or five days of deliberation this group of women could identify so accurately what would be the major issues several years hence. Surely it had to be the leading of the Holy Spirit.

Apparently, the Cabinet members felt that presence, for when the struggle was over and the plans were complete, the whole Cabinet spontaneously sang the Doxology. Almost two years later, when these studies that the Cabinet had developed appeared at local spring workshops, the excitement and sense of ownership was apparent. "That title was my idea!" exclaimed the president from Montana. Confessing that she had been terrified to come to Cabinet that first time, now this one individual saw the power of her presence.

Women leaders empowered other women leaders at every Cabinet meeting as new styles and methods were modeled. The primary style included a notable lack of emphasis on hierarchy. Those in leadership positions worked to include and empower everyone. Commented Marilyn, "Making the structures work demanded my best efforts. I wanted to support so many women in whom I believed.

The Cabinet is a tough group to lead but they bring so many talents. Invaluable was the support of Catherine [Broadus, ICWF vice president], the ICWF Executive Committee and the Church Women staff who always worked as a team. I greatly appreciated the way in which Fran Craddock made it clear that, while she was the executive, Catherine and I were the leaders and that our leadership carried responsibilities, but that she and the rest of the staff were there to enable that leadership. Therefore, the teamwork of the leadership was very good. There was not any tension but a commitment to what is best for the women of the church."[2]

Through the ICWF Cabinet, it became possible for women in regions and congregations to have direct impact on the goals, programming, and studies of the CWF. They had the time and resources to make more informed plans—which they did not have as a Commission. Strong representative, mutually accountable structures changed the life of the CWF. It widened the circle of participation and introduced the process of decision making by consensus.

The Cabinet became yet another training ground for women church leaders. The Cabinet proved to skeptics that such a large group could work together and produce something very specific. Even those frustrated with the time-consuming process saw value in the results: wide ownership and growth of leadership abilities. In 1975 Ann Dickerson, vice-moderator of the Disciples, had frequently observed that "the CWF is the most effective training ground for leadership in the Christian Church." It was still true a decade later.

Empowerment occurred as women shared the services of outstanding women leaders. The close working partnership between Church Women and Overseas Ministries became even closer as two women moved into powerful positions. On May 1, 1984, Luz Bacerra left the Department of Church Women to join the Overseas staff as the executive for Southeast Asia. Only three months later, Alice Langford, previously director for stewardship and worship, became the first female treasurer in Overseas Ministries. An excellent interpreter of finances in her former position, Alice had kept the financial records, encouraged and tracked giving, developed promotional materials for Christian giving, conducted a series of women and money workshops, and worked closely with Church Finance Council.

RESOURCES FOR LEADERSHIP AND SERVICE

One aspect of church life often taken for granted is the materials: the pamphlets, guidelines, leaflets, handbooks, and assorted other publications that bring information from one group to another. The CWF studies, determined by the Cabinet, continued to be carefully designed and widely used by groups in the congregations. They, like the programs for Quadrennial Assemblies, reflected the interests and issues of the times. Two study consultations were held, one in 1976 and another twelve years later. This first meeting produced two major changes. It was decided to match the action projects with the areas of study and to alter the format to have a leaders' book and learners' leaflets. This second change cut the cost to the learners yet provided them with the necessary material to engage in participatory study sessions.

The second consultation, called by Raye Feltner-Kapornyai, again evaluated the materials and format. Some changes had to be made. Modern women were busy women and demanded convenience. Many women now met in retreat settings and did the study in a weekend. They wanted material that could be adapted to different situations. They did not want a lot of separate leaflets. They wanted one flexible, all-encompassing resource that they could use in a variety of settings using a variety of methods for a variety of interests. Different formats were tried. In 1997–98, the three studies (mission, Bible, and current issues) were published in one volume with suggestions for diverse uses.

As always, leadership development was a primary concern and materials were needed to help current leaders function better. For example, CWF presidents and group leaders requested new guidelines for how to conduct business meetings. The CWF manual was also revised in order to help new leaders understand the network as it was and aid them in making changes to the organization at the local level. This manual was translated into Spanish. Although some materials such as the assertiveness training handouts of the Advocacy Years had been translated, few organizational materials were available until now. Hispanic women wanted to change this and were very interested in developing their network and linking into the wider framework of CWF.

These resources all spoke to the interests of select groups, but many were produced that sought a larger audience. One focused on the power of prayer to unite the church and aid its diverse causes around the world. The Prayer Calendar, designed by Raye Feltner-Kapornyai, presented a monthly theme and a daily prayer emphasis. The calendar asked owners to focus on diverse topics. With the help of John Humbert on the 1987 trip to Russia, I contributed to the calendar. During a Palm Sunday Eve worship service, I spied a group of babushkas—Russian grandmothers. Their faces poked out of black scarves and they carried small candles and pussy willow bouquets. The surrounding crowd limited my ability to capture the moment, until John took my camera, raised it high and snapped the picture. Although the Prayer Calendar has been a sporadic project with its prime years in the eighties, a new calendar was produced in celebration of the CWF anniversary in 1999.

CHURCH WOMEN'S COORDINATING COUNCIL

While the Christian Women's Fellowship leaders had significant impact on the church as a whole, it was important that the planning, decision-making bodies of women not be confined to this organization. Not everyone was a member of CWF. Nonmembers needed a way to empower themselves and the church. The Church Women's Coordinating Council was established to meet this need. But there was a problem. Because in a sense these women were "others," there was no network or source through which these women could be identified. Most of the female church leaders had a background in CWF. It was finally determined that women whose leadership was not currently in CWF would be sufficiently representative. On September 24, 1983, one thousand women attending the Women's Breakfast at the General Assembly in San Antonio elected the charter members of the Council.

Unfortunately, most Disciples were unaware of its existence, but this body did significant work that touched both the work of the women and the whole church. For instance, of the goals for 1984–1988 (1. To proclaim unity, value diversity; 2. To develop women leaders; and 3. To promote the advancement of women) the second goal was implemented through "Women as Effective Decision Makers," a training opportunity especially for women serving on all types of church boards. The design was tested with the women of the General Board of the Disciples and, at their request, became an annual time of mutual empowerment for several years.

General Assemblies always provided opportunities for women to forward their goals. Empowered by her participation at the 1984 Assembly of the World Council of Churches in Vancouver, Marilyn Moffett was excited by the idea of a "well," a meeting place for women. In 1985, The Well was added to the attractions for Disciples women during the General Assembly. It provided opportunities for dialogue with Assembly personalities, information gathering, interviews, quiet conversation, meetings with friends, and even a corner where mothers could privately nurse their babies. Always available was a cup of cold water (a most welcome oasis during the mid-summer). In the evenings, a key speaker of the day was brought into The Well for a question-and-answer period. This was usually the only opportunity that the participants had for any dialogue with the speakers, who have included poet Maya Angelou, Bishop Desmond Tutu, and other international celebrities.

Often ideas for programs and events initiated by women in the congregations and regions were developed and refined by the Council working closely with a member of the Church Women staff. *The Disciple Woman*, for example, reached out to each woman in order to speak to, about, and for her concerns, her involvement, her life, and her faith. Council members were delighted to discover that this quarterly publication became well known rapidly.

For about a decade this Council addressed women's issues and concerns, labored to increase the leadership of church women in areas and offices where they had not been before, and, in general, served as advocates for the leadership of women throughout the denomination. Often it was through the voice of the Council that search committees heard Disciples women. This was never truer than when the committee began its task of selecting a nominee for General Minister and President. In addition, women became participating members of the Council of Ministers; Claudia Grant was the first woman elected Deputy General Minister and President; Peggy Owen Clark was the first woman to be elected a regional minister. Increasingly, women were employed in executive positions and elected to decision-making bodies. Their success is clear.

But, for all their strides, it was obvious that some change was not happening fast enough. The year 1985 marked the end of the UN Decade for Women, and Disciples women took a look at what had happened during the ten years. A decade earlier, the Disciples' General Assembly had railed against the "obvious inadequate representation of women among executive positions"[3] in the church. Now they took another look at the situation and were not happy with what they saw. "In 1973 one woman was the chief administrative officer of a region and in 1985 one woman is serving as regional co-minister."[4] They reported three women staff executives in the Divisions of Overseas and Homeland Ministries.[5] Professional churchwomen listed in the denominational yearbook increased from 4 percent to 12 percent in the twelve years before 1985. Meanwhile, the number of women seminary students grew from 9 percent during the same period to 37 percent.[6] As a result of this, the Council wrote Resolution #8523, "Concerning the Leadership of Women in the Christian Church (Disciples of Christ),"which called for equal representation of women and men on all boards of the Christian Church.[7] It was adopted by the 1985 General Assembly in Des Moines, Iowa.

Further action was required and the Council worked to select and recommend the most qualified women in the Christian Church for the position of General Minister and President, the top employed executive of the church, plus other cabinet positions and regional ministers. As John Humbert prepared to retire, the Council drew up a list of women well qualified to succeed him. Among them was Joan Brown Campbell, ordained Disciples minister, then head of the United States Office for the World Council of Churches. Careful strategies were defined and followed, but the time was not right. Or was it? For the subsequent choice caused so much uproar in the General Assembly in 1991 in Tulsa, Oklahoma, that an Interim General Minister and President, William Nichols, was named to calm the roughened waters. In retrospect, perhaps the time was right—but we did not recognize it. Or, perhaps this was the time for a Disciples woman to become chief executive of the National Council of Churches in the United States, as Joan then did.

While not all action was successful, the fact that the three largest units of the church now have women presidents may give solace. Marilyn Moffett, former moderator of the church and former ICWF president has said of the Council: "I believe that the role of women has been greatly enhanced by that diverse group of women which was brought together by the Church Women's Coordinating Council. It had just become a viable advocacy force for women within the Christian Church when it was terminated."[8]

One may wonder why at such a crucial time, the program funds for this group were terminated. Was it really a matter of funding? Had it completed the task for which it was established in such a short period of time? Was there no further need for a widely representative group to advocate for church women among the Disciples? These questions remain unanswered. Certainly its influence continues long after its demise.

What Difference Does the Leadership of Women Make?

This was an era when women in both church and society were seeking to gain positions of power within the structures of the church. They believed not only that they had a right to be there but also that when they were not there, something was missing. Women's experiences and insights were missing and were important. The nurturing, caring sensitivity so frequently ascribed to women was not often found in the workplace. It *was* "a jungle out there" and there was a need to tame that jungle. Unfortunately, however, as women did achieve high management positions, many functioned in the same manner as their male counterparts.

After commenting on the need for more women church leaders, Dr. Anne Marie Oogaard, professor in the School of Theology at the University of Aarhus, Denmark, said that a male colleague retorted, "What difference does it make? The women function just like the men."[9] Anne Marie and I believed that when women make no obvious difference, women fail, rather than empower, one another.

Of course, styles of leadership are not identical. But, as those who "hold up the other half of the sky,"[10] women need to identify what unique styles are common to them but different from their male colleagues.

Aspiring to the Pulpit

Anna Jarvis Parker, in a 1985 *Discipliana* article, likened the church to "a large rambling, older house" surrounded by women diverse in age, size and complexion.[11] The women displayed quite an interest in the house and each had a different approach for entering and dwelling within. "The house seems to be closed but not barred or boarded up," the "door is stuck—but not completely unusable." The church, she implies, like the house "seems rather neutral, neither an impregnable fortress nor a welcoming home." Considering that at one time this house was locked and women barely allowed on the porch, the issue of women in the ministry had come a long way.

Cynthia Hale, Minister
Ray of Hope Christian Church
Decatur, Georgia

Women in the seminary certainly jumped a long way from the 1970s to the 1980s. LaTaunya Bynum writes in "Disciples on an Inclusive Quest" that in 1972, women who entered the seminary found themselves "very much in a small minority among the students. It was not unusual for women to report being the only woman in a class."[12] Fifteen years later, that situation was very different. In the 1986–1987 academic year, about 38 percent of full-time Master of Divinity students were women.[13]

Through the early and mid-1980s, the proportion of female seminary students hovered around one third.[14] The proportion of women pastors grew as well, but not to the same extent. June of 1984 saw 112 Disciples women pastors or 4.2 percent of the total, and 120 associate ministers, 32.8 percent of the total. While the associates had jumped more than 30 percent from 1972, the percentage of pastors was up less than 3 percent from a token half point.[15] Some women, it seems, did not even try to find places in the pulpits. The numbers of women seeking ordination for ministry increased, but those seeking placement as pastors in congregations did not increase in proportion.

Why were there not more women as pastors? Were they discouraged by the ongoing difficulty for a woman to secure a call from a congregation? Or, were the many specialized ministries better suited to their goals? Or were there other reasons? Prior to the mid-1980s, because they were going against the prevailing social expectation, women attended seminary only when their call was clear and definite. A trend then appeared among both women and men. Many who attended went seeking spiritual growth but without a call or a professional goal. This can strengthen congregations by providing theologically trained laypeople, but it may also reduce the availability of clergy seeking pastorates. Another possibility, the "graying" of the ministry, especially among women, may have played a role. Many women came to the ministry late because of a lack of early opportunities. They may have been more willing to take positions as associates or some other alternate ministry. Jarvis Parker writes of the Master of Religious Education students who "are more often women than men; they are second-career persons, mostly married, not right out of college, who want to be professionally trained for a form of ministry but who have no intention of moving cross-country to a church."

Despite the obstacles and ambivalence women continued to face, the small gains along the way cannot be denied. Homeland Ministries vice president Joyce Coalson listed three reasons why the number of clergywomen continued to grow.[16]

New regional ministers had attended seminary with women as full colleagues and had observed the pastoral ministry of women, the ways CWF and the Office of Disciples Women and other women leaders encouraged clergywomen and identified the correlation between their own leadership in the church and having a woman as pastor in their congregation. More and more congregations had experienced a woman serving as their pastor or associate pastor and recognized that, as with men, they could provide excellent as well as poor leadership.

Their worth increasingly recognized, women entered Jarvis' house and became clergy. They often felt isolated professionally, however. A series of pre-General Assembly gatherings of clergywomen and women seminary students held from the 1970s through the 1980s tried to ease that isolation. The gatherings, said Toni (La Taunya) Bynum, often included laywomen as full participants.[17] The two-day gatherings were usually held in a retreat center, or if absolutely necessary, in a hotel. Their purpose was to provide opportunities for women in ministry to meet one another, to hear from women theologians and other church leaders, and to learn about the "relocation [now the search and call] process." It was a rare chance for clergywomen to empower one another. Bynum said the pre-Assemblies eventually went out of existence because the women were torn between it and other pre-Assembly groups, which also had social welfare, peace and justice, and liberation content. The meetings were not forgotten. Later, in the 1990s, a clergywomen's association was established.

PROJECT ACE: EMPOWERMENT IN A LOCAL CWF

Inspired by its experience as a focus region during the Action Research Project, the CWF in Ohio decided to take a closer look at their congregations and determine what they were doing that worked and what needed to be changed. How could the CWF better meet the needs of its members whose lifestyles were changing? Women returning to work outside the home had little time for regular CWF meetings. At the same time, they were entering more fully into the total leadership of the church. Younger women had no history with the CWF and no desire to keep on doing the same old things in the same old way.

Working with the women in congregations, the Ohio CWF Commission set out to discover some answers. Ohio CWF president Carol Q. Murphy (later Cosby), Mary Alice Flynt (Ohio CWF staff), Rise Madden, and Joyce Savage developed a design for Project ACE (Activate, Celebrate, and Evaluate). It reflected the Ohio CWF Cabinet's enthusiasm and concern regarding the evident need for congregational resourcing and training. Project ACE provided a written guide that enabled congregational CWFs to examine their situation, envision a future, and develop a plan to move from one to the other. At each stage there was an opportunity to celebrate accomplishments.

Through the Department of Church Women, training for ACE has been and continues to be available, and the idea of ACE moved to other states. In Tennessee, it succeeded in drawing new members. "We learned that if we meet the need of our participants we do not have to work so hard to gain new members," said one churchwoman from that state.[18] "They simply see the excitement of the CWF and want to make it a part of their lives." Using what they learned through ACE, one Tennessee congregation began two new groups for mothers of young children, a day group for at-home moms, and an evening group for working moms. "The shot in the arm we received from ACE was a self-awareness and renewed enthusiasm for the Fellowship," said another woman.

GOING FORTH WITH VISION

In their article "Forty years of Choices and Changes," Martha Faw and Janice Newborn wrote "In 1985 women took a hard look at the record of giving over the years and concluded that the CWF was not doing the best it could to support the work of the church. Groups have been coasting long on a plateau of giving for many years. Not reaching for greater heights and certainly not living up to the calling as faithful stewards."[19] CWFs chose to change that by increasing the level of giving each year for five years. By 1990, the women would be offering at least five million dollars annually through the CWF to Basic Mission Finance. "Going Forth with Vision" was the title given this stewardship emphasis. Giving was substantially increased by 1990, and the CWF total offerings amounted to more than five million dollars, but the goal of that amount to Basic Mission Finance was not achieved.

Consequently, the 1986 Quadrennial Assembly "Because We Bear the Name..." carried a strong stewardship emphasis. In her stirring message, Kay White, associate regional minister in Florida, urged the women to dig deep into their pockets and reach the $5 million goal by 1990. Jean Woolfolk, president of the Church Finance Council, delivered her "family pocketbook" speech in which she

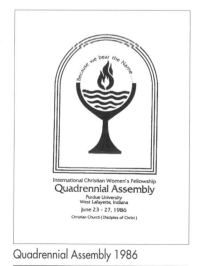

International Christian Women's Fellowship
Quadrennial Assembly
Purdue University
West Lafayette, Indiana
June 23 - 27, 1986
Christian Church (Disciples of Christ)

Quadrennial Assembly 1986

reminded Disciples that when the family needed money they often went to their mother's pocketbook. When Disciples need money, they go to Basic Mission Finance. But there will be great disappointment and inability to do the mission of the church, unless the Disciples keep their family pocketbook full.

Probably more women remember Jean at that Quadrennial for her role as Dorothy in the "Yellow Brick Road." What a shock went round the Music Hall when Kenneth Teegarden, General Minister and President, and his two deputies, John Humbert and Howard Dentler, appeared with Jean/Dorothy as the tin man, the scarecrow, and the cowardly lion respectively. Such spectacle certainly did not hurt Quadrennials during the Empowerment Years. While the largest attendance at a Quadrennial Assembly occurred in 1978, the period between 1982 and 1990 attained a consistently high attendance. The four assemblies attracted more than four thousand women each.[20] The mixture of entertainment, leadership development, social advocacy, and spiritual renewal served the participants and the greater church well as it inspired both social cohesion and action.

Women continued to go forth with vision outside the Quadrennials and outside the realm of fund-raising. Stewardship is not only a matter of money but also a matter of life. Never was this more evident than in the book of herstories, *Christian Women Share Their Faith*, published in 1986.[21] Among those in the Christian Board of Publication bookstore at Quadrennial to take part in the autograph sessions for this book was Julia Martin, then in her late nineties. When her daughter thought the experience might be too overwhelming, Julia exclaimed, "If those women want my signature, I am going to give it to them."

Typical of Disciples women across the years is that they had a clear vision of the mission of the church and were willing to give both their money and their lives to bring that vision to reality. One outstanding example is Alice Porter, a Canadian, who served in India as a nurse educator for forty years. At the same time, she made generous contributions to the capital campaign, "Embrace the Future," to the Pension Fund, and to the unit under which she once worked, Overseas Ministries.

In 1990, a new centralized fund would be established. The Women's Endowment Fund helped secure future financial support of leadership training, scholarships, outreach ministries, and faith development. After several years of floundering, the fund gathered great strength in late 1999. Although an outright gift to the fund is welcome, women are particularly encouraged to include the fund in their wills.

It's Okay to Be Different

As the 1980s progressed, leaders of Christian Women's Fellowship recognized the need to be more inclusive. This meant reaching out not only to minorities who often had strong participation but also to the disenfranchised within the mainstream. While in the past, the subtle message was, "You have to be like us to belong to our organization," Marilyn Moffett said, that changed and leadership put out the word that "it's okay to be different."[22] Jessie Trout, the founder of CWF, asserted that different methods were acceptable, that flexibility and inclusiveness were important. While differences vary according to the time, needs remain the same, leadership decided. Goals are the same, but methods can vary. Women stated a need for support from others. It was time to respond to more than a select few. Many members of Christian Women's Fellowship were finding ways to say with words, actions, and attitudes in non-matriarchal ways, "We want to help you find what you need from and within the church and it's OK if that is something different from our needs."

The goal of the woman's program was stated as: "Women care enough to seek out the uninvolved and with them discover what is needed and how the need can be met. Women who are flexible and who know the value of inclusiveness attract others." This outreach was important not only for the individual women it touched but for the church as well. As society changed and segmented, the women's organization and the church had to respond to the differing needs. "There is no typical women of the '80s," Brenda Osborn wrote in "Toward More Active Participation." "We have as women more choices than ever before and greatly varied lives and lifestyles. Reason dictates that a rigid program cannot respond to this variety."[23]

New Directions in Social Action

Disciples women in congregations continued to work through Church World Service on such projects as health kits, school kits, layettes, and blankets. Updates on information and political action related to issues and concerns about women came through ecumenical coalitions such as the Religious Network for the Equality of Women and the Religious Coalition for Abortion Rights. While most women heartily embraced such ecumenical endeavors, membership on the latter coalition was controversial. Participation of Homeland Ministries in this group was dependent on the fact that no funds were expended to support it. Therefore, the women's department was most grateful when Nancy Jo Wirth of Oklahoma provided a valuable service as the volunteer Disciples representative on the board of this coalition.

Women, always searching for sources of dependable information toward responsible action, enthusiastically engaged in peace seminars. At the first seminar in March 1984, forty-one participants from twenty-five regions gathered in Washington. They met with members of Congress and then traveled to New York City to learn from the Church Women United liaison staff stationed at the United Nations and to observe the business of that international body.

Other actions of the church had an international focus. In 1986, the Division of Overseas Ministries (DOM) made a decision to give token support of $1,000 to the World Council of Churches' Committee to Combat Racism. President William J. Nottingham of the DOM and board member Charles Bayer recommended that because of the volatility of the issue, the small grant was not worth the uproar. Maureen Osuga, board member and later ICWF vice president, gave a gripping speech supporting this gift, which would help the African National Congress (ANC), the party of Nelson Mandela. The board voted for the motion.

When Helen Spaulding, former Department of Church Women executive, heard of the decision, she immediately wrote out a check for another $1,000. She wanted to stand with the DOM board to help end apartheid in South Africa. The wisdom of the support was reflected when Mandela and the ANC became the elected leaders of South Africa with the end of apartheid. Although a major bloodbath was feared, the shift from all-white rule came with relative calm. In late 1998, Mandela surprised the World Council of Churches' General Assembly in Harare, Zimbabwe, by attending and expressing his personal gratitude for the support that churches gave the movement when it was a controversial thing to do.

At the end of the Empowerment Years, a new direction in social action was suggested. "By 1987 the ICWF Cabinet had determined that there should be a common social action emphasis, so that there would be more effective action with everyone doing the same thing at the same time...at least one thing in common. It was never determined that it would be everybody doing the same specific action but that it would all be around one particular topic," Carol Q. Cosby said.[24] Cosby came onto the scene in 1988. She pointed out that, once the topic was chosen, her task was to find "fifty different ways you can do something about this particular topic. Based on a survey on what people were interested in and what people thought they could do something about, they decided that the first one should be domestic violence. I suspect," continued Cosby, "that it had a lot to do with the fact that it became a really important issue at the 1986 Quadrennial Assembly."

One of the main speakers at that Assembly was Marie Fortune, founder and director of the Center for the Prevention of Sexual and Domestic Violence. Marie invited all those in the audience who had experienced domestic violence or known of anyone close to them who had experienced such violence to stand up. Who will ever forget how one by one women stood until, to the shock of everyone but Marie, almost the entire Assembly were on their feet? The Cabinet had made a wise and timely choice for the first common action topic.

The Cabinet's decision for a common social emphasis was not the only new direction during these last months of the Empowerment Years. Changes were on the horizon within the women's leadership of the Department of Church Women. Executive Fran Craddock retired at the end of 1987. Janice Newborn replaced her. With this new appointment, Janice became the first African American to serve as executive of a department within the Division of Homeland Ministries. She brought charm, grace, and strong commitment both to the church and to the task.

Upon assuming her post on January 1, 1988, Janice identified her primary goal as the affirmation of women by encouraging the increased involvement of young women, the development of clergywomen, and the greater participation of Hispanic and African American women. "It was an exciting time," she recalls, "and women greeted me with openness, acceptance and kindness. Of course, African American women were especially pleased that Dr. Compton had made it possible."[25] She looked forward to the future and what she could accomplish as executive, but Janice would face many challenges in the years ahead.

THE $\mathcal{S}$olidarity Years
1988–1992

As the title suggests, the short time between 1988 and 1992 meant a growing solidarity. On one level, there was the solidarity of North American women with women abroad, a global sisterhood. Ironically, there were challenges ahead in these years as much of the structure women had built was being torn down. Even this led to greater solidarity as women came together to save what they had worked so hard to create.

SOLIDARITY WITH WOMEN AND CHURCHES ABROAD: THE ECUMENICAL DECADE

In the spring of 1986 Dr. Paul A. Crow, president of the Council on Christian Unity, asked me if I would be interested in going to Bossey, an ecumenical institute in Geneva, Switzerland, to represent the Disciples women at a conference, "The Leadership of Women and the Church."

The timing was perfect; July and the Quadrennial would be over. At a week-long meeting women from around the world shared their needs and concerns, their joys and their sorrow. We found our solidarity as we sang, worshiped, laughed, and danced together. Although we could not walk in each other's shoes, we could stand beside our sister and support her, understand her, work with her, and love her. That is what solidarity is all about. That is the core of a global sisterhood. It was always my conjecture that the seeds of the ecumenical decade, "Churches in Solidarity with Women," were sown. Certainly the stories and strategies shared at Bossey indicated that the time had

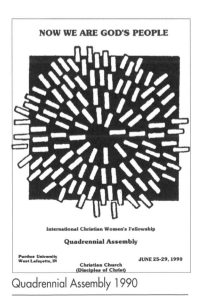

NOW WE ARE GOD'S PEOPLE

International Christian Women's Fellowship

Quadrennial Assembly

Purdue University
West Lafayette, IN

JUNE 25-29, 1990

Christian Church
(Disciples of Christ)

Quadrennial Assembly 1990

come to challenge the churches worldwide to recognize the issues confronting women in church and society and to claim these issues as their own.

The Ecumenical Decade followed close on the heels of The United Nations Decade for Women, which ended three years earlier. Sponsored by the World Council of Churches, it was launched at Easter of 1988. Leaders noted that the ministry of women began "as Jesus gave the message of new resurrected life first to the women, and said 'Go and tell.' So this Decade says to women: 'Tell your stories, help us to hear your voices.'" The Reverend Linda Daniels-Block explained the Ecumenical Decade and its spiritually based link to the women's movement. The Decade, she wrote, "grows out of a new theological awareness: of our global community, that we are all part of Christ's body; and out of a new look, by women and some men, at Jesus and how he reached out to women in everything he did. Jesus constantly and deliberately broke down the barriers and taboos set up against women."[1]

Earth Ball, 1990 Quadrennial Assembly

While churches interpreted the purpose through a variety of actions, the Reverend Daniels-Block suggested that, in general, it could be summarized in three emphases:

1. Full participation of women in the life of the church.
2. Justice for women in both church and society.
3. Theology and worship which includes women, their experiences and insight.[2]

Where were the women? This was a question that surfaced among those few women who attended the first meeting of the World Council of Churches in Amsterdam in 1945 and was later echoed at a similar assembly in Nairobi in 1975. That question might finally find an answer in the closing decade of the century. Was this a concept whose time had, indeed, come? Would the churches hear and understand the cries of the women among them? Could those Christians who had struggled with the recent study toward a "community of women and men in church" find the path to partnership?

Unfortunately, many Disciples women heard little or nothing of this decade. It impacted their lives, however. Reflecting on this time, Janice Newborn lists some of the church's related actions: preparation and approval of a special resolution (#8936) at the 1989 General Assembly; assurance that the Decade would be a central part of the planning for the ICWF Quadrennial Assemblies as well as any other activities and events taking place during the Decade; inclusion of the Decade program in all resources planned and distributed.[3] A special Bible study and guide, *To Speak or Not to Speak*, was prepared by June Doster of Georgia's regional staff and published in 1992.[4] This publication, which focused on women of the Bible, was shared with other denominational networks and became a valuable resource. Collections of poems and stories written by women were published as well, and several regions followed the lead of the Oklahoma Christian Women's Fellowship in compiling a packet for use in congregations.

There are always a few Disciples taking part in sometimes small, but significant, ecumenical meetings. For instance, in late April 1993, four Disciples women attended a small international mid-Decade meeting sponsored by the United Reformed Church in Windemere, England. Marilyn Moffett, moderator of the Disciples; Doris McCullough, then coordinator for the 1994 ICWF Quadrennial Assembly; and Kaye Murphy, staff of the Central Rocky Mountain region, joined me in England, where I was then a resident. Most of the other participants were from churches in Scotland, Northern Ireland, Germany, and the former Yugoslavia. Meetings such as this served to build a sense of solidarity with other countries.

As the Decade closed in the fall of 1998, the end was celebrated at the "Decade Festival" in Harare, Zimbabwe. Office of Department

Women staffperson Janis Brown attended, along with ten other Disciples women. At this meeting it was decided that work would continue because none of the goals had yet been met. It was suggested that the American churches had never accepted these goals or the ideals behind them. While there was a long way to go for churches to be in solidarity with women, one of the most valuable functions of the Decade was that it brought women into solidarity with women around the world.

WOMAN-TO-WOMAN WORLDWIDE: SOWING THE SEEDS

Founded to establish mission bases, train missionaries, and educate church people concerning mission work, the women's organization continued with this priority commitment throughout its history to date. By the mid-1980s, home mission virtually disappeared and work overseas was regarded as a venture in partnership with the host countries. Overseas staff, missionaries, were *invited* by the host country for a specific task for a limited time.

Yet, international travel was ever-increasing among church people. Meetings that had been routinely held in the United States or Canada were more frequently held in other countries, especially in developing countries, thus enabling a wider representation of people from those nations. As the number of ecumenical meetings on social issues increased, so did the demand for greater participation of women. Women were included among the delegates and there were more world events sponsored by women's organizations. Between 1975 and 1987, Disciples women were everywhere. Women went as delegates to the World Council Assembly in Nairobi, Kenya, and later to the one in Vancouver, British Columbia. Through Church Women United, women traveled to Cuba, China, and the USSR, and to meetings sponsored by the church in Minahasa, India; the Presbyterian women in Taiwan; the Disciples community in Zaire; the Puerto Rican CWF; the women of the Kyodan, Japan; and the Asian Church Women's Conference.

As we learned from these and other trips, the people we met abroad were just as interested in us as we were in them. Back home in the United States, some foreign friends reciprocated our interest as we returned their hospitality. When a team of Philippine Christian women visited Luz Bacerra, we found that they came to learn about us and our ways, our concerns and how we lived out our faith in our domestic context. International partnership went both directions. A plan unfolded as we searched for answers to questions such as:

"How can we most effectively provide similar experiences for a greater number of women? How can we bring the world more poignantly into more Disciples homes?" Because fewer people served overseas, and these for shorter periods of time, resources for personal stories and experiences diminished. Mission studies became more and more impersonal. The human link was missing.

As a staff member of the Department of Church Women, I had traveled to seven European countries in 1984 and found many common issues with church women there. North American Disciples, to truly understand their issues and concerns from a global perspective, had to set out into the world. Raye Feltner-Kapornyai, another staff member, visited Korea for that purpose. We learned such visits had tremendous impact, that lives were changed by this participation, as women in the rural or sparsely populated parts of North America saw how their issues were confronted and dealt with by other peoples.

It was particularly helpful for the specific mission studies that at least some women could visit the sites of study. They brought back knowledge for preparing materials and enthusiasm to share with the women engaged in study. Following consultations with the ICWF executive committee and regional staff in 1986, I drafted a proposal for a new program that would enable women to visit the areas of the mission study and would build a sense of global sisterhood with church women around the world. Conversely, it was necessary to enable women from other countries to visit Disciples women in their regions. Why not expand the number of overseas guests attending Quadrennial Assembly? Prior to the Assembly, regions could host a woman from overseas who would travel throughout the region sharing her story and learning about that region.

In 1987 the Woman-to-Woman Worldwide program was adopted by the ICWF Cabinet and two years later, two trips were held, one to the Philippines, the area of mission study, and one to Northern Ireland, an area of current interest. Because of funding restrictions, thereafter only the annual trip to the current mission study occurred, but the successful project continues to this day.

The purpose of the new program was:

1. To bring Disciples women in North America into contact with women around the world for greater understanding of each other and sharing of concerns.
2. To personalize the mission in the life of the congregation. The participants were expected to come back and share their experiences with regions and congregations.

As with all subsequent Woman-to-Woman trips, stories abound from this first experience which in itself was exemplary of partnership and solidarity. Barbara Weatherspoon, a member of the Overseas Ministries staff who had once lived in the Philippines, shared the leadership and planning of this trip with me. Fourteen women from nine regions went on the trip. "I couldn't believe it was me as I awoke early one morning on the floor in a tiny home placed on stilts in a rural village," exclaimed Mamie Townsend from Indiana. Marjorie Winnell, who was from a small town in upstate Michigan, commented that upon her return from the Philippines she could not read or watch the news in the same way. "Now that I have been there and know the people, I don't see things the same way I used to," she observed. If I were to choose the one universal phrase used to describe Woman-to-Woman across the years, it would be "a life-changing experience."

Friendships were formed and alliances made. Just recently, women who had been on the Woman-to-Woman trip to Indonesia in 1997 hosted some of their Indonesian sisters when they came to the 1998 Quadrennial Assembly. This situation is an excellent example of global sisterhood and Christian partnership in Christ's universal church. Both the American women and their guests discovered that they had something valuable to offer one another, and so new links were forged in the chain of solidarity.

Social and Political Action

CWF's social action emphasis "Domestic Violence" began in 1988 and continued until the end of 1990. This was the first and only social action emphasis that did not have a study book to support it or to give the background that led to the action. There was little need, with the barrage of reports from the mainstream media and the assistance of other denominations. Disciples shared material developed by their Presbyterian and United Church of Christ sisters.

In 1991 the focus changed to "Economic Justice for Women," an issue related to the biblical image of God's special concern for the poor because three fourths of the world's poor are women and children. A 1989 General Assembly resolution quoted statistics that pegged American women at 65 cents to every dollar men earn.[5] With black women and Hispanics the situation worsened: 60 cents and 57 cents respectively. Working closely through Church Women United, Disciples women supported government agencies, such as the Equal Employment Opportunity Commission, in their efforts to achieve equal pay and benefits for equal work. While the issue had originally been established for a two-year period of emphasis, it was soon apparent that more time was needed for effective action and the period was lengthened to four years. Furthermore, the Cabinet determined the CWF's issue study would support the emphasis for the upcoming two years, and Gretchen Eick wrote the study book *Women: Economic Exile in the Promised Land*.

The women went back to the General Assembly in 1991 and pushed for their concerns. They underscored the need for equitable salaries for women. They noted that pastors averaged $27,384 in salaries and housing, but women pastors received an average of only $21,215, or 77 percent of what their male counterparts did.[6] Regional ministers were urged to impress on search committees the need for equitable salaries for women clergy and the congregations served by women pastors to review their salary structures for fairness. Another issue that came to the 1991 General Assembly was that of gender equity in health research. Observing that less than 14 percent of the $7.6 billion research budget of the National Institutes of Health in 1990 went to women's health issues, that the National Cancer Institute shortchanges research into breast cancer, and that AIDS in women is virtually ignored, the Assembly urged the United States and Canada to put gender equity in the forefront of their funding requests.

In 1993 the Cabinet suggested that all CWFs engage in a single service project, and they chose sewing kits for the period January 1993 through June 1994. As Carol Cosby pointed out, "That was a project that tied in nicely with the economic justice emphasis because as women learned to do simple sewing projects they could earn money for their household."[7] The project was a success. They surpassed their goal of twenty thousand kits by at least six thousand, and the kits were dedicated at the next Quadrennial Assembly.

Following an impassioned plea concerning racism by Robin Hedgeman of the Ohio regional staff, the Cabinet selected "Ending Racism" as the social action emphasis for the 1995–1998 quadrennium, and Londia Granger Wright authored the study *Break the Dividing Wall*. Because the experiment in having a single service project for all CWFs had been so successful, the Cabinet devised a multicultural crayon project to support the emphasis. Crayons the color of skin tones of the world, together with five activity sheets, composed a packet that local CWFs were encouraged to provide to children within their congregations. Packets were also placed in any public location where children might wait restlessly, such as doctors' offices. Children were to draw their own hand and then find the crayon or combination of crayons that reproduced their own skin color—and then do it with a friend. Cosby pointed out that while "this is a simple thing to do, it causes the women who are going to do it to have to discuss how and why, what good it might do and for whom they are going to provide it. There were also ideas on how to use it for older children and adults."[8]

In 1995 Phyliss Hallman from the ICWF executive committee and Carol Q. Cosby represented the Disciples at the fourth United Nations Conference on Women held in Beijing, China. Out of the conference came the next social action emphasis, "Nurturing the Girl Child," which began in January 1999 and concludes at the end of 2002. This emphasis was introduced at the 1998 Quadrennial Assembly when the theme of that day was "Compassion for the Girl Child at Home and Around the World."

THE STRUGGLE FOR SURVIVAL: FROM DEPARTMENT TO OFFICE

While this period brought programs and goals that united women in solidarity, a behind-the-scenes downsizing movement within the church bureaucracy threatened all that women hoped to accomplish in the future. Ironically, the first woman president of Homeland Ministries, Ann Updegraff Spleth, led the change that some women felt would be the demise of their organization and their network in the church. In 1992, Updegraff Spleth instituted, with approval of the Homeland Ministries board and on the basis of recommendations of a professional consultant, a slimmed-down Homeland Ministries. The five departments converted into three ministry centers, with flexible staff. Abolished altogether were the departments of Church Women and Church in Society. Church Women's concerns were assigned to the Center for Leadership and Ministry. The upshot would be that the three Church Women staff members (down from a 1970s peak of six) would be separated, one in each of the three centers. Janice Newborn, situated in Leadership and Ministry, would have the primary responsibility for church women. The other two could be called on for whatever tasks the vice president in charge of the center determined.

Ann Updegraff Spleth, President
Division of Homeland Ministries

Announcement of this restructure came as a shock to women, especially those who were in the process of meeting with Ann to review and redefine agreements between Homeland Ministries and the International Christian Women's Fellowship. Less than two months before the announcement, the review group had been assured that no changes would be made without consulting them first.[9] They felt betrayed. Later Janice Newborn commented that she knew that there would be changes but "had no idea that they would be so drastic or so sudden."[10] It was ironic that women should feel such a sense of betrayal midpoint in the Ecumenical Decade which called for "Churches in Solidarity with Women."

The outcries from churchwomen were immediate. Letters began to pour into the office of the president. One complained that the Homeland Ministries restructure would "marginalize and disenfranchise" women. I personally believed there no longer would be a strong, informed, cohesive group of national women staff to work in partnership with women in congregations, districts, and regions. Sixteen Indiana CWF commissioners questioned whether Homeland Ministries had the right to unilaterally make such a major change. Hoosier women went to the General Assembly later that year with an emergency resolution to stop the divisional restructure. Their resolution was blocked, not on the basis of the issue, but on the technicality of its untimely filing. Mary Lou Canedy of Indiana complained that the change was effected without the advice and consent of the rank and file.[11] But, neither the ICWF officers nor the world CWF president even knew. The women's head of the United Church of Christ, Mary Sue Gast, spoke out in solidarity with her Disciples sisters, saying, "Autonomy of women's concerns is very important."[12] While this action threatened the autonomy of women and could cause the reduction of services, Updegraff Spleth told *The Disciple*: "We have no intention of reducing services to congregations. The point is to get the work done responsibly."[13]

Hired by Homeland Ministries in 1985 as executive vice president for program planning and staff development, Updegraff Spleth, it was understood, would plan for and carry out the restructure of the division. When she became president in January 1990, the board pressed her to reorganize.[14] Staff had already been reduced drastically from its heyday as part of the United Christian Missionary Society. Previous division leaders had worried about the unit's departments functioning almost independently, with some concern over accountability. This concern seemed somewhat ironic in light of the fact that the *divisions* themselves functioned independently and without much accountability. Outside consultant Loren B. Mead followed that up by saying that the division had overloaded people and understaffed jobs, and a situation now existed in which new programs were added and staff reduced but no tasks eliminated.

Mead called for new directions that would prove controversial. He cited the need for a Homeland Ministries that "does not create program for others to do, but operates in a variety of networks to identify needs, provide leadership and discover ways to respond."[15] The study recommended a new direction for Homeland Ministries, reducing the division's own programs and supporting congregational ministries. That change in style infuriated not only women, but all Disciples heavily involved in social action. Women were angry because they believed Mead did not grasp their method of partnership with women in congregations and regions. Programs, while administered through the Department of Church Women, were developed by local women responding to local needs. Historically, Homeland Ministries had been the origin of resolutions and public actions on peace and justice and domestic issues, informing the church of the issues, speaking prophetically to the general public, and probing the consciences of the powers-that-be in church, society, economics, and politics.

In May 1991 the Homeland Ministries board, with very little discussion, approved the restructuring. Two months later at a Futuring Conference both Bonnie Frazier, ICWF president, and Richard Hamm, then regional minister in Tennessee, presented papers in which they urged Homeland Ministries to reconsider the elimination of a department. During this conference, pressured by both the barrage of letters from women throughout North America and these presentations by Hamm and Frazier, the Division of Homeland Ministries compromised. While it did go ahead and abolish the Department of Church Women, and put the church women staff into the pool of the Leadership and Ministry center, it also created a new Office of Disciples Women, with specific staff dedicated to church women's work. Their focus would continue to be churchwomen, though they could be co-opted for other work in Leadership and Ministry.

Nevertheless, women were still angry. Meetings were held, and Updegraff Spleth was put on the spot for what some women felt were actions taken precipitously. Effective January 1, 1992, the new structure became official. Later that month, at a called meeting of the ICWF Cabinet, women regional leaders met with Updegraff Spleth and Joyce Coalson in Nashville, Tennessee. Some of those attending were unaware that it was "a done deal" and that the point of the meeting was to discover how to learn to live with it. They still could not believe that there was no room for further negotiation. All those in attendance remember that it was a "painful" experience. Frustration, rejection, defensiveness, and futility filled the air as people expressed themselves. No changes were made, but many of those there believe, in restrospect, that they did have their say.

Apparently this became something of a turning point because as one staff member put it, "We then needed to move on, even if it was within a different context." This overloaded, overworked staff had yet more to do. Now they faced double meetings and double responsibility because they belonged to two staffs (one in the Office of Disciples Women and one in the Center for Leadership and Ministry). They also wanted and needed to produce the resources of the CWF at the same level as before.

In March 1993 an evaluation meeting was held. Responses from twenty regions revealed that they did not perceive any change in the services they received, but tension and stress continued to be felt. The regions asked to be kept informed of any anticipated changes. They asked that there be secretaries provided to the Office of Disciples Women (ODW) and that the offices of the Disciple Women staff be closer in proximity. These steps would, they believed, help to relieve some of the pressure under which the staff was operating. Finally, even though the regions observed that it was too early to evaluate the new structure, the Evaluating Task Force determined that the Office of Disciple Women would remain in Homeland Ministries, perhaps because they anticipated that in 1995 another evaluation would take place. This evaluation has yet to occur.

By acting in solidarity one another, women discovered that they had at least limited power to effect change in their lives and to achieve some of their goals. A unified, identifiable staff for church women was necessary if the women in congregations and regions were to fulfill their mission effectively. With the establishment of the Office of Disciples Women they had such an administrative place. When the general offices were moved in 1995 from Missions Building to the Disciples Center in downtown Indianapolis, the three Office of Disciples Women staff offices were in one location so that they, again, could do their work together. They had gained some of what they had lost, but the voice of women still was missing from the central decision-making body of the division. Women as a group had lost their "place at the table."

THE $\mathcal{R}$eassessment Years
1993–1998

The Empowerment and Solidarity Years saw many changes. While the mid-to-late 1990s would see more major change, it was the time to prepare for the new millenium. As the twentieth century ended, it seemed natural to reassess recent history as well as how far the women and their organizations had come.

Women's Leaders Attend Closing Ceremony for Missions Building, January 30, 1995.
(Left to right) Fran Craddock, Executive, Department of Church Women, 1975–1987; Helen Spaulding, Executive Secretary, Department of Christian Women's Fellowship, 1961–1972; Department of Church Women, 1972–1974; Janice Newborn, Executive, Department of Church Women, 1988–1991; Senior Associate, Office of Disciples Women, 1991–1994; Ellen Frost, Senior Associate, Office of Disciples Women, 1995–.

Janice Newborn, head of the Office of Disciples Women, expended so much energy on the threat to abolish the women's department that she had little time to work on her goals. Right on the heels of that crisis came the preparation for the Office of Disciples

191

Women's move to a new location in downtown Indianapolis. When Newborn retired in December of 1994, Kentucky associate regional minister Ellen Frost came as the senior associate in the Center for Leadership and Ministry.

The Move Downtown

During the second half of the 1980s, there was a strong movement to move out of Missions Building and to establish a center to house all the Indianapolis-based units of the Christian Church (Disciples of Christ) in the heart of downtown Indianapolis. After an unsuccessful fund-raising attempt for a new building, Disciples leaders rented the top floors of an office building for a Disciples Center.

On January 30, 1995, Missions Building, with all its history, was closed. In an address at the closing ceremony, Dr. Joseph Smith, retired missionary and former staff of the Division of Overseas Ministries, talked about the place and the women who raised it:

> Missions Building can hardly lay claim to being the birthplace of the Disciples of Christ. However, a good case can be made for Missions Building as the Nazareth in which that segment of the Campbell-Stone reformation grew up and shaped an identity which distinguished it from other segments of the same movement. The two oldest units of the building testify to the Disciples' continuing emphasis on higher education as essentials for effective Christian leadership. One building is the former library of Butler University; the other was erected to house the College of Mission, the first graduate level institution for the preparation of missionaries founded by any Protestant denomination in America. And the women did it. Disciples women raised the money for erecting the College of Missions building. Pioneer women continued to play a major role in providing resources of money and leadership for the organizations housed in Missions Building long before their leadership role in local churches was widely recognized.[1]

While grateful that the staff for the ICWF and women's concerns would again be housed together in their new quarters, were any women present aware of the irony of their situation as they heard these words of Dr. Smith and considered the comments of Fran Craddock at the closing ceremony? "Over the arched east entrance to Missions Building are the words 'Christian Woman's Board of Missions,'" Craddock said. "Each time I pass under those words, I am reminded of my foremothers in the faith...for their spirit is ever-present [here]—nurturing, inspiring , and calling today's Disciples woman to the task of fulfilling God's mission for her."[2] One is compelled to wonder if we have really come such a long way? Women were instrumental in establishing Missions Building and had just concluded a struggle to keep an identifiable presence in the church structure.

REFLECTIONS ON RESTRUCTURE

In 1998, Ann Updegraff Spleth and I had a long reminiscence together of those moments of crisis in 1991 and 1992. She felt that the elimination of the Department of Church Women has not made a huge difference in Homeland Ministries' ministry to women. She thinks the creation of a "distinct Office for Disciples Women" in the new structure helped.[3] "Once we made that kind of course correction in the reorganization, I think, we have been able to maintain a strong presence. All leaders came together and worked hard on healing." She referred to meetings earlier in the decade as "extremely painful." At a widely attended gathering in Nashville, Tennessee, "maybe there were three people in the room who weren't mad at me."

Updegraff Spleth said she did not anticipate the loud negative response when she announced the structural change in May of 1991. There was a flood of mail, she said. There was some question by some women whether what she had said was not contradictory. Some women called it a "betrayal." "I can understand that," said Updegraff Spleth, looking back. "The board had a different opinion about that than I did. In fact, at my first board meeting in May 1990 about half the board asked, 'Well, where is it?'—meaning the reorganization plan. I think some people thought that because I had been there for five years I had it pretty well designed. So there was a greater sense of urgency than I had anticipated."

I asked her, "Are you saying that you didn't know the contents of the design six weeks before it was presented to the board?"

> *Ann*: The proposal that went to the board was about a week old. I had to fax it to Bonnie Frazier [the International CWF president] a page at a time because it wasn't written until a week before the board meeting.
>
> *Nancy*: Therefore the committee didn't have a chance to respond before it was announced as a fact. I was surprised that the board would vote to do away with two departments with so little deliberation.

194 *In the Fullness of Time*

Ann: Well, I think from their perspective they had been deliberating about it for a long time so it was way past due. While I probably was not at the time, I am aware now of what a different way of operating that was. You know, when you think about restructure, everything that happened, restructure of our church [or] our culture, our way of operating was to hash everything out ahead of time and then make changes—as opposed to announcing changes and then working out the implications, which was the way it happened with Homeland Ministries. But, you know, it was the response of the women that helped us refine the original proposal and build in the Office of Disciples Women to respond to their concerns. I suppose the original design could have worked if everybody had wanted it to, but there was almost no will for that.

Nancy: I had thought that it was still an open question at the time of the Nashville meeting, but I discovered that Nashville was to discuss "This is the way it is going to be. Now how are we going to live with it?"

Ann: Right.

Nancy: What did you learn regarding the women?

Ann: I learned what an extraordinary community of people it is, and I don't just mean in terms of a political network. I mean a fundamentally powerful group of people with gifts and the ability to turn those gifts loose. And there is also a sense in which I recaptured some knowledge, which I had been conscious of in the sense of being reconnected with a network of women's ministries that my mother had been a part of. I made some comments about this at the 1992 World Convention women's breakfast at Long Beach after which I heard from several women that they felt that there was hope for me after all. One of the things that happened through all that was that the things that we wanted as communities from each other were canceling each other out. One of the things that has happened with the laywomen leadership networks and the networks of clergywomen—and I think that some of what happened with us was an example of that—is that the community of clergywomen was longing for the community of laywomen to recognize them as people who could be their leaders, who had gifts to give the church and could be honored in that way. I think the community of CWF and larger groups of laywomen's ministries looked at the emerging group of clergywomen—and I include myself in that—and said, "You know you wouldn't be anywhere if it weren't for us." By the time we had gotten through all of that, some of the recognition that people had been longing for had been addressed. If you are never face-to-face, those affirmations cannot happen. I think we learned together that we weren't enemies.

Nancy: I think one of the things the laywomen learned was that they had the power. I don't think they believed that they had the power to make a difference.

Ann: Yes, I agree.

Nancy: And I think they learned the limits of that power. They could make a difference up to a point and beyond that point then you had the authority—so it was an understanding of authority.

Just as change in structures was painful, so it was with change in relationships. As women are able to be included in the decisions that shape their future, they may be better able to give strength and support to their sisters who have achieved positions of authority.

RE-IMAGINING, CONTROVERSY, AND QUADRENNIALS

While Ann Updegraff Spleth worked to rebuild trust in Homeland Ministries, another type of controversy would touch the church. In late 1993, a World Council of Churches event in Minneapolis, Minnesota, partly organized by Disciples lay theologian Rita Nakashima Brock, drew merciless attention from the conservative churches of North America. It was promoted as a "RE-imagining conference," in which women were to re-imagine life in a church and a world where women and men were equal. The focus naturally was on women, since it would be their initiative to make equality happen. The program lifted up the feminine side of God by focusing on Sophia, or the Wisdom aspect of God described in the Old Testament. That was met with horror by some women, goaded by the Religious Right, which declared that the Minneapolis meeting worshiped a "goddess," and showed how far the mainstream church had plunged into paganism.

Brock, a professor of women's studies and religion at Hamline University at the time, met one of the Religious Right on Ted Koppel's *Nightline* and defended the conference strongly. It was, she told the nation, "a profound affirmation of the global church." She said the conference succeeded in opening the doors "for re-imagining all of the central tenets of the Christian faith" and that there "was no strange idol worship, no goddess worship."

While some mainstream denominations were hit hard in the pocketbook by the controversy, and the Presbyterians suffered the loss of the head of their women's work, Disciples stayed fairly clear of the fallout, not having put any money into the event other than funds for Janice Newborn and others to attend. Newborn explained that it was not the role of the Disciples women to endorse what happened there, but to be aware of what was going on—and they had to attend to do that.

An element of the controversy, however, carried over to the 1994 Quadrennial Assembly in the person of speaker Chung Hyun Kyung, a young feminist theologian from Korea. She was a participant in the RE-imagining Conference, but first became a controversial figure at the 1991 World Council Assembly in Canberra, Australia. There she led a worship that incorporated Asian cultural elements, offending the more conservative in the World Council, who dubbed it syncretism—a mixture of Christianity and other faiths. Because of her background, the conservative group Disciple Renewal encouraged Disciples women to boycott Chung and the Quadrennial at which she would speak. But Disciples women leadership never wavered in their support of her as a speaker, whatever her views.

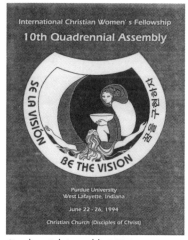

Quadrennial Assembly 1994

The attendance topped 3,600, which was higher by 300 than the previous Quadrennial. Following a most gracious introduction by Maureen Osuga, ICWF vice president, only a handful of women left as Chung rose to speak. The main body listened politely and gave her a standing ovation, though some had misgivings about her criticism of America's military policies in Korea. Chung declared that the United States and the Soviet Union forced the split into two Koreas. Now that the Soviet Union is gone, she said, the United States should withdraw from Korea as well and let the country solve its own problems. Chung read to the bemused audience some of the letters she had received, one calling her a wolf in sheep's clothing. She said she liked that one particularly because in Asian culture wolves are considered wild and free and sheep but gentle followers.

While Chung may have actually attracted a few more people than she discouraged, her presence did not overshadow the other business of the Quadrennial. Jackie Bunch of Columbus, Ohio, was elected the new CWF president. That tenth Quadrennial Assembly also honored clergywomen. They were presented ceremonial stoles made by churches throughout the denomination. While women around the country were making these colorful stoles, they were also providing twenty-six thousand sewing kits to women overseas, and the feat was noted.

The previous Quadrennial in 1990, with Martha Faw and Odatta Redd at the helm, provided several firsts. The joyous, enthusiastic team of Gail Murphy and Diane Mays from Mississippi Boulevard Christian Church in Memphis were the first African American song leaders at a Quadrennial. Another memorable occasion was the impassioned address presented by Lavinia Cano, a teacher, social worker and pastor's wife from Honduras who asked for donations for her work with the squatters in the DeMayo Colony. Immediately there was a rush from some of the audience to make an offering for Lavinia. This was a first, for there was an agreement with Purdue University that such spontaneous offerings would not take place. While that rule angered some of the more impetuous among the audience, most understood the necessity of such an agreement. To honor the desire of those who did wish to contribute, a channel for these offerings was provided through the financial office of Homeland Ministries. Meanwhile, three outstanding Disciples clergy spoke to and modeled the power of women: Joan Brown Campbell, Mary Jacobs, and Katherine Kinnamon who, in her closing sermon, challenged the women to "Go and do what you have the power to do."

The last Quadrennial of the millennium may be remembered for yet another first, the first time a rabbi (either male or female) was one of the presenters. Rabbi Sandy Sasso of Indianapolis shared in the Bible study dialogues with me. We were chosen to highlight both interfaith and intergenerational themes. We found that our theological perspectives, while different, blended to form a challenging conversation.

International Christian Women's Fellowship

11th Quadrennial
Assembly for Women

Reaviva la Llama

Purdue University
West Lafayette, Indiana

June 24-28, 1998

Christian Church (Disciples of Christ)

Quadrennial Assembly 1998

It might have been noted that while we entered our vocations at the same time, the Rabbi Sasso and I each belonged to a diferent generation, she being the younger. An intergenerational theme ran throughout the 1998 Quadrennial. The old cliché "We've come a long way, baby" came to mind as we listened to an intergenerational panel. Panelists were ICWF President Lenita "Jackie" Bunch and her daughters, Jamila and Jehan; Susan Gonzalez Dewey and her daughter, Leah; and a three-generation family: Sadie Lowery of Arizona with her daughter, Jean Mills, and granddaughter, Sadie Marie.

The assembly, presided over by Bunch and Peggy Gray, opened with a vibrant keynote address by the outstanding African American minister Cynthia Hale, pastor of Ray of Hope Christian Church in Decatur, Georgia, and closed with laywoman Susan Shank Mix's moving speech in which she incorporated her personal experience of the loss of her husband and her public experience as president of Church Women United. She gave her rationale for involvement in the ecumenical endeavor: "One primary reason I participate in CWU is because it allows me access to a wider faith community. I hear the concern of sisters in other churches. I worship and work side by side with sisters of other races. When we worship and work together I can no longer think in 'them' and 'us' terms. We become visibly one, united even in our diversity and able to be with one another in reconciliation and in love."

Looking to the future, members of the Quadrennial Assembly elected Jo Elkins and Kathy Jeffries as the 1998–2002 officers. These women will lead the first quadrennial of the new millenium.

CLERGYWOMEN: THE LONG, SLOW ROAD

The 1997 denominational yearbook listed more than 20 percent of Disciples clergy as women. That figure was certain to go higher as enrollment of women in seminaries passed the 50 percent mark. "The struggles for women in ministry continue in terms of salaries that too often are not equal to our male colleagues," said minister Toni Bynum. "There is still too much reluctance to call women to major leadership positions in all manifestations of the church. There is still too low pay. It is still too rare for women to be called to 'big steeple' pulpits. And there is still an unreal expectation of family, social life, and time in the church."[4]

There were some hopeful signs, however. In the 1990s Janet A. Long, pastor of the Washington Avenue Christian Church in Elyria, Ohio, became a role model for women pastors when she was elected the first clergywoman moderator of the Christian Church (Disciples of Christ). Long had for some time nurtured a close relationship among women in the church. Recognizing the CWF as an important force in congregational life, she attended as many CWF meetings as possible and encouraged their work and leadership, thus strengthening the whole congregation. Such efforts empower both the clergy and the laity. Her success is a testament to the network and its power.

Through CWF, women can enable one another's successes. There remain some clergywomen, however, who resist any contact with CWF because they don't want to be connected with traditional women's roles. This betrays a sense of insecurity among those clergywomen and possibly a lack of understanding about laywomen who could provide an atmosphere of affirmation. Women continue to be their own best friends as well as their own worst enemies as we slowly creep toward a time of full mutual encouragement and empowerment.

THE WORLD CWF MOVES STEADILY ON

Throughout the two decades since their twenty-fifth anniversary meeting in Hawaii, the women of the World CWF have met every four years during the World Convention of Churches of Christ in Jamaica, New Zealand, California, and Canada. In 2000, they will return to Australia after thirty years.

Central to the work of this group is its action project. The action project starts with a broad theme and then generally narrows so that real progress can be made to dent the problem faced. For instance, the emphasis for 1974 through 1980 was world hunger, and the World CWF focused on the hunger of people in the Sahel, a desert region in Africa. The decade of the 1990s centered on children: the street children in Latin America (1988–92) and the ending of child prostitution in tourism (1992–96); and the decade will close focused on the project the Khayelihle Children's Village in Zimbabwe (1996–2000).

Two newsletters a year keep women around the world abreast of the most recent news of their Christian sisters and provide information about these projects through which they remain in partnership.

WOMEN OF COLOR: LINKING INTO THE NETWORK

In the 1990s Hispanic women strengthened their organization on the national level. They had come a long way. A century before, Hispanic women in San Antonio, Texas, began to form women's organizations within their own congregations. Later, the women of the Northeast Florida region and other areas also formed women's organizations within their local churches. These Societe des Dames, as many were called, had their own programs and activities largely because materials were not available in Spanish. Little by little these groups discovered one another and some informal area associations emerged.

Hispanic women worked on their identity within the church. Slowly, CWF resources became available in Spanish. Leader training sessions were held triennially through the Department of Church Women. These were always planned and co-led by Hispanic women leaders. In 1978, black and Hispanic women leaders had met with general staff to identify specific needs and concerns. That led to the first Cross-Cultural Program in 1980.

Between 1970 and 1990 the Disciples of Christ began to recognize the growing leadership among Hispanic women. Elizabeth Rodriguez, Irma Delgado, Lily del Pilar, Wanda Gonzalez, and many others worked with Luz Bacerra and the Department of Church Women to forge a place for Hispanic women leaders within the whole church. Christian Women's Fellowship worked to encourage and train some women. Among the growing number of ordained

Hispanic and Bilingual CWF Officers, 1998–1999
Seated (left to right): Ellen Frost, Senior Associate, Office of Disciples Women; Arlene Pimentel, President. Standing (left to right): Lydia Velazquez, Adviser; Candida Gonzales, Vice President; Sue Arceo, Past President; Angelica Vilarreal, Treasurer.

Hispanic women, Daisy Machado has been a model, as she provided valuable leadership in both the worship and the business of the whole church.

Hispanic women have always had representation at the ICWF Cabinet, but the time had come for them to go national in their own way. In 1996, Hispanic women formed an official national organization. They elected Sue Arceo as president to replace Lily del Pilar, who had been a temporary leader of their previously loose-knit organization. In 1998, during the National Assembly of the Hispanic and Bilingual Fellowship in New York City, they asked that they be a recognized organization of that fellowship. This request was tabled for further discussion at the next Hispanic Assembly in 2000.[5]

At the Hispanic Assembly in San Antonio, Texas, in July 1998, Arlene Pimentel from Alvido, Florida, succeeded Sue Arceo. A member of the ICWF Cabinet by virtue of her office, Arlene is enthusiastic about all she is learning from that body. She is eager to promote leader training among the Hispanic women. Hispanic churches are organized into conventions rather than regions, and there are six conventions. As she looks to the future, Arlene hopes to have a major CWF leader training event with leadership from Janis Brown of the Office of Disciples Women in each convention. Although the language problem remains, Arlene pointed out that when women are willing to take resources not translated and adapt them in Spanish for their own use, it is "awesome." "What I would love to do right now is to take the word out to our local churches that there is material there that can be used and adapted by our women. While it would be great to have it in Spanish, at the moment having the leaders use it and adapt it would be good..." As Hispanic women, both lay and clergy, are providing more effective leadership in the churches, they look forward to the future when they will be a recognized part of the Hispanic and Bilingual Fellowship.

On the other hand, Asian women are at quite a different point in their relationship with the networks. As the millennium draws to a close, they are discovering one another within the Asian congregations. Not yet fully organized, they have representation on the ICWF Cabinet and in other significant churchwide leadership positions. Names such as Maureen Osuga and Rita Nakashima Brock are well known to all Disciples as they not only provide models for their Asian sisters but begin to provide visible wholeness to the church.

Janis Brown, African American laywoman and staffperson in the Office of Disciples Women, said that she believed it would be the women who would lead the church to wholeness. There is a sense in which this echoes Ann Dickerson's statement two decades ago that she believed CWF provided the best training ground for church leadership. To ensure the tradition of women as well-trained leaders, Janis has instituted a second level of the earlier Black Leadership Training events.

Even though the current situation among Homeland Ministries staff can be frustrating because all their time is consumed maintaining the essential programs and resources, leaving little time to think creatively, Janis has managed to develop a new Enablers in Ministry Program for women of color. While one class has completed this program, which is designed to encourage wider use of women's gifts and talents, Janis wants to mentor it further. Suggestions for potential leaders and current leaders from pastors and regional leaders provided the name of participants whose ages ranged from early twenties to fifties. A primary purpose of this program is to surface a key person in the congregation and develop her leadership skills; she, in turn, will identify other women in the congregation with leadership potential.

REASSESSMENT AND A NEW SURVEY

On paper, it looked as if interest in CWF waned. Between 1992 and 1995, the number of women in CWF groups declined precipitously. There was a reason for this drop and it was not a new disinterest. Just the opposite. After noting that the numbers had not changed much over the years, the ICWF Cabinet asked regions and congregations to take a careful count. They found the numbers were not accurate.

The year was one for reassessing. In anticipation of the fiftieth anniversary of CWF in 1999, the ICWF Cabinet decided to conduct a survey to find out what women in the congregations were doing and what they needed from the church. How could CWF, as it entered the new millennium, serve churchwomen more effectively?

A small task group appointed by the ICWF developed a set of questions, which were sent to women, not all of whom were in CWF, in fourteen regions and three interregional seminars. It soon became apparent, however, that this was not sufficient. In 1996 the ICWF executive committee hired their friend and consultant, Mary Sharer of the Institute for Organizational Research and Development.[6] In October, a survey was sent to 3,200 randomly selected Disciples women from all thirty-six regions and to the ICWF Cabinet. Another survey was sent to seventy-five randomly selected ministers and all regional ministers.

The research showed that CWF members were older, contributed more in time and money, and depended on the church more for support and fellowship. Members were concerned that more women in any congregation were in the CWF. No more than 30 percent of the women were in CWF in any congregation. Women not in CWF were younger, employed, had little time to offer outside work and the family, and felt that CWF did not speak to their needs.[7] A frequent reason for nonparticipation was "not enough time." This was an answer in 1980 as well, but while 20 percent of young women said it then, 40 percent checked that reason in 1995. Both CWF members and nonmembers said they needed fellowship and support. Bible study and local community service were the top interests sought through an organization such as CWF.

Mary Sharer, in her report to the ICWF Cabinet in January 1999, noted that flexibility was of paramount importance. Find ways, she suggested, to incorporate and recognize the actions of churchwomen. During the 1998 Quadrennial she talked with women about what was going on in their local CWFs. One woman she met at breakfast reported, "We have a lot going on in our congregation, but our young women just aren't coming to CWF, not even my daughter. Our focus for this year is 'making a difference in the lives of youth.' That is what we are working on, but our women aren't coming." Mary encouraged her to continue. "My daughter and her husband are running a youth group and they're going to be building a house in Mexico with the youth," the woman said. "They're just spending all their time on this and I just can't get her to come to CWF meetings." "But, isn't that making a difference in the lives of youth?" Mary asked. The woman realized it was and embraced her daughter's actions as a different way to go about the same goal.

Younger women want to have the opportunity for fellowship and support, but often do not have the time to attend traditional CWF meetings. Mary noted that some CWFs have stopped having any business at their regular meetings and others have stopped having regular meetings. Instead, they meet occasionally and provide diverse opportunities to meet. Ellen Frost reports that, as the research suggests, young women and older women are not communicating, especially about CWF.[8] At a meeting for mothers and daughters, she asked the mothers to tell what CWF meant to them. One of the younger women, after hearing her mother's testimony, said, "I knew that you had been going to CWF all my life and that you must have been getting something out of it, but I never once heard you talk about it the way you have today." There is a rich legacy that is often not passed to the next generation, perhaps because it is so obvious to the older generation that they think they have said it—over and over again.

The survey also revealed that retreats continued in popularity. They addressed contemporary issues, occurred only once or twice a year, and gathered diverse groups of women for worship and fellowship.

At the conclusion of her report to the Cabinet, Mary led the group in determining what the results might mean for future planning. She then indicated what it meant for leaders in CWF. Women need permission to do things in different ways and she pointed to the CWF Purpose Statement as an excellent place to begin. To move forward into the future will require courageous leadership, leadership of all ages. Leadership, Mary cautioned, is not "do-it-ship." Leaders may give ideas and then work in partnership with others.

Office of Disciples Women Staff 1999
First row (left to right): Laura Smith, Anne Hudson, Janis Brown.
Second row (left to right): Bonnie Gearlds, Ellen Frost, Carol Q. Cosby.

THE *Horizon Years*

1999 AND BEYOND

As the we enter the twenty-first century, Disciples women face a paradox: we have never been so different or so similar. Just as we celebrate the joys of a global sisterhood in which we meet other women and see they are not so different, we have also grown in power individually and taken individual, often diverse paths. On the one hand, we continue to connect with one another around the world. On the other, we face a great challenge as women, presented with more freedoms, diversify in their life choices and interests. The challenge is to encourage the connections, celebrate the differences, and meld the two to create stronger women, stronger women's organizations, and a stronger church.

Within the CWF, the primary challenge is to convince a younger generation that Christian Women's Fellowship, the women's organization of the Disciples of Christ, is relevant to their lives. I think it is. I see it as it continues to grow and change with women. At the 1998 Quadrennial Assembly, a woman approached and invited me to visit her church. During our conversation, she told me that the new women's group in her church had decided not to be a CWF. The Quadrennial had changed her mind. They were missing out, she said, pointing to the strength of the assembly and the network opportunities. I understood her group's original plan and her subsequent enlightenment. While the churchwomen probably thought the CWF was limiting, their group missed the strength of belonging to something larger. In the future, more and more women's groups who have decided not to be part of CWF will find they can join and not alter their way of operating.

Young women may not realize the power of CWF because their mothers never told them. That is a lapse we should regret, but it is not fatal to the organization. As young women decide to gather for Bible study, service projects, and fellowship, they begin to reach out to one another and find that these groups can assist one another. As they discover that there are groups just like theirs all over the country, they grasp the value in bonding and belonging. Resources are then developed for them and by them both on the regional and national levels. Why not be part of CWF? Thus the organization, which seems controlled and determined by their mothers, becomes theirs. As women rediscover the vision and vitality of their foremothers, they feel freed to exercise their own vision and vitality on behalf of their times. It is both regeneration and renewal—not the same old CWF but a new organization bonded and rooted in the past yet not bound by the past.

Little by little, women are grasping that they have, or do not need to have, permission to try new methods of organization, new leadership configurations, and new directions within CWF. Even a cursory glance at history reveals some significant differences between the Christian Woman's Board of Missions and CWF, and between the CWF of the early 1950s and the CWF of today. While decision making by the members of CWF has been severely decimated by the bureaucratic infrastructure in which it finds itself, it remains a remarkable force within the church. Always a significant locus of mission and agent for change within the total church, CWF will continue to call the church to account for its own values and virtues.

There is broad consensus that the women's organization will survive and continue to be an important part of the life of the church. Women who once thought CWF did not speak to their needs, so different from those of their mothers, might find they need the organization more than ever. "I am part of the CWF because I need a place to talk with other women. I can't do that on the job where I am in competition with other women for promotions and raises," a woman from Kingsway Christian Church in Memphis told Marilyn Moffett. As women work in the competitive workplace or stay at home in isolation, thanks to technological innovations change is inevitable, but women will still need support. Women will continue to need to network and to find strength in the community of CWF.

Increasingly, CWF will depend on smaller and smaller groups—not small groups of ten to twenty as in the past, but groups half that size. These groups will be more specialized according to the interests of small pockets of women. Some will focus on short-term social action. All will provide an intimate, safe environment for support and fellowship, sharing of faith and spiritual growth. That is at the local level. To bring everyone together, rejuvenate members spiritually, and build cohesion, regions will depend on retreats, and as always, ICWF will look to the Quadrennial. Retreats give the opportunity to discover and share new ideas. Quadrennial reminds women they are part of a wider sisterhood and how that can impact their individual lives.

The women's organization of the church is renewing itself. The decision has been made, at least for the immediate future, to keep the ICWF Cabinet. While it is expensive to fund such meetings, the extent to which the women have ownership of the decisions and programs empower them to provide more effective, knowledgeable leadership in the whole church. Thus, it becomes an investment rather than an expense. In their commitment to partnership and community, women will continue to witness to a wider, rather than a diminished, form of representative decision making—on the General Board, on regional boards, and in the congregations.

At the same time it supports and strengthens women, CWF draws strength and power from them. The church needs CWF as a strong, dependable source of information, service, and creative programming. The continuation of CWF is not just a nod to the past, but a gift to the future. As T. J. Liggett said,

> The conservation of heritage, without being enslaved to that heritage, is a major consideration as we think about the future of the CWF. In the Christian Church (Disciples of Christ), the CWF represents the best and most consistent expression of a missionary thrust, an orderly and systematic organization, a disciplined and fruitful program of study and enrichment, and a conscience about the important, cutting issues of the day. The whole church has been blessed by this heritage. Not just for the concerns of women but for the whole mission of the church. For the foreseeable future there is and will be, a need for such a movement within the Christian Church. I believe that the CWF has been and should continue to be that movement.[1]

In order to maintain the qualities Liggett mentions, strong leadership is needed. The regional CWF Cabinets and the ICWF Cabinet will need to be strong, clear, and courageous, especially in light of the growing trend for local CWFs toward smaller groups. As we look to the future, we need flexible leaders—those who work in willing partnership. There will be no place for the leader who says, "I can't get anyone to follow me in all the wonderful ideas I have."[2] The kind of leadership we will need are courageous women who are willing partners, guiding change step-by-step.

In 1998, I spoke with Homeland Ministries President Ann Updegraff Spleth about the past and future of women in the church. Ann went through a sort of "trial by fire" and reemerged with a greater understanding of our place. While most of this interview appeared in the chapter addressing the Reassessment Years, the following portion speaks to what's on the horizon.

Interestingly, much of what Ann said underscores the need for a strong woman's organization. "I don't know if CWF is what it will be called, but that is a pretty good name," she said.[3]

> I think the historic women's organization of our church will have a future as significant as the past has been. Because there is no question that it provides a significant and meaningful place for women to discover and explore their gifts. Or, if they are people who already have a sense of what their gifts are, it provides a resting-place where they can enjoy their gifts as opposed to feeling on the hot seat all the time. You know, I think about that Nashville meeting [at which the restructure was discussed] and how uncomfortable I was, and really frightened, of being there. But, in the past few years, one of my favorite places to go is CWF staff fellowship because there is a sense in which I am a member of that group—in a sense it is my home.
>
> Personally, I feel that there is no part of the church that is more important than what is in the women's organization, in terms of leadership development, strengthening the whole church, continuing to lift up the issues which the church needs to address. I have an extraordinary appreciation for that body and for the fact that it is rebuilding itself, it's building its own future even as we speak. We can't say to each other that we know what it is going to be, but we can say that it is going to be there. It's an organization that has the authority and the will to remake itself. It has done that before and will do it again. So I am committed to that happening, not just because it is a good idea, but because it is my community too.

Ann worries that the momentum of the participation of women could be endangered in the next ten to twenty years. "That has a lot to do with what we can accomplish now. Bright, capable, engaged people who have choices may very well choose to use their gifts elsewhere. I think it is time for the paradigm to shift again or the brightest and best are not going to be attracted to ministry." She warned further that the church could look at women's accomplishments and decide that "we have done that."

> I think that is a real possibility. Women have not been given the opportunity to make mistakes and move on as men have.

Women get one mistake. Subtle ways of equipping haven't happened for women, and as a result, we elect women into positions of leadership where they are more vulnerable than their brothers—both emotionally and with what they are expected to know and do.

In terms of clergywomen—it is overwhelming to see how the community has responded to Ellen's [Frost] leadership and all of a sudden the vast sense of agenda and purpose that is there among the clergywomen of our church. We must find a way to address that more completely. Not a full-time staff person—not that we couldn't use one—but Ellen has entirely too much for her to have that whole assignment. One of the gifts to me about the emerging clergywomen community is that Toni Bynum, the staffperson whose portfolio was eliminated, is a volunteer on the steering committee of the Disciples Women Clergy organization. So that is another place where we have been able to come through painful times and still recognize that we have a shared mission to pursue.

There has never been any doubt, at least to clergywomen, that there is a shared mission—whether one is talking about the mission to the organizations, the congregations, the church, or to God. While some, both men and women, have stood and continue to stand in the way, women with a vision will persevere. As Ann Updegraff Spleth said, Toni Bynum is one of the dedicated. And, as Toni pointed out earlier, we have a long way to go before female clergy enjoy the same respect and the same opportunities to serve that men take for granted.

The goal is that one day women in ministry will be taken for granted. While their number is diminishing, there are still too many people who believe it is not God's will that a woman is called to the ministry. Too many congregations refuse to consider a woman as a primary candidate. While many congregations agree to consider a woman and to have a woman's name submitted by a regional minister, they know she will not make it through to the final few. Joyce Coalson observed that it is apparent that women are beginning to serve some of the larger congregations, but men still receive the higher salaries. It has long been a practice for smaller congregations to opt for a full-time clergywoman rather than a part-time clergyman.

Meanwhile, the associations among clergywomen are strengthening. In 1997, under the guidance of Ellen Frost, an association of women in ministry (clergywomen) and its membership broadened to include licensed as well as ordained clergy. Such actions indicate that women clergy are becoming increasingly comfortable with their position among the clergy and can risk opening their community to those who may have different but similar certification. Such attitudes give room for growth not only among the members but also within the individual members themselves. This association will strengthen as clergywomen come together to share their concerns, and it will provide a voice for those concerns.

Clergywomen will continue their dialogue with laywomen. After nearly four decades of steadily increased participation in all the areas of church leadership, women are still on trial. The stronger the solidarity among churchwomen, lay and clergy, the more powerful will be their witness and the more effective will be their presence.

From the early 1970s to 1991, articles appeared periodically updating the statistics of the participation of women in church life, especially those of clergywomen. Such updates were helpful in identifying progress and noting areas where more energy was needed to increase the numbers of women leaders. Significant progress was revealed in these pieces, and women celebrated their acceptance in many new areas of church life. Church people may believe that women have arrived, that the increased sensitivity to employing or electing women can be maintained or increased without any further monitoring or advocacy, but the numbers could decline without anyone perceiving it. New studies and statistics must be published at regular intervals to show women how far they have come and how far they have yet to go. Without vigilance, there is still the danger that churches may believe that "we have done the woman thing" and now it is time to return "normal."

At present, it appears that the church will enter the twenty-first century amid a "healthy" economy. The stock market continues to climb, unemployment is declining, and there is little inflation. It is difficult to determine the impact of all this on the church. One would hope that as the economy's health increases, giving to the church will increase. As usual, the church reflects the society in which it finds itself. The United States has a surplus, yet increasingly, funding for the arts, for poverty programs, and for education comes from the private sector. Similarly, some segments of church life, once supported by general funds, are now expected to be self-supporting. Increasingly, regional budgets no longer include a full or even half-time staff for women's programming. Women's issues and CWF responsibilities are either a very small percentage of a staffperson's portfolio or relegated to a volunteer. Volunteers will play a larger role in the coming years. The restructure of Homeland Ministries also has meant that regions and congregations have had to assume financial responsibility for their own programming and leader training. In the future this may mean that it will be necessary for women in local CWFs to raise their own funds and develop their own budgets. However, this situation may limit the networking and the partnerships among the three manifestations of the church. As women responsible for CWF and women's concerns are eliminated from regional staff positions, the voice of women speaking for women to and through church structures is threatened.

While staff working on women's concerns diminishes, there are, at the same time, more opportunities than ever before for advancement in other areas of the church. More women will be regional ministers, more women will pastor large churches, more women will be elected to key offices, and more women will become powerful laywomen within congregations. We should rejoice in the number of women who are taking significant staff and ministry positions. However, to maintain this momentum it is necessary to have advocates for women present on all decision-making bodies. It would be very easy for the presence of women in visible, decision-making positions to fade as rapidly as they appeared. The centuries of acculturalization and socialization that kept women in the home and in a dependent situation have not yet been overcome. This is still an experimental stage. To date we have had but a taste of partnership. Still all too rare are the instances of full partnership in all areas of church life. There remains the perception that because the leadership of women is increasing and women are the "weaker" sex, the church is weakening—that there is a "feminization" of the church, rather than an attempt at a community of equals.

This future community of equals depends on a language of equals. Language is not a matter of political correctness; it is a matter of mutual respect. While critics worry about the "feminization" of the church, we face historic "masculinization." For example, as long as we refer to "elders" and "women elders" we betray our continuing belief that male is the norm. As long as we believe that male is the norm, then we see the current movement toward a true partnership of equals as a brief detour of civilization.

We can say what the future ought to be, but it is difficult to say what it will be. We stand at the brink. We have the chance to build a stronger partnership. We have the chance to go forward and build a new community. In the next millennium, women will continue to break down the barriers—race, age, economic status, and, most recently, profession—that have separated them. What is true of women is also true of other voices that have been marginalized in the past. Too often women have to carry advocacy responsibility for two or even three groups, thus diminishing the impact of any one concern. Recognition of all peoples, their differences and their gifts to the church, is essential to its well-being. However, all humanity has a basic partnership: male and female. So obvious, so simple, and yet so difficult to achieve. In the next millennium, it is our hope that a balance will appear.

Former ICWF Staff and Officers who attended the 1999 ICWF Cabinet meeting for the 50th birthday party
Seated (left to right): Helen Spaulding, Fran Craddock, Janice Newborn. Standing (left to right): Peggy Gray, Odatta Redd, Martha Faw, Virginia Bell, Sybel Thomas, Maureen Osuga, Catherine Broadus, Bonnie Frazier, Betty Mohney, Jackie Bunch, Marilyn Moffett. Those not able to attend: Hazel Rudduck, Mary Louise Rowand, and Ann Burns.

Appendices

Fran Craddock

Appendix I
Officers and Staff of Women's Organizations
Christian Church (Disciples of Christ)

Appendix II
Christian Women's Fellowship

Appendix III
Publications and
The National Benevolent Association

Appendix IV
Women in Leadership
in the Christian Church (Disciples of Christ)

Appendix V
Timeline

Appendix I

Officers and Staff of Women's Organizations
Christian Church (Disciples of Christ)

Historical Purposes of the Women's Organizations

Christian Woman's Board of Missions

United Christian Missionary Society
Women on Executive Committee
Department of Auxiliary Organizations
Department of Missionary Organizations
Department of Missionary Education
Conference on Women's Organizations
Department of Christian Women's Fellowship

Division of Homeland Ministries
Department of Church Women
Office of Disciples Women

International Christian Women's Fellowship
Officers
Advisory Council
Executive Committee
CWF Staff Fellowship
Church Women Staff Fellowship

National Christian Missionary Convention
Women's Missionary Society Field Staff
Christian Women's Fellowship Field Staff

National Convocation of Christian Church

Hispanic and Bilingual CWF

World Christian Women's Fellowship

Clergy Women
Staff
Clergy Women and Clergy Development

Church Women's Coordinating Council

Historical Purposes of the Women's Organizations

CHRISTIAN WOMAN'S BOARD OF MISSIONS (1874)
"To cultivate a missionary spirit, to encourage missionary effort in our churches, to disseminate missionary intelligence, and to secure systematic contributions for missionary purposes."

WOMEN'S MISSIONARY ORGANIZATIONS (1928)
"To develop a trained Christian womanhood; to unite them in worldwide service for Christ; to encourage systematic giving for missionary work through The United Christian Missionary Society."

CHRISTIAN WOMEN'S FELLOWSHIP (1949)
"To develop all women in Christian living and Christian service."

CHRISTIAN WOMEN'S FELLOWSHIP (1960)
"To develop all women in Christian living and Christian service as part of the witnessing church of Jesus Christ."

CHRISTIAN WOMEN'S FELLOWSHIP (1973)
"To provide opportunities for spiritual growth, enrichment, education and creative ministries to enable women to develop a sense of personal responsibility for the whole mission of the church of Jesus Christ."

Christian Woman's Board of Missions

Formed October 21, 1874, in Cincinnati, Ohio
Office Established in Private Homes
1888—160 N. Delaware, Indianapolis, Indiana
Later—152 E. Market Street, Indianapolis, Indiana
1910—222 S. Downey Avenue, Indianapolis, Indiana

PRESIDENTS

Maria Jameson	1874–1880
Nancy "Nannie" Burgess	1880–1881
Maria Jameson	1881–1890
Nancy "Nannie" Burgess	1890–1902
Nancy E. Atkinson	1902–1906
Helen E. Moses	1906–1908
Anna R. Atwater	1908–1920

STATE REPRESENTATIVES

(Organizational Meeting)
Mrs. J. B. Thomas, Baltimore, Maryland
Charlotte M. King, Allegheny, Pennsylvania
Mrs. W. T. Moore, Cincinnati, Ohio
Mrs. Nancy E. Atkinson, Wabash, Indiana
Mrs. S. E. Jones, Newtown, Kentucky
Elmira Dickinson, Eureka, Illinois
Mrs. Enos Campbell, St. Louis, Missouri
Mrs. James E. Garton, Des Moines, Iowa
Mrs. T. F. Campbell, Monmouth, Oregon

VICE PRESIDENTS

Nancy "Nannie" Burgess	1887–1890
Mary Armstrong	1890–1892
Nancy E. Atkinson	1892–1902
Effie L. Cunningham	1902–1904
Anna R. Atwater	1904–1908
Ida Withers Harrison	1908–1920

CORRESPONDING SECRETARIES

Caroline Neville Pearre	1874–1875
Sarah Wallace	1875–1880
Maria Jameson	1880–1881
Sarah E. Shortridge	1881–1890
Lois A. White	1890–1899
Helen E. Moses	1899–1906
Mrs. M. E. Harlan	1906–1913

SECRETARIES

Effie L. Cunningham	1913–1920
Josephine M. Stearns	1913–1920
Ellie K. Payne	1913–1920
Daisy June Trout	1916–1920
Affra B. Anderson	1918–1920
Esther Treudley Johnson	1918–1919
Lida B. Pearce	1919–1920

RECORDING SECRETARIES

Sarah Wallace	1874–1876
Marie Cole	1876–1878
Naomi Tomlinson	1878–1880
Lizzie A. Moore	1880–1887
Sarah Wallace	1887–1889

Annie B. Gray	1889–1910
Helen L. Dungan	1910–1913
Ellie K. Payne, Recorder	1913–1920

TREASURERS

Nancy "Nannie" Burgess	1874–1878
Mrs. R. T. Brown	1878–1880
Mary C. Cole	1880–1890
Mrs. J. R. Ryan	1890–1892
Mary J. Judson	1892–1916
Susanne Moffett	1916–1920

SECRETARIES OF YOUNG PEOPLE'S DEPARTMENT

Charlotte M. King	1884–1893
Ida C. Black	1893–1896
Mattie Pounds	1896–1912
Harriet R. Longdon	1912–1913
Ellie K. Payne	1913–1919
Lida B. Pearce	1919–1920

SUPERINTENDENTS OF MISSION CIRCLES

Allena Grafton	1913–1916
Esther Treudley Johnson	1918–1919
Lola B. Conner	1919–1920

United Christian Missionary Society

Formed June 22, 1920
1920—15th and Locust Street, St. Louis, Missouri
1922—425 DeBaliviere Avenue, St. Louis, Missouri
1928—222 S. Downey Avenue, Indianapolis, Indiana
1995—130 E. Washington Street, Indianapolis, Indiana

Women on Executive Committee

PRESIDENTS

| Ann Updegraff Spleth | 1993–1995 |
| Patricia Tucker Spier | 1996–1999 |

ACTING PRESIDENT

| Jessie M. Trout | July 1–
Sept.1, 1951 |

VICE PRESIDENTS

| Anna R. Atwater | 1920–1925 |
| Josephine M. Stearns | 1926–1928 |

Mary Campbell Metcalf	1928–1933
Lela E. Taylor	1933–1938
Mary Lediard Doan	1940–1949
Jessie M. Trout	1950–1961
Mae Yoho Ward	1961–1967
Kathleen Bailey Austin	1967–1974
Marilynne Hill	1974–1985
Julia Brown	1986–1987
Ann Updegraff Spleth	1988–1992
Patricia Tucker Spier	1994–1995
Ann Updegraff Spleth	1996–1999

RECORDERS

Lela E. Taylor	1920–1924
Effie L. Cunningham	1924–1927
Helen Goodrick	1927–1928
Hazel Scott Payne	1928–1947
Mayble Epp	1947–1965
Nancy Wilson	1966–1980
Mary Collins	1984–1993
Jennie A. King	1994–1999

Department of Auxiliary Organizations
Formed 1920

Affra B. Anderson, Executive Secretary	1920–1927

Department of Missionary Organizations
Formed July 1, 1927

Daisy June Trout, Executive Secretary	1927–1929
Alma Evelyn Moore, Associate Secretary	1928–1929
Alda Teachout, Executive Secretary	1930–1932
Ora Leigh Shepherd, Associate Secretary	1930–1932
Ora Leigh Shepherd, Executive Secretary	1932–1940
Thelma Marx, Executive Secretary	1940–1945
Jessie M. Trout, Executive Secretary	1946–1952
Velva Dreese, Associate Secretary	1948–1952
Anna M. Clarke, Superintendent of Youth	1922–1934
Nora Darnall, Superintendent of Junior Work	1925–1931
Helen Spaulding, Director, Youth and Children	1935–1943
Kathleen Shannon, Director, Youth Work	1943–1945

Lillian B. Harness, Director, Children's Work	1944–1947
Jane Ellen Horner, Director, Youth Work	1945–1949
Alma Scott, Department Associate	1946–1952
Carrie Dee Hancock, Children's Work	1948–1950
Katherine Schutze, Director, Business	1949–1952
Florence Sly, Program Coordinator	1950–1952

Department of Missionary Education
Formed 1920

STAFF

Josephine M. Stearns, Executive Secretary	1920–1928
Affra B. Anderson, Associate Secretary	1919–1920
Joy F. Taylor, Executive Secretary	1927–1932
Grace McGavran, Executive Secretary	1933–1934
Genevieve Brown, Executive Secretary	1934–1959
Russell Harrison, Executive Secretary	1959–1969
Nora Darnall, Superintendent, Boy's and Girl's Work, Editor of *King's Builders*	1921–1924
Edith Eberle, Director, Adult Work	1927–1942
Grace McGavran, Executive Secretary	1933–1935
Genevieve Brown, Executive Secretary	1934–1959
Rose Wright, Director, Youth Work	1935–1943
Mabel Niedermeyer, Director, Children's Work	1936–1948
Frances Hill, Children's Work	1948–1961
Mary Mondy, Director, Adult Work	1942–1944
Lois Anna Ely, Adult Work	1943–1952
Muriel Watkins, Director, Adult Work	1951–1955
Marilynne Hill, Director, Adult Work	1955–1970
Lester McAllister, Director, Youth Work	1944–1945
Mareta Smoot, Director, Youth Work	1945–1964
Bernice LeMaster, Editorial Associate	1947–1965
Marilynne Hill, Research Associate	1953–1955
Christine Siefke McNelly, Research Associate	1957–1960
Anita Newsome, Research Associate	1960–1964
Leta Bradney, Research Associate	1964–1972

Conference on Women's Organizations
Turkey Run State Park, Indiana
January 8–17, 1949

REPRESENTATIVES

| Alabama | Elma Conwell, Irene Stuart |
| Arizona | Susan Moomaw |

Arkansas	Wilma Ruth Maledon
California, North	Elizabeth Kratz, Mary Pollard
California, South	Luella Bridenstine
Canada	Ina McCully, Hazel Wright
Colorado	Mrs. A.H. Munday, Carrie M. Howland
District of Columbia	Nell Swett, Bessie Atwood
Florida	Hazel Sears
Georgia	Elizabeth Brodmann, Anne Beach
Idaho, South	Elsie Fuller, Mrs. Norman Rowe
Illinois	Lorraine Close, Mabel Crown
Indiana	Pauline Johnson, Pearl M. Jones (Sisson)
Iowa	Mary C. Metcalf, Elsie H. Purdy
Kansas	Erma Lewellyn, Helen Schwab, Gladys Irwin
Kentucky	Elizabeth Watt, June Stanley
Louisiana	Betty S. Burns, Agnes Plopper
Maryland	Mary Longfellow, Lena Hofrichter
Michigan	Corrine Tweddale, Gertrude Hersee
Minnesota and North Dakota	Edith Evans, Mildred Hautzenrader
Mississippi	Margaret Windsor, Myra Bloomfield
Missouri	Martha Gibson
Montana	Velma Beaumont, Alice Meyers
Nebraska and South Dakota	Mrs. Fenner King, Mary E. White
New Mexico	Alice Corn
New York and New Jersey	Marie Bridwell, Ruth DeBoer
North Carolina	Margaret Haney, Agnes S. Settle
Ohio	Freda Putnam, Bertha Park Wyker
Oklahoma	Naomi Taylor, Agnes Henderson, Margaret Edwards
Oregon	Ola Smith, Edna Burke
Pennsylvania	Verla M. Ross
Tennessee	Nina Hardy, Evylin R. Gribble
Texas	Mary Jo Hearn, Bessie Hart
Utah	Lynn V. Carpenter
Virginia	Nelle Stanger, Ina Miller Rau
Washington and Idaho, North	Mrs. Merle Price, Allie W. Lorimer
West Virginia	Alice Biddle, Edna Bruner

National Christian Missionary Convention: Alva Shackelford Brown

Missionary Organizations Department, UCMS: Jessie M. Trout, Velva Dreese, Katherine Schutze, Carrie Dee Hancock, Jane Ellen Horner, Alma Scott

Department of Christian Women's Fellowship
Formed July 1, 1952

STAFF

Jessie M.Trout, Executive Secretary	1952–1961
Velva Dreese, Associate Secretary	1952–1967
Katherine Schutze, Director	1952–1971
Alice Rist Langford, Director	1952–1955
Alma Scott, Associate	1952–1957
Martha Whitehead Faw, Director	1955–1961
Mildred Smith, Associate	1958–1962
Leta Bradney, Director	1960–1964
Helen Spaulding, Executive Secretary	1961–1973
Jane Heaton, Director	1961–1972
Lois Mothershed, Director	1961–1963
Olive Trinkle, Associate	1965–1972
Eunice B. Miller, Director	1965–1968
Rosemary Roberts, Associate Secretary	1967–1972
Lois Clark, Director	1971–1972
Pauline Thames, Interim Director	1972–1972

Division of Homeland Ministries
Department of Church Women
Formed January 1, 1973

STAFF

Helen Spaulding, Executive	1973–1974
Rosemary Roberts, Associate Executive	1973–1973
Jane Heaton, Director	1973–1974
Lois Clark, Director	1973–1982
Margie Richardson, Director	1973–1978
Itoko Maeda, Associate	1973–1974
Laura Luz Bacerra, Director	1974–1983
Frances "Fran" Craddock, Executive	1975–1987
Nancy Heimer, Director	1975–1991
Alice Langford, Director	1976–1984
Janice Newborn, Director	1983–1988
LaTaunya "Toni" Bynum, Director	1984–1986
Raye Feltner-Kapornyai, Director	1984–1991

Janice Newborn, Executive	1988–1991
Carol Q. Murphy, Director	1988–1991
Marilyn Moffett, Assembly Coordinator	1988–1990

Office of Disciples Women
Established January 1, 1992

STAFF

Janice Newborn, Senior Associate	1992–1994
Carol Q. Murphy Cosby, Associate	1992–
Raye Feltner-Kapornyai, Associate	1992–1995
Doris McCullough, Assembly Coordinator	1993–1994
Ellen Frost, Senior Associate	1995–
Janis Brown, Associate	1995–
Claudia Grant, Assembly Coordinator	1995–1998
Maurica Thompson, Assembly Coordinator	1999–

International Christian Women's Fellowship
Organized in Portland, Oregon
July 4, 1953

Officers

Freda Putnam, President, Ohio	1953–1957
Hazel Rudduck, Vice President, Ind.	1953–1957
Jessie M. Trout, Secretary-Treasurer*	1953–1961
Edith Evans, President, Minn.	1957–1961
Elizabeth Landolt, Vice President, Mo.	1957–1961
Lucille Cole, President, Ohio	1961–1966
Helen Pearson, Vice President, Tex.	1961–1966
Helen Spaulding, Secretary-Treasurer*	1962–1974
Betty Fiers, President, Ind.	1966–1970
Ann Burns, Vice President, Ky.	1966–1970
Mary Louise Rowand, President, Tex.	1970–1974
Frances "Fran" Craddock, Vice President, Ill.	1970–1974
Carnella Barnes, President, Calif.	1974–1978
Virginia Bell, Vice President, Tenn., Ky.	1974–1978
Frances "Fran" Craddock, Secretary-Treasurer*	1975–1987
Betty Mohney, President, Kans.	1978–1982
Sybel Thomas, Vice President, Ill.	1978–1982
Marilyn Moffett, President, Ind.	1982–1986
Catherine Broadus, Vice President, Ky.	1982–1986

Martha Faw, President, Ga.	1986–1990
Odatta Redd, Vice President, Va.	1986–1990
Janice Newborn, Secretary-Treasurer*	1988–1994
Bonnie Frazier, President, Okla.	1990–1994
Maureen Osuga, Vice President, Ohio	1990–1994
Lenita "Jackie" Bunch, President, Ohio	1994–1998
Peggy Gray, Vice President, Mo.	1994–1998
Ellen Frost, Secretary-Treasurer*	1995–
Josephine "Jo" Elkins, President, Ky.	1998–2002
Kathy Jeffries, Vice President, Tenn.	1998–2002

*Staff

Advisory Council
1953–1982

1953–1957

Freda Putnam, Ohio
Hazel Rudduck, Ind.
Mrs. Thomas Dodson, Ark.
Elizabeth Landolt, Mo.
Mildred Hautzenrader, Minn.
Ona Lee Bowen, Ky.
Verla Ross, Pa.
Mary Dale, Tex.
Mrs. Arthur J. Culler, Ohio
Agnes Henderson, Okla.
Mary Ellen Larue, Ky.
Berniece Holmes, Okla.
Mrs. John FitzGerald, Calif.
Shirley Muir, Iowa

Mrs. V. E. Lemon, Canada
Kitty Huff, Kans.
Lenore Rolla, Tex.
Lelia Jewsbury, Ill.
Marjorie Massey, Miss.
Esther Underwood, Ind.
Helen Schwab, Kans.
Evelyn Nicholas, Ind.
Mrs. Karl Adams, D.C.
Mrs. Chester Mitchell, Tenn.
Hazel McAfee, Ark.
Mrs. Harold Barr, Kans.
Winifred Hillyer, N.C.

1957–1961

Edith Evans, Minn.
Elizabeth Landolt, Mo.
Jessie M. Trout, Ind.
Mrs. Carl Adams, D.C.
Clara Blacklock, Canada
Mrs. Harold Barr, Kans.
Winnifred Hillyer, D.C.
Lelia Jewsbury, Ill.
Mrs. Chester Mitchell, Tenn.
Hazel McAfee, Ark.

Mrs. Verle Safford, Ill.
Ruth Ingram, N.C.
Evelyn Nicholas, Ind.
Mate Gray Hunt, Mich.
Helen Schwab, Kans.
Zellie Peoples, Ind.
Nina Faye Calhoun, Tex.
Mrs. O. H. Hopkins, Va.
Helen Gilbert, Iowa
Lola Delehoy, Nebr.

Lanie Davis, Ga.
Bonnie Updegraff, N.Y.
Mrs. Neil Christensen, Wyo.

Genevieve Wills, Canada
Mate Graye Hunt, Mich.
Anne Beach, Ga.

1961–1966

Lucille Cole, Ill.
Helen Pearson, Tex.
Jessie Trout, Ind.
Helen Spaulding, Ind.
Anne Beach, Ga.
Hilda Beachin, Canada
Pauline Bence, Ala.
Ann Burns, Ill.
Mrs. Lester Childers, Ky.
Edith Evans, Minn.
Martha Faw, Ind.
Nancy Fowler, Ga.
Essie Gandy, Okla.
Margaret Hociota, W.Va.

Mrs. Richard James, Fla.
Janet Moffett, Ariz.
Mrs. Howard Moye, N.C.
Mrs. Oscar Olson, Colo.
Beulah Palmer, Mich.
Freda Putnam, Ohio
Katherine Schutze, Ind.
Mrs. Richard Saunders, N.Y.
Esther Underwood, Ind.
Marguerite Webb, Ill.
Mrs. Glen T. Welin, Calif.
Essie Gandy, Okla.
Myrta Ross, N.Y.

1966–1970

Betty Fiers, Ind.
Ann Burns, Ky.
Louise Allen, Miss.
Lucille Cole, Ill.
Edith Bristow, Ky.
Edith "Tevie" Grooms, Ky.
Frances "Fran" Craddock, Ill.
Mary Dale, Ind.
Ora Dunn, Canada

Jane Heaton, Ind.
Blanche Lillie, Nebr.
Harriett McEuen, Ohio
Kathleen Owens, Iowa
Dorothy Richeson, Minn.
Pauline Thames, Tex.
Avis Thompson, Oreg.
Erma Toler, Calif.
Mary Helen Wyman, N.C.

1970–1974

Mary Louise Rowand, Tex.
Frances "Fran" Craddock, Ill.
Helen F. Spaulding, Ind.
Anne Alexander, N.C.
Carnella Barnes, Calif.
Loma Mae Chalfant, Ind.
June Christensen, Pa.
Betty Fiers, Ind.
Bettie Griffith, Kans.
Middy Harvey, Ga.
Jane Heaton, Ind.

Betty Hurst, N.Mex.
Loma Mae Jones, Ind.
Bonnie Kirkman, Ky.
Lois Layman, Kans.
Marvelle McCoy, Fla.
Virginia Moorehead, Idaho
Louise Pratt, La.
Edieth Richardson, Tex.
Jean Rolfe, Canada
Connie Shannon, Ind.

1974–1978

Carnella Barnes, Calif.
Virginia Bell, Tenn.
Frances "Fran" Craddock, Ind.
Clara Black, S.C.
Effie Burford, Ind.
Sally Dyer, Nebr.
Jo Henry, Ga.
Christi Hershberger, Ill.
Lois Hodrick, Calif.
Mickey Hunter, Ill.
Linda Kemp, Ill.
Muriel Luton, Canada

Hazel McAfee, Ark.
Pat Moore, Va.
Marilyn Moffett, Ind.
Margaret Ann Rousseau, Tenn.
Phyllis Russell, Oreg.
Mary Bethel Robinette, Mich.
Dale Shreeves, Md.
Martha Lee Sugg, Colo.
Lois Thompson, Mo.
Mildred Watson, Ala.
Gretchen Wharff, Minn.

1978–1982

Betty Mohney, Kans.
Sybel Thomas, Ill.
Frances "Fran" Craddock, Ind.
Stephanie Boughton, Ga.
Ellamae Bowers, Pa.
Eliza Cave, S.C.
Giley Griffin, Tex.
Margaret Hociota, W.Va.
Lynne Hood, La.
Maldonia Jackson, Ala.
Louise Klingerman, N.C.

Jean McArthur, Canada
Benita Lopez, N.Y.
Ernestine Mrozinski, Calif.
Mary Bethel Robinette, Mich.
Narka Ryan, Md.
Maribeth Blackman Sexton, Okla.
Ivyl Sims, Iowa
Jody Vanderkolk, Ariz.
Eula Woodall, Tenn.
Marcella Young, Miss.

Executive Committee

1982–1986

Marilyn Moffett, Ind.
Catherine Broadus, Ky.
Frances "Fran" Craddock, Ind.
Evelyn Cartmill, Tenn.

Gwendolyn Chambliss, Miss.
Ernestine Mrozinski, Calif.
Jane Parker, N.C.

1986–1990

Martha Faw, Ga.
Odatta Redd, Va.
Janice Newborn, Ind.
Kathy Helseth, Okla., Wash.

Doris McCullough, Calif.
Maureen Osuga, Ohio
Kay White, Fla.

1990–1994

Bonnie Frazier, Mo.
Maureen Osuga, Ohio
Janice Newborn, Ind.
Doris Bennett, Calif.

Cindy Beyer, Ohio
Eliza Cave, S.C.
Kaye Murphy, Colo.

1994–1998

Lenita "Jackie" Bunch, Ohio
Peggy Gray, Mo.
Ellen Frost, Ind.
Frankie Gay, Fla.

Phylis Hallman, Ariz.
Gloria F. Hernandez, Ill.
Kitty Polk, Mo.

1998–2000

Josephine "Jo" Elkins, Ky.
Kathy Jeffries, Tenn.
Ellen Frost, Ind.
Georgia Traylor-Julien, Tex.

Martha Williams, Calif.
Sue Arceo, Ariz.
Judy Row, Calif.

CWF Staff Fellowship
Formed 1952
Church Women Staff Fellowship
Renamed 1975

PRESIDENTS

Lucille Schaefer, Mich.	1952–1953
Agnes S. Settle, N.C. and S.C.	1953–1954
Mary E. White, Tenn., Mich., La.	1954–1955
Edna Bruner, Ind.	1955–1956
Chloe Kelly, Ohio	1956–1958
Anne Beach, Ga.	1958 1960
Pauline Thames, Tex.	1960–1962
Edith Baker, Ill.	1962–1964
Essie Gandy, Okla.	1964–1965
Elizabeth Hartsfield, Ky.	1965–1968
Ethel Darling, Colo.	1968–1970
Mary Alice Flynt, Ohio	1970–1972
Louise Allen, Miss.	1972–1974
Anne Beach, Ga.	1974–1976
Evelyn Hay, Tenn.	1976–1977
Alva Brown, Tex., N.Mex.	1977–1978
Jane Nesby, Kans.	1978–1979
Doris V. McCullough, Calif.	1980–1981

Mary Alice Flynt, Ohio	1982–1983
Jo Hill Snyder, Okla.	1984–1985
Alice Bolen, Iowa	1986–1987
Evelyn Hale, Ark.	1988–1989
Ellen Frost, Ky.	1990–1991
Marge Green, W.Va.	1992–1993
Marilyn Taylor, Va.	1994–1995
Sylvia Mills, Ind.	1996–1997
Phyllis Hallman, Ariz.	1998–1999

National Christian Missionary Convention
Organized 1917
Women's Missionary Society Field Staff

Sarah Lou Bostick, Organizer	1896–1948
Rosa Brown Bracy, Secretary	1916–1938
Carnella Jamison, Secretary	1938–1945
L. Ruth Rotten Patterson	1945–1946
Alva Shackelford Brown	1946–1948
Dorothy Greene	1948–1949

Christian Women's Fellowship Field Staff

Berniece A. Holmes, Director	1949–1950
Anna Belle Jackson, Director	1951–1960

National Convocation of the Christian Church
Formed 1969

CWF PRESIDENTS

Eunice Miller, S.C.	1970–1974
Mary Harris, Kans.	1974–1976
Giley Griffin, Tex.	1976–1978
Eliza Cave, S.C.	1982–1986
Odatta Redd, Va.	1986–1988
Isabel Smith, Miss.	1988–1992
Joyce Mims,Tex.	1992–1994

Mary Anne Williams, D.C.	1994–1996
Betty Jo Brown, Tex.	1996–1998
Susie Cobb, S.C.	1998–2000

Hispanic and Bilingual CWF
Formed 1996

Sue Arceo, Ariz., President	1996–1998
Candida Gonzales, N.Y., Vice President	1996–2000
Lydia Velazquez, Fla., Secretary	1996–1998
AngelicaVilarreal,Tex., Treasurer	1996–1998
Mary Muniz Andujar, Puerto Rico, Adviser	1996–1998
Arlene Pimentel, Fla., President	1998–2000
Candida Gonzales, N.Y., Vice President	1998–2000
Sandra Del Bilar. Calif.. Secretary	1998–2000
Angelica Vilarreal, Tex., Treasurer	1998–2000
Lydia M. Velazquez, Fla., Adviser	1998–2000
Sue Arceo, Ariz., Adviser	1998–2000

World Christian Women's Fellowship
Formed August 20, 1955
Toronto, Ontario, Canada

OFFICERS

Hilda Green, England, President	1955–1960
Juliana Banda, Philippines, Vice President	1955–1960
Jessie Trout, United States, Secretary/Treasurer*	1955–1961
Esther Maldonado, Puerto Rico, President	1960–1965
Clarice Digweed, Australia, Vice President	1960–1965
Helen Spaulding, United States, Secretary/Treasurer*	1961–1974
Kathleen Lawton, Australia, President	1965–1970
Magdalena Parrilla, Argentina, Vice President	1965–1970
Magdalena Parrilla, Argentina, President	1970–1974
Stella Salisbury, New Zealand, Vice President	1970–1974
Marjorie Black, Canada, President	1974–1980
Shernett Smith, Jamaica, Vice President	1974–1980

Frances "Fran" Craddock, United States, Secretary-Treasurer*	1975–1987
Freida Reid, Jamaica, President	1980–1985
Marjory Blampied, New Zealand, Vice President	1980–1985
Marie Wills, New Zealand, President	1985–1988
Lucy Godoy, Paraguay, Vice President	1985–1988
Janice Newborn, United States, Secretary-Treasurer*	1988–1994
Sybel Thomas, United States, President	1988–1992
Joy Sansome, Australia, Vice President	1988–1992
Sheila Bailey, Canada, President	1992–1996
Iris Ruth Melecio, Puerto Rico, Vice President	1992–1996
Ellen Frost, United States, Secretary-Treasurer*	1995–
Marj Dredge, Australia, President	1996–2000
Yvonne Davidson, Jamaica, Vice President	1996–2000

* Staff

Clergy Women
Staff

Katherine Schutze, Consultant, Women's Ministries	1974–1974
Deborah Casey, Consultant in Women's Ministries	1976–1978
Susan Robinson, Director, Women in Ministry	1979–1982
LaTaunya Bynum, Director, Senior Associate	1983–1994

Clergy Women and Clergy Development
Ellen Frost, Senior Associate, Office of Disciples Women 1997–

Church Women's Coordinating Council
Established July 1, 1982

1982–1986

Catherine Broadus, Ky.	Carol Q. Murphy, Ohio
Janet Casey-Allen, Ind.	Isabell Smith, Miss.
Joyce Foulkes, Ind.	Deborah Thompson, Colo.
Janet Fountain, Canada	Jan Womack, Okla.
Ellen Frost, Ky.	Luz Bacerra, Ind.
Wanda Gonzalez, N.Y.	Alice Langford, Ind.
Margaret Harrison, Tex.	Nancy Heimer, Ind.
June Jacobs, Calif.	Frances "Fran" Craddock, Ind.
Marilyn Moffett, Ind.	Janice Newborn, Ind.

1986–1990

LaTaunya Bynum, Ind.
June Doster, Ga.
Martha Faw, Ga.
Raye Feltner-Kapornyai, Ind.
Marge Green, W.Va.
Betty Hall, Okla.
Nancy Heimer, Ind.
Claudia Highbaugh, Conn.
Kiyo Kamikawa, Wash.
Marilyn Moffett, Ind.

Carol Q. Murphy, Ind.
Constance Nealey, Ala.
Janice Newborn, Ind.
Mary Maxine Palmer, Tex.
Mica Pereira, Tex.
Odatta Redd, Va.
Joann Ross, Ohio
Pat Rumble, Canada
Lois Ward, N.C.

1990–1994

La Taunya Bynum, Ind.
Noris Cabrera, N.Y.
Bonnie Frazier, Mo.
Marge Green, W.Va.
Betty Hall, Okla.
Claudia Highbaugh, Mass.
Kiyo Kamikawa, Wash.
Constance Nealey, Ala.
Maureen Osuga, Ohio

Mary Maxine Palmer, Tex.
Joann Ross, Ohio
Pat Rumble, Canada
Lois Ward, N.C.
Raye Feltner-Kapornyai, Ind.
Carol Q. Cosby, Ind.
Janice R. Newborn, Ind.
Doris McCullough, Calif.

Appendix II

Christian Women's Fellowship

CWF Studies, 1950–2000
CWF Giving, 1950–1998
ICWF Quadrennial Assemblies
Themes and Attendance
Committees

CWF Studies
1950–2000

1950–51   Theme   And So, Forth
    Group Studies   Town and Country Church
    The Near East

1951–52   Theme   Commissioned to Serve
    Group Studies   Churches for Our Country's Needs
    Latin America

1952–53   Theme   Bridges of Fellowship
    Group Studies   Home Missions and Human Rights
    Africa

1953–54   Theme   Lift Thine Eyes
    Group Studies   The Life and Task of the Church
    around the World
    Spanish-Speaking Americans

1954–55   Theme   And Gladly Give
    Group Studies   The City
    India, Pakistan, and Ceylon

1955–56   Theme   Light unto Our Path
    Group Studies   Indian Americans
    The Christian Mission in a Revolutionary Age

1956–57   Theme   That Thy Way May Be Known
    Group Studies   Mission Field: USA
    Southeast Asia

1957–58   Theme   The Greatest of These Is Love
    Group Studies   Christ, the Church, and Race
    Japan

1958–59   Theme   Women on World Highways
    Group Studies   Christian Concerns of North American
    Neighbors
    Middle East–South America

1959–60   Theme   Thy Mission High Fulfilling
    Bible Study   Every Time I Feel the Spirit
    Group Studies   Disciples of Christ in Town and
    Country
    Africa

1960–61   Theme   Set Our Feet on Lofty Places
    Bible Study   Lord, Teach Us to Pray
    Group Studies   Heritage and Horizons in Home
    Missions
    Into All the World Together

1961–62   Theme   Doorways to Decision
    Bible Study   That Timeless Purpose
    Group Studies   Churches for New Times
    Latin America

1962–63   Theme   Christian, Rise and Act Thy Creed
    Bible Study   Paul's Roman Sandals
    Group Studies   The Church's Mission and Persons of Special
    Needs
    The Christian Mission on the Rim of East Asia

1963–64   Theme   God's Voice in Crowded Ways
    Bible Study   Channels of His Spirit

Group Studies   The Changing City Challenges the Church
The Christian Mission in Southern Asia

1964–65   Theme   God's Family on Earth
Bible Study   Letters of Trial and Triumph
Group Studies   Spanish Americans
The Christian Mission among New Nations

1965–66   Theme   Partners in Faith and Action
Bible Study   The Word with Power
Group Studies   Mission: The Christian's Calling
Mission as Decision

1966–67   Theme   The Challenge of Change
Bible Study   Acts: Then and Now
Group Studies   Affluence and Poverty: Dilemma for
Christians
Canada

1967–68   Theme   Christians Unlimited
Bible Study   Creative Obedience
Group Studies   Japan
Christ and the Faiths of Men

1968–69   Theme   And What of Our Faith?
Bible Study   And What of Ourselves?
Group Studies   Winds of Change
Southeast Asia Kaleidoscope

1969–70   Theme   The Church Mobilizing for Mission
Bible Study   Interpreted by Parables—The Church's
Mission Viewed from Parables of Jesus
in Luke
Group Studies   Set Free for Others
Change in China

1970–71   Theme   The Christian's Response to Change
Bible Study   Christian Communicators
Group Studies   Where Tomorrow Struggles to Be Born—
The Americas in Transition

1971–72   Theme   A Time to Listen…A Time to Act
Bible Study   Jonah
Group Studies   Technethics: Christian Mission in an
Age of Technology
Shinny Down Your Sycamore

1972–73	Theme	Interdependence—An Uneasy Alliance
	Bible Study	To Resist or Surrender
	Group Studies	Six Hundred Million Neighbors Lighting Up Life

1973–74	Theme	Release…the Year of the Lord
	Bible Study	Four Parts of a Whole
	Group Studies	Where in the World Are We Going?
		How a Christian Uses Power

1974–75	Theme	Shalom
	Bible Study	For Such a Time as This
	Group Studies	Danger and Hope in the Holy Land
		The Christian and the Changing Family

1975–76	Theme	Caring
	Bible Study	Faith in Action
	Group Studies	Dignidad: Hispanic Americans and Their Struggle for Identity
		Little Land on Which to Build a Fire
		Canada's Native Peoples

1976–77	Theme	Called to Be…a People under God
	Group Studies	New People…New Nation: The American Experiment
		The Untold Story, A History of the Black Disciples
		Lands of Faith and Ferment, Southeast Asia

1977–78	Theme	God's Kingdom Has No End
	Bible Study	You May Enter the Unending Kingdom
	Group Studies	Witness in the Caribbean
		No Skeletons in Our Closet

1978–79	Theme	Set Free by the Spirit
	Bible Study	Questions for Christians
	Group Studies	China Speaks to Our Time
		A Rewarding Look…Christian Women Celebrate Progress

1979–80	Theme	All God's Children
	Bible Study	Luke: A Search for Wholeness
	Group Studies	Born to Be Free
		Let the Children Come

1980–81   Theme   Trusting
        Bible Study   New Life in Christ: The Ephesians
        Goup Studies   Latin America: Witness and Risk
                Caring Enough to Confront

1981–82   Theme   Partners in New Possibilities
        Bible Study   Nehemiah: A Leader of Courage
        Group Studies   To Whom Much Is Given
                Old Roots, New Shoots: Christians in
                    Europe Today

1982–83   Theme   Put Love First
        Bible Study   Love Beyond Barriers: The Story of Ruth
        Group Studies   Christian Unity: Matrix for Mission
                Pacific People Sing Out Strong

1983–84   Theme   Compelled by Faith
        Bible Study   Women of Faith
        Group Studies   Stress and Unstress—Beyond Coping
                Journey of Struggle, Journey of Hope

1984–85   Theme   …Therefore Choose Life
        Bible Study   John: The Word of Life
        Group Studies   Prayer—A Way of Life
                Fire beneath the Frost

1985–86   Theme   The World Is My Neighborhood
        Bible Study   Minor Prophets—Major Messages
        Group Studies   The Walls Can Fall
                Stories of Survival

1986–87   Theme   Transformed by Christ…Filled with Power
        Bible Study   The Power of a Transformed People
        Group Studies   Churches for Our Country's Needs
                Linking Spirit and Struggle in Southern Asia

1987–88   Theme   Who Then Is the Faithful and Wise Steward?
        Bible Study   The Word for Stewards
        Group Studies   Churches for Our Country's Needs
                It's a Question of Money
                One Thousand Years—Christianity in
                    the USSR 988–1988

1988–89   Theme   Dare to Be Courageous
        Bible Study   Living Stones: Study of 1 Peter

Group Studies   Courageous Peacemakers
                South Africa's Moment of Truth

1989–90   Theme   Celebrating the Family of God
     Bible Study   Every Family in Heaven and on Earth
  Group Studies   The Family Album
                    Rice in the Storm: Faith and Struggle
                        in the Philippines

1990–91   Theme   Decisions? Decisions!
     Bible Study   Alive in Christ
  Group Studies   To Be or Not to Be…Faithful
                    Seeds of Promise: Central America

1991–92   Theme   Faithfulness: A Spiritual Quest
     Bible Study   Philippians: Letter to a Faithful People
  Group Studies   Patterns of Faith
                    Christians in Japan

1992–93   Theme   Women in Covenant with God
     Bible Study   Women Who Witnessed: Luke
  Group Studies   Faith in the Midst of Struggle: Middle East
                    Women/Men/Church: Strength in Unity

1993–94   Theme   How Can We Sing the Lord's Song?
     Bible Study   Hope in the Wilderness—Ezekiel
  Group Studies   Women: Economic Exile in the Promised Land
                    The Other Side of Paradise—Caribbean

1994–95   Theme   Cherish the Children
     Bible Study   1 John: God Is Love
  Group Studies   Children: Loved or Lost?
                    African Churches Speak

1995–96   Theme   No Longer Strangers
     Bible Study   Acts: God Shows No Partiality
  Group Studies   Letters from Europe
                    Break the Dividing Wall

1996–97   Theme   Disciples: Identity, Faith, and Mission
     Bible Study   Training Yourself in Godliness
  Group Studies   Unity, Liberty, Charity
                    China and Hong Kong: Congregations and
                        Meeting Points

	1997–98	Theme	Church Alive
		Bible Study	Biblical Women
		Issue	Creative Evangelism and Witness
		Mission	Brazil

	1998–99	Theme	Called to JAM—Justice, Action, Mercy
		Bible Study	Esther
		Issue	Justice, Action, Mercy
		Mission	Indonesia

	1999–2000	Theme	Spiritual Inheritance: Claim it! Live It!
		Bible Study	Romans
		Issue	Critical Formation of Personal Spirituality
		Group Studies	Cuba

Christian Women's Fellowship
Offerings, 1950–1998

Year	Number of CWFs	Offerings
1950–1951	3,967	1,008,401
1951–1952	3,827	1,087,412
1952–1953	3,692	1,163,975
1953–1954	3,961	1,325,807
1954–1955	4,072	1,428,306
1955–1956	4,154	1,548,761
1956–1957	4,248	1,445,406
1957–1958	4,641	1,773,995
1958–1959	4,325	1,786,577
1959–1960	4,279	1,941,276
1960–1961	4,248	1,985,121
1961–1962	3,940	2,137,455
1962–1963	4,062	2,181,806
1963–1964	4,331	2,298,464
1964–1965	4,087	2,232,722
1965–1966	4,246	2,345,107
1966–1967	4,065	2,375,087
1967–1968	4,070	2,342,148
1968–1969	3,946	2,321,180
1969–1970	3,857	2,279,035
1970–1971	3,500	2,301,270
1971–1972	3,356	2,278,833
1972–1973	3,412	2,303,578
1973–1974	3,562	2,287,875

1974–1975	3,506	2,498,703
1975–1976	3,501	2,402,139
1976–1977	3,336	2,483,336
1977	3,322	2,509,968
1978	3,327	2,547,068
1979	3,189	2,555,309
1980	3,181	2,608,961
1981	3,057	2,454,933
1982	3,119	2,956,929
1983	3,245	2,937,118
1984	3,152	3,016,605
1985	3,150	3,043,724
1986	3,206	3,175,224
1987	3,148	3,177,348
1988	3,029	3,210,123
1989	3,052	3,225,360
1990	3,079	3,204,416
1991	3,058	3,179,223
1992	3,014	3,144,740
1993	3,007	3,039,064
1994	3,126	3,013,756
1995	2,783	2,940,427
1996	1,988	2,817,126
1997	1,825	2,757,271
1998	*1,166	2,409,818

(*—number reporting)

Total Giving to Missions **$117,488,294**

ICWF Quadrennial Assemblies
Themes and Attendance

Year	Theme	Attendance
1957	Constrained by Love	3,575
1961	Choose Ye This Day	2,885
1966	Courage to Be Christian	3,773
1970	We Ask in Faith And Miracles Occur	3,466
1974	God Is! Rejoice	4,166
1978	Behold the New Day	4,914
1982	Hope for the Journey	4,659
1986	Because We Bear the Name	4,450
1990	Now We Are God's People	3,859

| 1994 | Be the Vision | 3,557 |
| 1998 | Rekindle the Flame | 3,545 |

Committees

1957

Freda Putnam, President, Ohio
Hazel Rudduck,
   Vice President, Ind.
Mary Dale, Tex.
Jessie M. Trout, Executive, Ind.
Velva Dreese, Ind.
Martha Whitehead, Ind.
Golda Bader, N.Y.
Clara Blacklock, Canada
Muriel Brown, Calif.
Mrs. R. A. Burghart, Colo.
Alberta Craggett, Calif.
Mrs. John B. Dalton, Ohio
Carmen Dobbs, Ga.
Betty Fiers, Ind.
Regina Glasco, Ohio

Elizabeth Hartsfield, Ky.
Lelia Jewsbury, Ill.
Vivian Johnson, Ky.
Pauline Johnson, Va.
Elizabeth Landolt, Mo.
Alice Langford, Va.
Lillian Lantz, Ind.
Shirley Norris, Ind.
Frances Reed, N.Y.
Myrta Ross, N.Y.
Lucille Schaefer, Mich.
Katherine Schutze, Ind.
Mrs. H. J. Shonts, N.C.
Ola Smith, Oreg.
Esther Underwood, Ind.
Mary Ellen White, Tenn.

1961

Edith Evans, President, Minn.
Elizabeth Landolt,
   Vice President, Mo.
Jessie Trout, Executive, Ind.
Velva Dreese, General Director, Ind.
Katherine Schutze, Ind.
Martha Faw, Ind.
Mildred Smith, Ind.
Leta Bradley, Ind.
Mrs. Ted Bartlett, Mo.
Hilda Beachin, Canada
Lucille Cole, Ohio
Mrs. Ralph Cook, Oreg.
Ethel Darling, Colo.
Mrs. L. V. Dennis, La.
Louise DePew, Fla.
Miriam Fonger, Calif.

Mrs. J. L. Galbreath, Calif.
Urith Gill, Ind.
Irene Goulter, Okla.
Marian F. Hall, Minn.
Maxine Harber, Ga.
Mrs. Joseph B. Hunter, Ark.
Goldie Kelly, Kans.
Mary Ellen LaRue, Mich.
Dorothy Lindsay, Okla.
Naomi Osborn, Ind.
Helen Pearson, Tex.
Mrs. James Pippin, Va.
Freda Putnam, Ohio
Violet Raloff, Ill.
Mary Louise Rowand, Tex.
Hazel Rudduck, Ind.
Helen Schwab, Kans.

Winnifred Smith, Ind.
Pauline Thames, Tex.

Marguerite Webb, Ill.
Connie Wick, Ind.

1966

Lucille Cole, President, Ill.
Helen Pearson, Vice President, Tex.
Helen F. Spaulding, Executive, Ind.
Velva Dreese, General Director, Ind.
Olive Trinkle, Ind.
Alice Wright, Ind.
Elizabeth Hartsfield, Ky.
Jane Heaton, Ind.
Pearl Harms, Ind.
Eunice Miller, Ind.
Essie Gandy, Ind.
Middy Harvey, Ind.
Katherine Schutze, Ind.
Pauline Bence, Ala.
Ann Burns, Ky.
Mrs. Wayne Doolen, Ind.
Nancy Fowler, Ga.
Mrs. Roy Gumm, Wash.
Maxine Johnson, Ill.

Mrs. H. F. Kaufman, Miss.
Martha Gibson, Mo.
Bess Kenne, Tex.
Lorraine Lollis, Ky.
Helen Lyddon, N.Mex.
Mrs. Herman Marts, Nebr.
Mrs. C. B. Meininger, Iowa
Janet Moffett, Tex.
Mrs. Russell Palmer, Fla.
Lenora Rolla, Tex.
Mrs. W. G. Spearman, Fla.
Mrs. E. R. Snyder, Tenn.
Mrs. S. II. Stroud, N.C.
Sybel Thomas, Ill.
Mrs. Clifford Weare, Oreg.
Leslie Weesner, Ind.
Mrs. J. T. Uzzle, N.C.
Jessie Reid, Canada

1970

Betty Fiers, President, Ind.
Ann Burns, Vice President, Ky.
Helen F. Spaulding, Executive, Ind.
Rosemary Roberts, Ind.
Olive Trinkle, Ind.
Margaret Katter, Ind.
Ethel Darling, Colo.
Alpha Blackburn, Ind.
Jane Heaton, Ind.
Mildred Baltzell, Tex.
Essie Gandy, Ind.
Katherine Schutze, Ind.
Martha Baker, Ohio
Martha Bissex, Tex.
Maxine Burch, Nebr.
Mrs. Gilbert Davis, Jr., La.
Kay Davison, Ill.
Virginia Dixon, Tex.

Mrs. Edward Kennedy, Ohio
Alice Langford, Ind.
Hattie Belle Lester, Ala.
Susan Mix, Colo.
Marilyn Moffett, Ind.
Darlene Olson, Iowa
Mrs. E. Phil Dubbs, Nebr.
Mrs. William Gibble, Mo.
Janice Hassig, W.Va.
Mrs. James Henderson, Canada
Hazel Jolly, Ga.
Mrs. Cadwallader Jones, Okla.
Mrs. Hazel Rasbury, N.C.
Rebecca Riley, Ky.
Mrs. John Rousseau, Tenn.
Amy Tabor, Mo.
Erma Toler, Calif.
Betty Young, Va.

1974

Mary Louise Rowand,
   President, Tex.
Frances "Fran" Craddock,
   Vice President, Ill.
Helen F. Spaulding, Executive, Ind.
Pauline Thames, Ind.
Margie Richardson, Ind.
Janet Blickenstaff, Ind.
Louise Allen, Miss.
Jane Heaton, Ind.
Lois Clark, Ind.
Laura Luz Bacerra, Ind.
Itoko Maeda, Ind.
Kaye White, Ohio
Virginia Bell, Tenn.
Lorraine Briggs, Mo.
Mrs. J. H. Brady, Calif.
Minnie Dorman, Okla.
Martha W. Faw, Ill.

Faye Feltner, Oreg.
Georgetta Gilford, W.Va.
Margaret Grzeszkiewicz, Md.
Virginia Hargraves, Kans.
Delores Highbaugh, Ill.
Ann Hockaday, Iowa
Mrs. A. R. Jablonsky, Mo.
Mrs Wade Jones, Mich.
Dollie Louder, Idaho
Mrs. James Maris, Ind.
Georgia Meece, Fla.
Molly Pekar, Canada
Virgie Reed, Kan.
Carol Sallee, N.Mex.
Mrs. William T. Shirey, Tex.
Mrs. James Turner, Tenn.
Wilma Tye, N.Y.
Kaye White, Ohio

1978

Carnella J. Barnes, President, Calif.
Virginia Bell, Vice President, Ky.
Frances "Fran" Craddock,
   Executive, Ind.
Alice E. Langford, Ind.
Margie Richardson, Ind.
Martha Million, Ind.
Laura Luz Bacerra, Ind.
Catherine Broadus, Ky.
Martha W. Faw, Ill.
Nancy Heimer, Ind.
Jane Nesby, Kans.
Carol Sallee, N.Mex.
Linda Austin, Ohio
Stephanie Boughton, Ga.
Marion Matthews, Mo.

Eliza Cave, S.C.
Page Miller, Md.
Marian Cowan, Calif.
Anna Lou Finney, Utah
Miriam B. Gibbons, Pa.
Darlene Goodrich, Iowa
Shirley Lucey, N.C.
Betty Mohney, Kans.
Charlotte Noe, Ill.
Frances Oliver, Va.
Kathleen Jones, Tenn.
Kay Jones, Ariz.
Barbara Pierce, Nebr.
Virginia Liggett, Ind.
Ethel Roberts, Ark.
Suzanne Webb, Tex.

1982

Betty Mohney, President, Kans.
Sybel Thomas, Vice President, Ill.

Frances "Fran" Craddock,
   Executive, Ind.

Alice Langford, Ind.
Mary Payne, Ind.
Gwen Daniel, Ind.
Elaine Alsobrook, Ga.
Laura Luz Bacerra, Ind.
Bonita Bergman, Canada
Barbara Boyte, Mich.
Marilyn Carter, Mont.
Shirley Christopher, Pa.
Lois Clark, Ind.
Martha Faw, Ga.
Bonnie Frazier, Okla.
Marie Gordon, Ill.
Jackie Grinstead, Ohio
Nancy Heimer, Ind.
Delores Highbaugh, Ill.
Lynne Hood, La.

Enid Jones, Ariz.
Shirley Lucey, N.C.
Nita Matthews, Calif.
Hazel McAfee, Ark.
Doris McCullough, Calif.
Jean Myers, Nebr.
Jensene Goodwin Payne, N.Y.
Gwen Reid, Va.
Mavis Rusinak, Minn.
Narka Ryan, D.C.
Bettie Sabin, Oreg.
Nancy Saenz, Tex.
Mildred Stone, Kans.
Eula Woodall, Tenn.
Alice Wright, Ind.
Esther Zepf, Ohio

1986

Marilyn Moffett,
    ICWF President, Ind.
Catherine Broadus,
    Vice President, Ky.
Frances "Fran" Craddock,
    Executive, Ind.
Janice Newborn, Ind.
Mary Payne, Ind.
Mary Lou Curtis, Ind.
Janet Helme, Mich.
Mary Jacobs, Ariz.
Martha Faw, Ga.
Nancy Heimer, Ind.
Gloria Jeffery, Tenn.
LaTaunya Bynum, Ind.
Mary Alice Flynt, Ohio
Maureen Osuga, Ohio
Gwen Reid, Va.
Marie Gordon, Ill.

Raye Feltner-Kapornyai, Ind.
Suzanne Tumblin, Tenn.
Joanne Verburg, N.C.
Dudley Seale, Tenn.
Bertha Gilchrist, Ind.
Cleda Cox, Kans.
Jean McArthur, Canada
Isabell Smith, Miss.
Betty Heltzel, W.Va.
Ginger Jarman, Tex.
Bernice Mazeau, Fla.
Vickie Holland, Ind.
Mary Ann Williams, D.C.
Gayle Martin, Tex.
Jody Vanderkolk, Ariz.
Janet Blickenstaff, Ind.
Lois Ann Alber, Iowa
Carolyn Simpson, Okla.
Irma Delgado, Tex.

1990

Martha Faw, ICWF President, Ga.
Odatta Redd,
    ICWF Vice President, Va.

Janice Newborn, Executive, Ind.
Marilyn Moffett, Ind.
Susan Shank Mix, Va.

Raye Feltner-Kapornyai, Ind.
Alberta Jones, Mich.
Cynthia Winton-Henry, Calif.
Eula Woodall, Tenn.
Nancy Heimer, Ind.
Gloria Hernandez, W.Va., Ky.
Carol Q. Murphy, Ind.
Gwen Daniel, Ind.
Carolyn Simpson, Tex.
Alice Bolen, Iowa
Norma Doremire, Ind.
Rise Madden, Ohio
Jackie Kennedy, Ala.
Jane Parker, N.C.

Esther Brown, Okla.
Margaret Morrison, S.C.
Jeanne O'Neal, Ind.
Doris Bennett, Calif.
Mary Crow, Ind.
Janet Hoyt, Mich.
Ann Denton, Ky.
Wendy Miles, Colo.
Sarah Webb, Pa.
Gail Beck, Ind.
Rebecca Cruz, Ill.
Sue Merritt, Ga.
Joyce Schrader, Ill.
Joyce Stewart, Kans.

1994

Bonnie Frazier,
    ICWF President, Okla.
Maureen Osuga,
    ICWF Vice President, Ohio
Janice Newborn,
    Senior Associate, Executive, Ind.
Doris McCullough,
    Coordinator, Calif.
Georgia Taylor, Tex.
Lillian Nunnelly, Ky.
Debra Barnes, Ind.
Amy Madison, Fla.
Norweida Roberts, Miss.
Miriam Cruz, D.C.
Grace Kim, Calif.
Ann Pickett, Miss.
Nancy Brewer, Tenn.
Raye Feltner-Kapornyai, Ind.
Doretta Philpott, Colo.
Brenda Etheridge, Mich.
Sue Dowler, Ala.
Carol Q. Cosby, Ind.
Ruth Bosserman, Wash.
Karen Smith, Ill.

Susan Shank Mix, Va.
Frankie Oliver, Ariz.
Charlotte Hackley, Tex.
Karen Yount, Mo.
Janet Adams, Ind.
Freida Armstrong, Ind.
Joyce Beloat, Ind.
Norma Roberts, Ill.
Millie Park, Ind.
Judith Finley, Ohio
Terry Tribe, Canada
Rise Madden, Ohio
Alice Langford, Ind.
Carol Galbraith, Ind.
Leora Walton, Iowa
Norma Doremire, Ind.
Judith Kares, Ariz.
Deborah Bailey, Ohio (UCC Rep.)
Mary Crow, Ind.
Betty Duhon, La.
Claudia Thomas, Ohio
Kitty Polk, Mo.
Ruth Tiffany, Calif.

1998

Lenita "Jackie" Bunch,
  ICWF President, Ohio
Peggy Gray, Vice President, Mo.
Ellen Frost, Senior Associate,
  Office of Disciples Women, Ind.
Claudia Grant, Ind.
Sarah Riester, Ind.
Susan Shank Mix, Va.
Penny Shorow, Oreg.
Bonnie Cole, Tex.
Claudia Thomas, Ohio
Betty Duhon, La.
Georgia Traylor, Tex.
Carol Q. Cosby, Ind.
Deborah Bailey, Ohio (UCC Rep.)
Judith Kares, Ariz.
Jane Harnden, Okla.
Leona Griggsby, Mo.
Daisy Chambers, N.C.
Lillian Nunnelly, Ky.
Cindy Dougherty, Mo.

Judy Dunson, Ind.
Judy Row, Calif.
Mary Ann Williams, D.C.
Janine Ishee, Ohio
Marty Hamilton, Tex.
Kathy Jeffries, Tenn.
Betty Jo Brown, Tex.
Janis Brown, Ind.
Wendy Miles, Iowa
Virginia Krebs, Oreg.
Donna Muiller, Kan.
Betty Mowery, Ind.
Marilyn Taylor, Va.
Brenda Etheridge, Mich.
Carolyn Day, Ind.
Mindy Hamm, Ind.
Evelyn Hale, Ark.
Carole Montgomery, Miss.
Linda Klein, Ark.
Sarah Kennerly, Ill.

Appendix III

Publications and
The National Benevolent Association

Publications

Missionary Tidings
Published by the CWBM, 1883–1918

EDITORS

Marcia Bassett Goodwin	1883
Sarah Shortridge and Mrs. L. S. Moore	1883–1884
Sarah Shortridge	1884–1890
Lois White	1890–1899
Helen Moses	1899–1905
Anna R. Atwater	1905–1909
Effie L. Cunningham	1909–1918

World Call
Missionary Tidings merged with *The Missionary Intelligencer*,
The American Home Missionary, *Business in Christianity*, and
The Christian Philanthropist to form *World Call* in 1919.
Published by Christian Board of Publication.

EDITORS

W. R. Warren	1919–1929
Bess White Cochran	1929–1932
Harold Fey	1932–1935
George Walker Buckner	1935–1961
Samuel F. Pugh	1961–1971
James Merrell	1971–1974

The Disciple

The Christian and *World Call* merged to form
The Disciple on January 1, 1974.

EDITORS

James Merrell	1974–1989
Robert Friedly	1990–1998
Patricia Case	1998–

The National Benevolent Association

Established at St. Louis, Missouri
January 10, 1887

FOUNDERS

Elizabeth Hodgen, President
Judith E. Garrison, Vice President
Mrs. Wheeldon, Vice President
Mrs. O. B. Harris, Vice President
Mrs. S. M. McCormack, Vice President
Mrs. J. E. Cash, Vice President
Fannie Shedd Ayars, Corresponding Secretary
Landonia Hansborough, Recording Secretary
Cecilia Wiggin, Treasurer
Sophia Roberson Kerns
Rowena Mason
Emily Meier
Ida Harrison
Mattie Hart Yunkin

Appendix IV

Women in Leadership
in the Christian Church (Disciples of Christ)

International Convention

National Christian Missionary Convention

Commission on Brotherhood Restructure

Christian Church (Disciples of Christ)
Moderators of the General Assembly
Vice Moderators of the General Assembly
Presidents of General Units
General Cabinet
Office of the General Minister and President
Regional Ministers

**National Convocation of the Christian Church
(Disciples of Christ)**

National Hispanic and Bilingual Fellowship

World Convention of Churches of Christ

Church Women United

National Council of Churches

International Convention of Disciples of Christ
renamed **International Convention of Christian Churches (Disciples of Christ)** in 1956

VICE PRESIDENTS

Mary Latshaw, Mo.	1917
(No Assembly)	1918
Florence Miller Black, Ky.	1919
Mrs. W. B. Craig, Iowa	1920
Ida Withers Harrison, Ky.	1921
Mrs. O. H. Greist, Ind.	1922
Mrs. A. R. Strang, Ohio	1923
Elizabeth Ross, Iowa	1924
Mrs. Howard Scott, Kans.	1925
Mercy Kendall, Ohio	1926
(No Assembly)	1927
Mrs. Hugh Morrison, Ill.	1928
Louella St. Clair Moss, Mo.	1929
Leila Rothenburger, Ind.	1930
Mrs. H. N. Lester, Calif.	1931
Mrs. Kent Hughes, Ohio	1932
Mary Campbell Metcalf, Mich.	1933
Mrs. W. B. Clemmer, Mo.	1934
Mrs. George Stewart, Canada	1935
Mrs. J. T. Ferguson, Mo.	1936
Mrs. E. C. Smith, Iowa	1937
Mrs. E. V. Pugh, Calif.	1938
Mrs. C. O. Stuckenbruck, Kans.	1939
(No Assembly)	1940
Mrs. Marvin O. Sansbury, Iowa	1941
(No Assembly)	1942
Ona Lee Bowen, Ky.	1943
Adelaide Adams, Mo.	1944
(No Assembly)	1945
Mrs. A. C. Ragsdale, Mo.	1946
Mrs. Henry G. Harmon, Iowa	1947
Mildred Hamilton, Ohio	1948
Helen Pearson, Tex.	1949
Mossie Wyker, Mo.*	1950
(Regional Assemblies)	1951

*Acting President

Kathleen Bailey, Tex.	1952
Maxine Miller, N.Y.	1953
Jean McGowan, Calif.	1954
(Regional Assemblies)	1955
Ola Smith, Oreg.	1956
Hazel Rudduck, Ind.	1957
Zellie Peoples, Ind.	1958
Dorothy Bicks, Canada	1959
Thelma Hastings, D.C.	1960
Carnella Barnes, Calif.	1961
Freda Putnam, Ohio	1962
Elizabeth Landolt, Mo.	1963
Winnifred Smith, Ind.	1964
(Regional Assemblies)	1965
Mary Louise Rowand, Tex.	1966
Jean Woolfolk, Ark.	1967

National Christian Missionary Convention
Organized 1917

VICE PRESIDENTS

Berniece Holmes, Okla.	1953–1954
Edith Bristow, N.Y.	1953–1954
Mrs. J. E. Walker, Tenn.	1953–1954
Lois Mothershed, Ark.	1953–1955
Lenora Rolla, Tex.	1954–1955
Zellie Peoples, Ind.	1955–1957
Mary McElroy, Mo.	1955–1957
Oneida Reed, Mo.	1956–1957
Rosa Brown Haynes, Tenn.	1957–1959
Edith Richardson, Tex.	1957–1959
Barbara Gill, Miss.	1957–1959
Zellie Peoples, Ind.	1959–1965
Margarette Webb, Ill.	1960–1961
Mrs. R. L. Saunders, N.Y.	1961–1963
Dorothy Witten, Va.	1961–1963
Justine Sutton, Mo.	1963–1965

Bessie Garner, Ky.	1963–1965
Edith Bristow, Ky.	1966–1967
Lucille Compton, Ohio	1966–1968
Edith Grooms, Ky.	1967–1968
Stacy Evans, Ind.	1967–1968
Eunice Miller, Ind.	1968–1969
Lydan Range, Ohio	1968–1969
Amelia Webb, Ill.	1968–1969
Ann Dickerson, Tenn.	1968–1969

Commission on Brotherhood Restructure
1962–1968

Carnella Barnes, Calif.
Mrs. S. W. Breeland, S.C.
Martha Carpenter, Tenn.
Rosemary Brooks, Ky.
Edith Evans, Minn.
Lucille Cole, Ill.
Mrs. John T. Fitzgerald, Calif.
Mrs. Carl Gast, Mo.
Ruth Johnson, Ind.
Shirley Muir, Canada
Mrs. Glen D. Post, W.Va.
Freda Putnam, Ohio
Dorothy Richeson, Minn.
Mrs. F. W. Rowe, Nebr.
Mrs. C. S. Schoverling, Tex.
Ola Smith, Oreg.
Helen Spaulding, Ind.
Mrs. Howard Stover, Utah
Mrs. O. G. Thomas, Ala.
Mae Yoho Ward, Ind.
Marguerette Webb, Ill.
Jean Woolfolk, Ark.

Christian Church (Disciples of Christ)
Provisional Design adopted in 1968

Moderators of the General Assembly
Jean Woolfolk, Ark.	1973–1975
Joy Greer, Ark.	1981–1983
Marilyn Moffett, Ind.	1991–1993
Janet Long, Ohio	1995–1997

Vice Moderators of the General Assembly
Sybel Thomas, Ill.	1968–1969
Margaret Wilkes, Calif.	1971–1973
Ann Dickerson, Tenn.*	1975–1975
Delores Highbaugh, Ill.	1975–1977
Joy Greer, Ark.	1977–1979
Charlotte Emel, Ill.	1979–1981
Margaret Buvinger, Okla.	1983–1985
Donna Albright, Wash.	1985–1987
Audrey Anderson, Calif.	1987–1989
Frances "Fran" Craddock, Ind.	1989–1991
Mary Jacobs, Ariz.	1991–1993
Cynthia Hale, Ga.	1993–1995
Joyce Blair, Tenn.	1993–1995
Saundra Byrant, Calif.	1995–1997
Zola Walker, Tex.	1997–1999

*Died shortly after elected

Presidents of General Units
Jean Woolfolk, Church Finance Council	1976–1983
Ann Updegraff Spleth, Division of Homeland Ministries	1990–
Patricia Tucker Spier, Division of Overseas Ministries	1994
Cynthia R. Dougherty, National Benevolent Association	1997
Lois Artis Murray, Church Finance Council	1997

General Cabinet

Kathleen Bailey Austin, Assistant to the President	1970–1973
Helen Spaulding, Assistant to the President	1974–1974
Jean Woolfolk, President, Church Finance Council	1976–1983
Carolyn Day, Vice President for Communication	1987–1988
Claudia Grant, Deputy General Minister and President	1987–1993
Ann Updegraff Spleth, President, Division of Homeland Ministries	1990–
Patricia Tucker Spier, President, Division of Overseas Ministries	1994–
Cynthia R. Dougherty, President, National Benevolent Association	1997–
Lois Artis Murray, President, Church Finance Council	1999–

Office of the General Minister and President

Claudia Grant, Deputy General Minister and President	1987–1993
Shirley Cox, Managing Editor, Year Book and Directory	1978–1995
Linda McKiernan-Allen, Program Director, General Assembly	1994–1997
Lori Adams, Staff Minister for Discernment	1996–
Lois Artis Murray, Church Finance Council President and Associate General Minister	1999–

Regional Ministers

Mabel Figgs, Arizona, Administrator	1970–1977
Anne J. Beach, Interim, Georgia	1982
Doris McCullough, Acting Regional Minister, President	1982
Margaret Owen Clark, Pacific Southwest	1987–1990
Margaret Harrison, Southwest	1990–1994
Martha A. Williams, Regional Minister, Vice President	1990–
M. Jane Nesby, Interim, Arizona	1992
Karen Frank-Plumlee, Montana	1993
Darlene Goodrich, Co-Interim, Tennessee	1993–1994
Darlene Goodrich, Co-Interim, North Carolina	1994–1995
Susan Bowman, Co-Minister, California, North and Nevada	1995–1996
Barbara Jones, Arkansas	1996–
Narka Ryan, Co-Interim, Virginia	1996
Patsie Sweeden, Kansas	1998–
Dawn Stemple, Co-Interim, Nebraska	1998

National Convocation of the Christian Church (Disciples of Christ)

PRESIDENTS

Cynthia Hale, Ga.	1985–1986
Lenita "Jackie" Bunch, Ohio	1989–1990
Sybel Thomas, Ill.	1993–1994
Della January, Ohio	1996–1998

National Hispanic and Bilingual Fellowship

PRESIDENTS

Daisy Machado-Sanchez, Tex.	1991–1994
Dinah Negron-Serrano, Fla.	1995–1996
Maria C. Perez, N.Y.	1997–1998

World Convention of Churches of Christ

PRESIDENT

Marjorie Black, Canada	1991–1996

Church Women United

PRESIDENTS

Mossie Wyker, Ohio	1950–1955
Mary Louise Rowand, Tex.	1977–1980
Susan Shank Mix, Va.	1996–2000

SPECIAL REPRESENTATIVE

Mossie Wyker, Ky.	1960– 1967

AMBASSADOR OF GOOD WILL

Rosa Page Welch, Ill., Colo., Miss.	1950s–1970s

National Council of Churches

<small>GENERAL SECRETARY</small>

Joan Brown Campbell, Ohio, N.Y.   1990–

∼

The church is blessed by a "great cloud of witnesses" whose names may not be found in this book. They are women who have given strong leadership and quiet service, and have lived the good news of Jesus Christ. To all named and un- named, we express our gratitude.

Appendix V

Historical Timeline
1800–1999

Christian Church (Disciples of Christ)

Disciples Women

Ecumenical Developments

Events in Society

	1800 to 1900		
CHRISTIAN CHURCH (Disciples of Christ)	1801 Cane Ridge Camp Meeting 1832 Campbell's Disciples and Stone's Christians unite 1843 Canadian Disciples hold first annual meeting	1849 First National Convention at Cincinnati, Ohio 1849 Organization of American Christian Missionary Society 1855 Anti-slavery convention in Cleveland, Ohio	
DISCIPLES WOMEN			1874 Caroline Neville Pearre's vision 1874 Christian Woman's Board of Missions founded 1874 Maria Jameson elected first president 1874 CWBM national office located in Indianapolis 1874 Woman's Christian Temperance Union formed
ECUMENICAL DEVELOPMENTS		1861 Woman's Union Missionary Society established	
EVENTS IN SOCIETY		1848 Women's Rights Convention, Seneca Falls, N.Y. Abolitionist movement World trade increased	Employment of women and children in factories 1861–1865 Civil War Transcontinental telegraph completed

1800 to 1900 (continued)

Missionaries sent:
1850—Jerusalem
1853—Liberia
1858—Jamaica
1864—no funds
1883—Japan and India
1886—China

1887 First Canadian
Convention of
Cooperation of
Disciples

1876 CWBM sent
their first
missionary to
Jamaica

1881 Began Home
Mission work in
Jackson, Miss.

1883 Published
first issue of
Missionary Tidings

1883 CWBM sent
missionaries to
India

1886 CWBM
established Hazel
Green School

1887 Canadian
CWBM organized

1887 Women
established National
Benevolent
Association

1889 Clara
Babcock
ordained

1887 First World Day
of Prayer

Child labor increases

1898 U.S.
participates in first Peace
Conference at the Hague,
the Netherlands

World trade increased

	1900 то 1950		
CHRISTIAN CHURCH (Disciples of Christ)	1900 Negro work transferred to CWBM 1909 Centennial Convention at Pittsburgh, Pa.	1917 Organization of the International Convention of Disciples of Christ 1917 Organization of the National Christian Missionary Convention	1920 Creation of The United Christian Missionary Society 1928 UCMS headquarters moved to Indianapolis
DISCIPLES WOMEN	College of Missions, 222 S. Downey Ave, Indianapolis, Ind. dedicated, 1910 Network developed with women in state and local missionary organizations		Bible Chairs opened in many state universities
ECUMENICAL DEVELOP- MENTS	1908 Federal Council of Churches formed 1910 World Missionary Conference of Protestant Churches in Edinburgh, Scotland		
EVENTS IN SOCIETY	World War I		

1930 First World
Convention of
Churches of Christ

1941 Emergency
Million

1946 Crusade for a
Christian World
launched

1935 Unified Promotion
established

1949 Conference of State
Presidents and
Secretaries, Turkey Run, Ind.

1949 Mrs. George Stewart
elected chair of All Canada
Committee

1913–1949 Variety of independent congregational women's groups increase
(Ladies Aids, missionary societies guilds, councils)

1941 United Council of
Church Women formed

1948 World Council
of Churches formed

Dust Bowl

1945 United Nations formed

1948 Universal
Declaration of
Human Rights

Depression

World War II

Atom Bomb

Women in workplace
increase

	1950 TO 1999			
CHRISTIAN CHURCH (Disciples of Christ)	1950 Council of Agencies formed		1960 Committee on Brotherhood Restructure commissioned	1968 Provisional design for Christian Church (Disciples of Christ) approved
DISCIPLES WOMEN	1949–50 CWF launched	1953 ICWF organized 1955 WCWF organized	1957 First ICWF Quadrennial Assembly 1957 CWF offerings go to total church	1968 Consultation on Women in the Church
ECUMENICAL DEVELOP- MENTS	1950 National Council of Churches established		1960 Consultation on Church Union formed	
EVENTS IN SOCIETY			Urban Crises US–Super Power Racism	Vietnam War Drugs

1973, '77, '79, '85 General Assemblies passed resolutions regarding inadequate representation of women in church leadership

1995 General Offices moved to 130 E. Washington, Indianapolis, Ind.

1978 Consultation on Asian Disciples

1973 Jean Woolfolk elected first woman moderator

1981 First National Hispanic Assembly

1973 CWF Department became Department of Church Women

1980 Action Research Project

1997 Survey of Women

1977 First Convocation for Women in Ministry

1982 ICWF Restructure

1989 First Woman to Woman Worldwide Program launched

1992 Office of Disciples Women established

1974 100th Anniversary of the Christian Woman's Board of Missions

1982 Church Women's Coordinating Council established

CWU Responsibility Workshops

1988–1998 Ecumenical Decade The Churches in Solidarity with Women

Women's Ecumenical Coordinating Committee

World Council of Churches Consultation on Sexism in the Churches

Justice for Women Committee

Religious Committee on the Equal Rights Amendment

1974 UN International Women's Year World Conference, Mexico City, Mexico

1980 Mid-Decade World Conference, Nairobi, Kenya

1995 World Conference on Women, Beijing, China

1975–1985 United Nations International Women's Decade

Organ Transplants

Landed on moon

Internet

Notes

INTRODUCTION

[1]Betty Fiers, "Women in the Church Today and Tomorrow," *Discipliana*, Winter 1973.

[2]Helen Spaulding, "Foreword," *Discipliana*, Winter 1973.

[3]Turning points in history that demand decision because they are specially appointed times in the purpose of God, as in the appearance of Christ.

Part I

THE VENTURING YEARS, 1874–1919

[1]Minutes of the American Christian Missionary Society, 1870, Indianapolis, UCMS microfilm.

[2]Some sources show the date as April 9; most show April 10, which is generally accepted.

[3]Caroline Neville Pearre, "Our Beginning," *Missionary Tidings* 17 (August 1899).

[4]R. Pierce Beaver, *All Loves Excelling*, American Protestant Women in World Mission (Grand Rapids: Eerdmans, 1968), 87.

[5]Caroline Neville Pearre, "Our Beginning," *Missionary Tidings* 17 (September 1899).

[6]No official roster of all those in attendance was made. States represented were Illinois, Indiana, Iowa, Kentucky, Missouri, Maryland, Ohio, Oregon, and Pennsylvania.

[7]Minutes of American Christian Missionary Society, UCMS microfilms.

[8]First Constitution of the Christian Woman's Board of Missions, 1874, Article II.

[9]Ida Withers Harrison, *The Christian Woman's Board of Missions, 1874–1919*, 28.

[10]As recorded in Ida Withers Harrison's history, 42.

[11]Ibid., 44–45.

[12]Bailey, Fred Arthur, "The Status of Women in the Disciples of Christ Movement, 1865–1900," unpublished thesis, 1979, vii.

[13]"Zerelda Wallace: Death Today of a Notable Indiana Woman," *Indianapolis News*, 19 March 1901, 2.

[14]Jamaica was one of three missionary posts established in 1858. Support was withdrawn in 1864 because no funds were available from its parent organization, ACMS.

[15]Lorraine Lollis, *The Shape of Adam's Rib* (St. Louis: Bethany Press, 1970), 65–69.

[16]Imogene M. Reddel, "The Story of 60 Years," *Christian Evangelist* (August 23, 1934): 1092.

[17]Debra B. Hull, *Christian Church Women, Shapers of a Movement* (St. Louis: Chalice Press, 1994), 123.

[18]William E. Tucker and Lester G. McAllister, *Journey in Faith: A History of the Christian Church (Disciples of Christ)* (St. Louis: Bethany Press, 1975), 333.

[19]Ida Withers Harrison, *The Christian Woman's Board of Missions, 1874–1919*, 123.

[20]Ibid.

[21]Tucker and McAllister, 255.

[22]*National* was later inserted in the official title of this agency.

[23]For a more complete history of the National Benevolent Association, see Hiram and Marjorie Lester, *Inasmuch...The Saga of the NBA* (St. Louis: National Benevolent Association, 1987).

[24]William T. Moore, *A Comprehensive History of the Disciples of Christ* (New York: Fleming H. Revell, 1909), 767.

[25]Ida Withers Harrison, 145.

[26]Edith Eberle, "The Talking Woman," *World Call* (March 1948): 33.

[27]Richard L. Harrison, Jr., *From Camp Meeting to Church: A History of the Christian Church (Disciples of Christ) in Kentucky* (St. Louis: Christian Board of Publication, 1992), 180.

[28]J. B. Lehman, "Looking Over Half a Century," *World Call* (September 1925), 6–8.

[29]Oma Lou Myers, *Rosa's Song: The Life and Ministry of Rosa Page Welch* (St. Louis: CBP Press, 1984), 8.

[30]From correspondence between Anna R. Atwater and W. R. Warren.

[31]Lorraine Lollis, *The Shape of Adam's Rib*, 12.

[32]M. R. Warren, "The Last President," *World Call* (April 1920), 29–31.

[33]Lela E. Taylor, "She Led in Untried Ways," *World Call* (May 1948), 33.

[34]The Gospel of John 17:21. The "unofficial" scriptural basis of CWBM, as reflected in its publications and private correspondence.

[35]*Missionary Tidings* (November 1918): 245–46.

THE UNIFYING YEARS, 1920–1949

[1]William E. Tucker and Lester G. McAllister, *Journey in Faith: A History of the Christian Church (Disciples of Christ)* (St. Louis: Bethany Press, 1975), 348.

[2]W. E. Garrison and A. T. DeGroot, *The Disciples of Christ, A History* (St. Louis: Bethany Press, revised 1958), 429.

[3]*Golden Jubilee, 1874–1924, Christian Woman's Board of Missions* (St. Louis: United Christian Missionary Society, October 1924), 16. The front cover featured the title and a sketch of the Jubilee pin: the world in blue, with "For Christ" emblazoned across it in gold.

[4]"The Women Lead the Way," *World Call* (October 1922): p. 3.

[5]Loren E. Lair, *The Christian Churches and Their Work* (St. Louis, Bethany Press, 1963), 246.

[6]Genevieve Brown was head of the Missionary Education Department, UCMS, for more than 25 years, beginning in 1935.

[7]Lorraine Lollis, *The Shape of Adam's Rib* (St. Louis: Bethany Press, 1970), 134, 135.

[8]*Year Book 1947* (Indianapolis: International Convention, Disciples of Christ), 55.

[9]Jessie M. Trout, "On the Crusade Road," *World Call* (July–August 1948): Indianapolis, 33.

[10]Lorraine Lollis, 142.

THE RESURGENT YEARS, 1950–1968

[1]*World Call* (March 1949): 34.

[2]*World Call* (September 1950): 5

[3]Mossie A. Wyker, *Church Women in the Scheme of Things* (St. Louis: Bethany Press, 1953), Foreword, x.

[4]Ibid., 14–15.

[5]Spencer P. Austin, in an "Open Letter to Christian Women's Fellowship," included in the program book for the 1957 Quadrennial Assembly.

[6]A. Dale Fiers, *Leaven*, monthly bulletin, UCMS.

[7]Willard M. Wickizer, *Ideas for Brotherhood Structure*, Indianapolis, 1958.

[8]*Broadcaster*, ICWF Quadrennial Assembly, West Lafayette, Indiana, Vol. 9, no. 1. (June 25, 1990).

[9]Lorraine Lollis, *The Shape of Adam's Rib* (St. Louis: Bethany Press, 1970), 187.

[10]The stated purpose of Christian Women's Fellowship, rewritten and adopted following the name change of the women's department on January 1, 1973, to Department of Church Women.

Part II

INTRODUCTION TO PART II

[1]Personal papers of Fran Craddock, notes from consultation.

[2]Transcript of address.

THE SELF-REALIZATION YEARS, 1968–1973

[1]*Year Book and Directory of the Christian Church (Disciples of Christ)* (Indianapolis: The General Office of the Christian Church, 1968).

[2]*Year Book and Directory of the Christian Church (Disciples of Christ)* (Indianapolis: The General Office of the Christian Church, 1974).

[3]Marilyn Breitling, personal interview, May 1999.

[4]Helen Spaulding, personal interview, 1974.

[5]Jean Munro Gordon, personal correspondence to author, May 19, 1999.

[6]Purpose statement, ICWF Quadrennial Assembly Program Book, 1970.

[7]ICWF Quadrennial Program Books, 1957–1974.

[8]ICWF Quadrennial Assembly Program Book, 1982.

[9]ICWF Quadrennial Assembly Program Book, 1970.

[10]*1974 Year Book and Directory of the Christian Church (Disciples of Christ).*

[11]Ibid.

[12]Roger Heimer, personal notes, May 1999.

[13]*Year Book and Directory of the Christian Church (Disciples of Christ)*, "Resolution No. 7524: Concerning Individual Freedoms in Abortion" (Indianapolis: The General Office of the Christian Church, 1974), 198.

[14]Equal Rights Amendment.

[15]*Year Book and Directory of the Christian Church (Disciples of Christ)*, "Resolution No. 7342: Concerning Women in the Church (Indianapolis: The General Office of the Christian Church, 1974), 161.

[16]*Year Book and Directory of the Christian Church (Disciples of Christ)*, "Resolution No. 7337: Concerning Women in the Ministry" (Indianapolis: The General Office of the Christian Church, 1974), 155.

[17]*Year Book and Directory of the Christian Church (Disciples of Christ)* (Indianapolis: The General office of the Christian Church, 1973). Reporting to the denominational yearbook is voluntary, as is every other activity of the Disciples.

The Advocacy Years, 1974–1982

[1]*Year Book and Directory of the Christian Church (Disciples of Christ)*, "Resolution No. 7342: Concerning International Women's Year" (Indianapolis: The General Office of the Christian Church, 1974), 161.

[2]*Year Book and Directory of the Christian Church (Disciples of Christ)*,"Resolution No. 7526: Concerning International Women's Year" (Indianapolis: The General Office of the Christian Church, 1975), 199.

[3]*Year Book and Directory of the Christian Church (Disciples of Christ)*, "Resolution No. 7737: Concerning Salary Support of Women Pastors" (Indianapolis: The General Office of the Christian Church, 1977), 228.

[4]*Year Book and Directory of the Christian Church (Disciples of Christ)*, "Resolution No. 7748: Concerning Professional Clergy Couples in the Order of Ministry" (Indianapolis: The General Office of the Christian Church, 1978), 234.

[5]*Year Book and Directory of the Christian Church (Disciples of Christ)*, "Resolution No. 7769: Concerning Women in the Pastoral Ministry" (Indianapolis: The General Office of the Christian Church, 1978), 262.

[6]Ibid.

[7]*Year Book and Directory of the Christian Church (Disciples of Christ)*, "Resolution No. 9140: Concerning Equitable Salaries for Women Clergy" (Indianapolis: The General Office of the Christian Church, 1992), 302.

[8]Luz Bacerra, telephone conversation with author, fall 1998.

[9]Ellen Frost, personal interview, fall 1998.

[10]Office of Disciples Women staff interview, fall 1997.

[11]One attempt was made to correct some of this ignorance through the 1976–77 CWF/CMF group study *The Untold Story*, the story of the black Disciples. One interesting revelation to many was that both African American and white Disciples had founders named Alexander Campbell: one a refugee, the other a slave.

[12]Katherine Schutze, Homeland Ministries survey results, 1974.

[13]Ibid.

[14]Ibid.

[15]Jarvis Parker, "The Situation and Trends in the Ministry of Disciple Clergywomen in the Last Seven Years," *Discipliana* (Spring 1985).

[16]Joyce Coalson, personal interview, September 1998.

[17]Ibid.

[18]Winifred Smith, personal recollections, taped for the author, summer 1998.

[19]Fran Craddock, personal papers.

[20]*Community of Men and Women in the Church: The Sheffield Report*, ed.Constance Parvey (Geneva: World Council of Churches, 1983).

[21]*Year Book and Directory of the Christian Church (Disciples of Christ)* "No. 7750: A Study Document of Homosexuality and the Church" (Indianapolis: The General Office of the Christian Church, 1992), 236–44.

[22]Jackie Bunch, taped interview, Quadrennial Assembly, June 1994.

[23]Fran Craddock and Marilyn Moffett, conversation with the author.

[24]Women in Transition. "Report: Action Research Project" commissioned by the Christian Church (Disciples of Christ), Department of Church Women.

THE EMPOWERMENT YEARS, 1983–1987

[1]Marilyn Moffett, personal interview, fall 1997.

[2]Ibid.

[3]*Year Book and Directory of the Christian Church (Disciples of Christ)*, "Resolution No. 7342: Concerning Women in the Church" (Indianapolis: The General Office of the Christian Church, 1974), 161.

[4]*Year Book and Directory of the Christian Church (Disciples of Christ)*, "Resolution No. 8524: Concerning the Leadership of Women in the Christian Church (Disciples of Christ)" (Indianapolis: The General Office of the Christian Church, 1986), 255.

[5]Ibid.

[6]Ibid.

[7]Ibid.

[8]Marilyn Moffett, personal interview, fall 1997.

[9]Ann Marie Oogaard, conversation with the author, June 1984.

[10]Chinese proverb.

[11]Anna Jarvis-Parker, "The Situation and Trends in the Ministry of Disciple Clergywomen in the Last Seven Years," *Discipliana* 45:1 (Spring 1985): 7–10.

[12]LaTaunya Bynum, "Disciples on an Inclusive Quest," *The Disciple* (October 1987). 14.

[13]Ibid.

[14]Information from both Jarvis and Bynum articles.

[15]Bynum, "Disciples on an Inclusive Quest."

[16]Joyce Coalson, personal interview, September 1998.

[17]LaTaunya "Toni" Bynum, unpublished paper, "Reflections on Women in Ministry" sent to the author in 1998.

[18]Carol Cosby, personal notes given to the author.

[19]Martha Faw and Janice Newborn, "Forty Years of Choices and Changes," *Discipliana* 51:1 (Spring, 1991): 3.

[20]1994 Quadrennial Program Book "Be the Vision," 9.

[21]*Christian Women Share Their Faith*, 1986.

[22]Marilyn Moffett, notes given to the author.

[23]Brenda Osborn, unpublished paper, "Toward More Active Participation," c.1987.

[24]Carol Q. Cosby, personal interview, fall 1998.

[25]Janice Newborn, personal interview, fall 1998.

THE SOLIDARITY YEARS, 1988–1992

[1]The Reverend Linda Daniels-Block, "What Is the Decade? And Why Should I Care?" (Commission for Women, Evangelical Lutheran Church in America, 1989).

[2]Ibid.

[3]Janice Newborn, "Reflections on 1988–95," written for the CWF 50th Anniversary packet.

[4]Published by Atlanta's Prisca Press.

[5]*Year Book and Directory of the Christian Church (Disciples of Christ)*, "Resolution No. 8931: Concerning Economic Justice for Women" (Indianapolis: The General Office of the Christian Church, 1990), 295.

[6]*Year Book and Directory of the Christian Church (Disciples of Christ)*, "Resolution No. 9140: Concerning Equitable Salaries for Women Clergy" (Indianapolis: The General Office of the Christian Church, 1992), 302.

[7]Carol Cosby, personal interview, fall 1998.

[8]Ibid.

[9]Elizabeth Hartsfield, personal interview, November 1998.

[10]Janice Newborn, personal interview, fall 1998.
[11]Robert L. Friedly, "What Will Become of the CWF?" *The Disciple* (January 1992).
[12]Ibid.
[13]Ibid.
[14]Ann Updegraff Spleth, personal interview, November 4, 1998.
[15]Loren B. Mead and Ann Updegraff Spleth, "A Report to the Board of Directors, Division of Homeland Ministries, Christian Church (Disciples of Christ): Self-Study and Recommendations," April 19, 1991.

THE REASSESSMENT YEARS, 1993–1998

[1]Joseph Smith, address given at Missions Building closing ceremony, January 30, 1995.
[2]Fran Craddock, address given at Missions Building closing ceremony, January 30, 1995.
[3]Ann Updegraff Spleth, personal interview, November 4, 1994.
[4]Toni Bynum, unpublished paper, "Reflections on Women in Ministry."
[5]Arlene Pimentel, personal interview, January 1999.
[6]Mary had worked with the women in 1980 as they conducted the Action Research Project and again in 1988 for the second studies conference.
[7]"Christian Church (Disciples of Christ) Women in Congregations: Survey," fall 1996.
[8]Ellen Frost, personal interview, fall 1998.

THE HORIZON YEARS, 1999 AND BEYOND

[1]T. J. Liggett, "What Is the Future of CWF?" *The Disciple* (March 1987).
[2]Mary Sharer, taped verbal report to ICWF Cabinet, January 1999.
[3]Ann Updegraff Spleth, personal interview, November 4, 1998.

Index